BLOODY APRIL 1917

BLOODY APRIL 1917

AN EXCITING DETAILED ANALYSIS OF ONE OF
THE DEADLIEST MONTHS IN THE AIR IN WWI

**NORMAN FRANKS
RUSSELL GUEST
& FRANK BAILEY**

GRUB STREET | LONDON

Published by
Grub Street
4 Rainham Close
London
SW11 6SS

An expanded and updated paperback edition, with new photography, of Part One
of *Bloody April, Black September* (published by Grub Street in 1995)

Copyright © 2017 Grub Street, London
Text copyright © 2017 Norman L R Franks, Russell Guest and Frank Bailey

A CIP record for this title is available from the British Library

ISBN 978-1-910690-41-3

Cover and book design by Daniele Roa

Printed and bound by Finidr, Czech Republic

Our friend and co-author of *Bloody April, Black September*, Frank 'Bill' Bailey,
died in December 2010. He was a great WW1 aviation researcher, especially
concerning the French air force. A WW2 US Marine veteran (awarded two
Purple Hearts), in his post-war career in the USN he spent some years in Paris
where he was able to indulge his passion by spending long hours in the French
archives. We still miss him.

Contents

APRIL 1917

Acknowledgements

The authors wish to thank and acknowledge the help given by a number of friends and fellow historians, together with advice, support and photographs. Since the original work on *Bloody April* ended in 1995, a number of our pals have departed this life, but we remember them all. Neal O'Connor, George Williams, Ed Ferko, Richard Duiven, August Blume, Stewart Taylor, Stuart Leslie, Mike O'Connor, Greg Van Wyngarden, D MacGuinness, Russell Manning, Ola Sater, Dennis Connell, Paul Chamberlain, Dr Gustav Bock, Alex Imrie and Jörg Mückler.

Special acknowledgement must go to Trevor Henshaw not only for his massive work on WWI flying casualties with his book, *The Sky Their Battleground II,* (Fetubi Books, 2014) but for his generous help over the years with this tremendous undertaking of recording the events of WWI in the air.

Also to the keeper and staff at the Public Archives at Kew, Surrey, and the Bureau Central d'lncorporation et D'Archives, de l'Armée de l'Air, the Service Historique de l'Armée de l'Air (SHAA), France.

Introduction

Military aviation in World War One was new. Only six years before the war began in August 1914, the Frenchman Louis Blériot became the first man to fly the English Channel, and only two years before the conflict did the Army grudgingly acknowledge the aeroplane by creating the Royal Flying Corps in May 1912. For its part, the Royal Navy had its own air-arm from the same date, the Naval Wing which in turn became the Royal Naval Air Service in July 1914.

In less than two years of armed conflict, the war had ground to the stalemate of the Western Front trench systems that stretched from the North Sea coast near Nieuport to the Swiss frontier. The generals that commanded the various armies in France had grown up with the ideals of open land warfare wherein cavalry not only made the occasional dramatic charge with lance and sabre gleaming, but as tradition had shown, were the eyes of those generals in finding out what the enemy were doing on 'the other side of the hill'. The trenches, with their barbed-wire entanglements, not to mention the quagmires of 'no man's land', made cavalry scouting patrols impossible. Almost overnight the generals turned to the aeroplane to be their eyes, for in flight they could not only see the other side of the hill, but photograph it as well.

Thus reconnaissance and aerial photography changed the whole nature of military flying in that both sides suddenly needed the means of both stopping the enemy from carrying out its reconnaissance sorties and ensuring its own aeroplanes were able to operate over the lines. Thus the struggle for air supremacy began.

This is not a book covering the study of wartime aviation development. Suffice it to say that over the period of 1915-16, both sides tried many means to achieve their aims in the air, and each side began producing fighting aeroplanes equipped with machine guns to try to shoot down enemy two-seaters and oppose the single-seaters that were endeavouring to do the same thing to their own side's two-seaters.

Initially, the Germans assigned two or three fighters to each of its reconnaissance units, known as Feldflieger Abteilung (FFA, later shortened to FA, Flieger Abteilung), to fly both protection sorties and hunting sorties against the British and French. The British and French, meantime, formed complete fighting units which they used in much the same way, although the Royal Flying Corps consciously adopted an offensive attitude under its overall commander, Major General Hugh Trenchard.

The Germans, for their part, with slightly fewer aeroplanes than the combined numbers of the British, French and Belgian air forces, were content to take on a more defensive posture, letting the enemy come to them so that they were generally able to dictate the terms of battle. Though this doctrine, in time, was proved wrong, by late 1916 that was the 'status quo' within which they had to operate.

The period known as the Fokker Scourge – the Germans using the nimble Fokker monoplanes with a forward-firing machine gun, which covered the approximate period August 1915 to June 1916 – created many of the early fighter aces among the German Fokker Eindekker pilots. Immelmann, Wintgens, Parschau, Berthold, von Mulzer, Frankl and Boelcke took their place in aviation history during this period, but the most well known was Boelcke. This was not just due to his successes in early air combat, but also to his foresight and help in creating the fighting squadrons of the German Air Service, the Jagdstaffeln, known individually in the abbreviated form of Jasta.

The German Jasta units were created in the autumn of 1916. The first seven were formed by the beginning of October and over the next few months more were established, so that by the early spring of 1917, 37 Jastas were in existence. Their birth coincided with the arrival of new single-seat biplane fighters, the Albatros DII and Halberstadt DII Scouts, each having machine guns that fired through the propeller. These greatly outclassed the existing British and French fighters such as the DH2 and FE8 pusher-types and could give a good account of themselves against the FE2b two-seat pusher, and the single-seat Nieuport Scouts, Sopwith Pups and two-seater Sopwith 1½ Strutter.

As spring arrived on the Western Front in that fateful year of 1917, two things happened which together brought the air war to a head during April. Firstly, the German Jastas had begun to hone themselves into an aggressive fighting force during the winter months, when generally the chances of proving themselves and their aeroplanes against the Allied air forces were limited due to the weather. With the arrival of spring and better weather came at last the opportunity they'd been waiting for. Secondly, the Allied commanders had plans for a huge offensive as soon as the weather improved. The plan was to mount the offensive along a 100-mile section of the Western Front between Arras in the north and the Aisne River in the south. If it succeeded, British troops would attack at Arras while the French armies would make an assault from the southern end of the line. This, of course, was nothing new: such assaults had happened before, such as the disastrous Somme offensive in July 1916, but Allied commanders were nothing if not optimistic of success as each subsequent offensive came onto the drawing board. In hindsight, their perseverance and constant belief in success as each new battle was planned was something to behold.

Field Marshal Sir Douglas Haig would command the British, General Robert Nivelle, hero of Verdun, the French. Tasked with providing the necessary air support, Trenchard was well aware of the shortcomings of his aircraft, especially now that the Germans had reorganised their fighter force and had received superior aircraft. He had requested and been promised new types but nothing much had yet arrived in France. Some new types were on the way, such as a two-seater Bristol Fighter, and a new single-seater called the SE5, but the former had only just arrived (one squadron) and had yet to fly their first operational patrols, while the SE5 (again just one squadron) would not arrive until the second week of April and not be operational for another two. Meanwhile, Trenchard would have to start the battle with old DH2s, the FE2 squadrons, French Nieuports and the handful of Sopwith Pup squadrons. He did have the added support of some RNAS squadrons which had Sopwith Pups and Sopwith Triplanes, while the French had a lively little fighter, the Spad VII, some of which had been given to the British, but only two squadrons had them. The French were naturally more keen to get rid of their Nieuports than their new Spads.

The German Jastas became more aggressive during the first weeks of 1917 and it was obvious to Trenchard that with their new aircraft and therefore their new-found prowess, retaining air superiority over the coming offensive would be difficult. It made it even more essential that his airmen fly even more aggressively in an attempt to overwhelm the Germans, who were still, in the final analysis, inferior in numbers. However, aggression was one thing, the ability to be aggressive another.

Haig was kept well aware of the situation, and to his credit he wrote several times to the War Cabinet urging them to hurry along the new types promised, but these could not be produced overnight so Trenchard and his force would have to do the best with what they had.

Even before the April offensive, the Germans had the latest version of their Albatros Scout – the DIII – begin to make its appearance over the front. Boelcke, of course, had died in a collision on 28 October 1916, but his name lived on in several of his pupils, not the least of whom was a young cavalry officer, Baron Manfred von Richthofen. In January 1917 he was given command of Jasta 11, which would soon become the highest scoring of all the Jastas. By the end of March, von Richthofen would have a personal score of 31 victories, only nine short of the number his mentor Boelcke had achieved.

So, on the eve of battle, Trenchard knew that having survived the Fokker Scourge of the previous year, the tide of supremacy would soon turn against his airmen once more – and at a most critical time. At first he thought of conserving his forces, but the amount of information needed to plan the offensive made it necessary for photo and visual reconnaissance missions to be flown in number, which in turn increased the aerial activity over the front. Overall monthly personnel casualties since October 1916 had been in double figures, with 75 in October the highest. Now, in March 1917, the figure shot up to 143 airmen dead or missing. The number of sorties also increased, to 14,500, the highest recorded in any month so far.

The Arras offensive would see the British forces take the brunt of the fighting. For its part the RFC had 25 squadrons along this section of the front, with around 365 serviceable aeroplanes, of which about a third were fighter types. Other units covered the more northern sectors, opposite Lille and Ypres. Across the lines, the German 6 Armee covering the area Lille in the north to Cambrai in the south had 195 aircraft, of which half were fighters. But numbers were not totally relevant when one considered the quality of the German fighter force: in many respects the relationship between German fighters, Allied fighters and Corps aircraft would be akin to sharks among minnows in the coming battle.

This book will record in detail the air Battle of Arras and the air fighting which developed through that fateful month of April 1917 – which would later be called Bloody April.

We have attempted to be accurate in both recording the air actions and making the analysis of losses and claims. Reference to all the surviving RFC/RAF loss records has produced much information, but due to the period of time and so on, one cannot vouch for total accuracy or completeness. Some records we know are no longer available and have been lost, even over recent years.

Claims by both sides are as accurate as can be achieved, but the reader must realise the difference between claims and verified losses on either side. It doesn't take too much intelligence to realise there was over-claiming on both sides of the lines, mostly in good faith, and an awful lot of things can come between a claim and a confirmed victory. Many of course are in no doubt, while others might be queried by the reader due to some other previous publication saying something quite different.

In this particular respect, we have tried our utmost to study closely the relationship between a claim and a victory, taking into account time, location, and close scrutiny of maps, something which some people in the far or even more recent past seem to have taken little interest in. Even so, we are fallible, but generally we have good reasons for saying what we do but would welcome constructive comment should we have failed in one or two instances, for the sake of future reference if nothing else.

Generally speaking, the German claims are very good, one reason being that with the majority of the air fighting taking place over their own territory, aircraft or wreckage fell where it could be seen and recorded. The RFC/RAF on the other hand had generally to go on eyewitness verifications of what they saw – or thought they saw – and usually had no wreckage to inspect. The French, and later the Americans too, had a different system, being far more stringent in verification of claims, but this could still lead to a claim having no apparent corresponding loss. In the final analysis, we can only say what was claimed at the time, given credit for, and show what losses are known.

It has been difficult to verify all the German claims. Even so-called official sources note no losses whereas there is not the slightest doubt losses occurred – even aircraft having come down on the Allied side, that had to be a loss. However, we have had access to all the German personnel casualties – at least fatalities – so we can be fairly certain they are all correct. With aeroplanes it might be different. We do not know for certain if when an aircraft came down and, say, was destroyed by fire, but the pilot or crew scrambled clear unharmed, whether a pure aircraft loss was recorded, as opposed to an aircraft and crew. There is strong evidence to suspect that in some records, if there were no personnel losses, even if an aircraft was destroyed or sub-sequently written-off, that no loss record occurs. Therefore, in the German loss column at the end of each day, we have had to produce a figure from what we know, and this has no verification from any official source, but is given for information and comparison.

With Allied claims in these daily lists, we show the 'out of control' victories by the British, but as the French airmen had no comparable type of combat claim, there will be no figure for them under that heading.

Throughout the daily reporting we have tried to work chronologically but some-times we do not know for certain the timing of a combat or a loss so these, while mentioned, will appear generally in the daily loss notes.

We have made little reference to losses due to non-combat sorties, or where an aircraft may have crashed returning from a sortie, but where the accident was not attributable to combat damage. Anyone reading through the daily aircraft loss reports will see just how many aircraft were lost, certainly by the British, through flying accidents and pilot error. To have included all those would have made the book unwieldy, so only crashes where combat damage was involved have been noted.

Where personnel casualties have been recorded, but the aircraft was not lost, even though damaged (which includes aircraft recovered from forced landings behind the front lines), a * will appear far right of the daily casualty entry to denote the aircraft was not a loss. Also, in the case of two-seater crews, the first named will always be the pilot; where only one crewman is recorded a (P) or (O) appears to denote pilot or observer.

In the narrative, during the periods where Allied and German times differed by one hour, reference to this will be emphasised by an (A) or (G) next to an Allied or German time, although generally the time attributable to an Allied or German action/report will, of course, be the time relevant to the side involved.

Royal Flying Corps Order of Battle 1 April 1917

Brigade	Wing	Sqdn	A/C	Base	Corps
GHQ	9th	35	AWFK8	Savy	Cavalry
Savy		27	Martinsyde G100	Fienvillers	
		55	DH4	"	
		57	FE2d	"	
		70	Sopwith 1½ Strutters	"	
		19	Spad VII	Vert Galant	
		66	Sopwith Pups	"	
I	1st	2	BE2	Hesdigneul	I
Château du Reveillon		5	BE2	La Gorgue (a)	XIII
		10	BE2	Chocques	XI
		16	BE2	Bruay	I Canadian
	10th	25	FE2b	Lozinghem	
		40	FE8	Treizennes (b)	
		43	Sop 1½ Strutters	"	
		8N	Sop Triplanes	Lozinghem (c)	
II	2nd	53	BE2	Bailleul	IX
Cassel		6	BE2	Abeele	X
		42	BE2	Bailleul	
		46	Nieuport XII	Droglandt (d)	VIII
		21	RE8	"	II Australian
	11th	1	Nieuport XVII	Bailleul	
		20	FE2d	Boisdinghem (e)	
		41	FE8	Abeele	
		45	Sop 1½ Strutters	St Marie Cappel	
III	12th	8	BE2	Soncamps	VII
Château de Sains		59	RE8	Bellevue	XVIII
		12	BE2	Avesnes	VI
		13	BE2	Savy	XVII
	13th	11	FE2b	Le Hameau	
		29	Nieuport XVII	"	
		48	BF2a	Bellevue	
		60	Nieuport XVII	Le Hameau	
		6N	Nieuport XVII	Bellevue (f)	
		100	FE2b	Le Hameau	
IV	3rd	7	BE2	Nesle	IV
Miséry		9	BE2	Morlancourt	XIV
		34	RE8	Foucaucourt	III
		52	BE2	Meaulte	XV
	14th	22	FE2d	Chipilly	
		24	DH2	" (g)	
		54	Sopwith Pups	" (h)	
		1N	Sop Triplanes	" (i)	

Brigade	Wing	Sqdn	A/C	Base	Corps
V	15th	4	BE2	Warloy	I Australian
Albert		3	Morane Parasol	Laviéville	I Australian
		l5	BE2	Léalvillers	V
	22nd	18	FE2b	Bertangles	
		23	FE2b/Spad VII	Baizieux	
		3N	Sopwith Pups	Marieux	
		32	DH2	Léalvillers	

Notes:

(a) 5 Squadron moved to Savy 7 April; (b) 40 Squadron moved to Auchel 25 April, then to Bruay 29 April; (c) Two flights of 8 Naval moved to Flez 26 April; (d) One flight 46 Squadron moved to Boisdinghem 16 April; followed by the main body on 25 April; (e) 20 Squadron moved to St Marie Cappel 16 April; (f) 6 Naval Squadron moved to Chipilly 11 April; (g) 24 Squadron moved to Flez 18 April; (h) 54 Squadron moved to Flez 18 April; (i) 1 Naval Squadron moved to Bellevue 11 April.

Wing Headquarters Locations

9th at Fienvillers

1st at Chocques

2nd at Eecke

10th at Lozinghem, moved to
  Château de Reveillon, Chocques 18 April

11th at Bailleul

12th at Avesnes, moved to Agnez-lès-Duisans 24 April

13th at Le Hameau

3rd at Bouvincourt

14th at Chipilly, moved to Guizancourt 29 April

15th at Arqueves

22nd at Toutencourt

German Jastas attached to each Armee, April 1917

1 Armee – Jastas 2, 17, 29, 36

2 Armee – Jastas 2, 5, 20, 26

3 Armee – Jastas 9, 21, 29, 31

4 Armee – Jastas 8, 18

5 Armee – Jastas 7, 10, 13

6 Armee – Jastas 3, 4, 6, 11, 12, 27, 28, 30, 33

7 Armee – Jastas 1, 13, 14, 15, 17, 19, 22, 32

Abt 'A' – Jastas 24, 37

Abt 'B' – Jastas 16, 26, 35

Abt 'C' – Jastas 23, 34

German Jasta Bases, April 1917

Unit	Base	Armee	Location
Jasta 1	Vivaise	7	10 km NW Laon
Jasta 2	Pronville	1 and 2	15 km W Cambrai
Jasta 3	Guesnain	6	5 km SE Douai
Jasta 4	Douai	6	
Jasta 5	Boistrancourt	2	10 km SE Cambrai
Jasta 6	Aulnoy	6	2 km S Valenciennes
Jasta 7	Procher	5	
Jasta 8	Rumbeke	4	2 km S Roulers

Unit	Base	Armee	Location
Jasta 9	Leffincourt	3	50 km NE Reims
Jasta 10	Jametz – then Aincrevillers	5	30 km SE Stenay 14 km SE Stenay
Jasta 11	Douai-Brayelles – then Roucourt	6	5 km SE Douai
Jasta 12	Épinoy	6	8 km NW Cambrai
Jasta 13	Reneuil Ferme	5 and 7	
Jasta 14	Boncourt – then Marchais	7	15 km ENE Laon 8 km E Laon
Jasta 15	La Selve	7	48 km N Reims
Jasta 16	Eisenheim – then Habsheim	Abt 'B'	5 km SE Mulhouse
Jasta 17	St Quentin le Petit	7 and 1	
Jasta 18	Halluin	4	1 km SE Menin
Jasta 19	Thour	7	30 km N Reims
Jasta 20	Guise	2	30 km NE St Quentin
Jasta 21		3	
Jasta 22	Laon	7	
Jasta 23	Mars-la-Tour	Abt 'C'	15 km W Metz
Jasta 24	Morchingen – then Annelles	Abt 'A' and 1	
Jasta 26	Habsheim – then Guise-Ost – then Bohain-Nord	Abt 'B' 2	5 km SE Mulhouse 25 km ENE St Quentin 20 km NE St Quentin
Jasta 27	Ghistelles	6	15 km S Ostende
Jasta 28	Wasquehal	6	1 km SW Roubaix
Jasta 29	Juniville	3 and 1	15 km W Leffincourt
Jasta 30	Phalempin	6	10 km S Lille
Jasta 31	Mars-sous-Bourcq	3	10 km E Leffincourt
Jasta 32	Chéry-les-Pouilly	7	10 km N Laon
Jasta 33	Villers-au-Tertre	6	10 km SE Douai
Jasta 34	Mars-la-Tour	Abt 'C'	15 km W Metz
Jasta 35	Habsheim – then Colmar-Nord	Abt 'B'	5 km SE Mulhouse
Jasta 36	Le Châtelet	1	
Jasta 37	Montinghen- Metz	Abt 'A'	

01 APRIL 1917
M T W T F S **S**

British Front

There was not the slightest portent of things to come as the new day's grey light cast out the previous night's shadows across the shattered landscape of the Western Front on this first day of April 1917. There was no spring dawn, only scudding cloud that would bring rain on and off all day.

Deep in their trenches, the fighting soldiers of both sides tried to keep warm in their underground bunkers. Others began to move about, brewing the inevitable billy of tea, while making sure yesterday's leftover bread had not been 'got at' by the rats during the night. Outside, the luckless men who had been on guard duty in the chill of pre-dawn stood on the parapet woodwork. Occasionally they would peep out through a sand-bagged spy hole, or into those extended see-over parapet eyeglasses at the enemy lines.

What they saw was the familiar barbed wire entanglements in front of their trenchworks, the lifeless churned-up mud and earth of no man's land, then the German wire, with some parapet sandbags or pieces of timber beyond it. There was little growing other than perhaps the odd clump of grass, or a new weed. Trees and bushes had long since gone, smashed and shattered in countless bombardments. There might be the odd stubborn tree stump, but little else.

For the men in the trenches – on both sides – the day would be much like any other. Those on guard duty would turn out for their period of time-on, then time-off. The others would stay under cover, attending to household or personal chores. Perhaps a bit of urgent repair to their underground living quarters, replacing worn or broken duck-boards in the trenches, darning socks, washing a shirt or some item of underwear; fetching food and water from the rear, cleaning one's rifle, while all the time trying to think of anything other than their present soul-destroying lifestyle.

One could just about get used to trench-life. Nothing had ever prepared the men who fought World War One for such an existence, but like most things, once it was understood to be inevitable, then it could be endured – by most of them. Occasionally a sniper, British, French or German, might fire at a fleeting target. Minds would then be concentrated for a few minutes on the possible implications, but when it remained silent, things would return to normal. Occasionally something would disturb the tranquillity and a machine gun might rattle out. Men would rush to the gun-slits, fire off a few rounds in panic, followed by other machine guns. Suddenly it would stop, and after a few minutes, peace reigned once more.

There was no constant, daily fighting. Generally speaking unless some field commander decided that today was the day to launch yet another offensive to try and break the deadlock that was the Western Front, all would remain quiet. All quiet on the Western Front; it was often so. As the soldiers noted, it was only those intrepid aviators who 'went over the top' every day – and good luck to 'em. Leave us in peace and we'll be more than happy.

Yet on this day there was little flying also; the weather saw to that. But between the rain showers, the ever aggressive doctrine of the Royal Flying Corps saw to it that aeroplanes were sent up to make sure the Germans knew the war was still on. The artillery flyers went up to the front in order to guide shellfire onto any enemy gun positions noted the previous day, or even during the current day, by overzealous officers at the front who, as far as their men were concerned, couldn't leave well enough alone. It usually started with a 'tit-for-tat' episode. Someone would spot a likely target and after a wireless call, a gun battery would be ordered to lob a few shells at it. This would bring a response from the other side. Positions of guns would be noted and radioed back to headquarters, who would then send up aircraft, or tethered kite balloons, both to range for the guns and to record the fall of shot. This might then escalate as each side sent up fighting aircraft to try to drive off the artillery flyers. Sometimes it all ended with everyone going home, sometimes all hell was let loose. War is sometimes like that. It just takes someone to stir up trouble.

Even so, on quiet days too, it was essential to keep an eye on the enemy. If either side seemed exceptionally quiet it could mean they were up to something. Planning an attack, bringing up troops and equipment, ammunition and guns. Each side needed to keep watch on the other, especially in the rear areas. Any unusual movements would in all probability mean something was afoot, then the other side would begin to move up troops to counter the threat, transferring men and equipment from another part of the front. And so it went on.

There were two ways of keeping an eye on the opposition – by aircraft being flown over the rear areas, or by observers being hoisted aloft in a basket beneath a static-line balloon. The balloon lines were some way back from the immediate front, so as not to be in danger of light ground fire, and the observers in the dangling baskets could observe their section of the front through powerful binoculars. They could see both movement and flashes or smoke from gun batteries. It followed, therefore, that the balloons too would be attacked, to be either destroyed if possible, or at least forced down. It took a while to haul them down and then get them back up, so forcing them down was a good second-best. Forcing the observer to jump out of his basket with the aid of a rudimentary parachute at least stopped him working – and he might even break a leg!

Time on the Western Front at this period was the same for both the Allied and German forces. It would not change until 16 April, when the German time would be advanced by one hour.

At this particular juncture on the British front, much of the area to the south-east of Arras was rather more fluid than usual, as German troops were gradually withdrawing to their Hindenburg Line positions. As British troops eased forward, there was some brisk fighting for the shattered remains of a few villages before they were forced to halt in front of the mighty German defence line.

On the British front the balloons were up early and so were the artillery flyers. Such were the conditions that the balloon of No. 10 Kite Balloon Section (10th Section, 2nd Company, 1st Wing), supporting the Canadians, was struck by lightning and destroyed. One of the section's ground personnel, Private A Simpson, was also struck, and killed instantly.

Meanwhile, others were reporting German gun batteries, so RFC aircraft were up ranging the guns along the fronts of the 1st, 3rd and 4th Armies. A few German fighter pilots were called to take off and see if they could disrupt proceedings.

Jasta 2 (now called Jasta Boelcke in memory of the dead air hero) based at Pronville, 16 km due west of Cambrai, sent up a patrol, led by Leutnant Otto Bernert, who would command this Staffel in June. Taking advantage of the cloud, Bernert and his wingman nipped across the front line, and attacked the balloon of the 4th KB Section (4th Section, 13th Company, 5th Wing) at Villers-au-Flos at 1045, Bernert sending it down in flames; the two observers, Second Lieutenants Cochrane and Hadley, parachuted down. It was Bernert's 11th victory and the British had suffered their first air loss of April to the German fighter pilots.

While all this had been happening, a two-seat BE2c of No. 15 Squadron RFC was engaged on artillery work in approximately the same area. Captain A M Wynne and his observer, Lieutenant A S Mackenzie, of 15 Squadron, based at Léalvillers, 12 km north-west of Albert, had taken off at 0925 that morning, so at way past 1130 they were just about to head for home after ranging for guns of V Corps, when they were spotted by a German pilot, again from Jasta Boelcke. Unfortunately for the two British airmen it was another expert fighter ace, seated in the cockpit of his Albatros DII, and he had twice as many victories as Bernert. Leutnant Werner Voss had spotted them and kept above some cloud so as to approach unobserved. Between Ecoust and Saint-Léger, he swooped down through the cloud, diving down on the BE which was at 800 feet. Wynne saw the danger and headed west, Mackenzie opening fire with his Lewis gun. He fired two drums with no apparent effect, as Wynne headed down. At 100 feet, Mackenzie was hit in the heart and died instantly. Wynne immediately prepared to put down but was then hit in the leg by another burst from Voss. The BE scraped over the front-line trenches, watched by soldiers who always knew no good would come of flying, and crunched into the ground near Saint-Léger. Wynne was thrown out which was just as well, as Voss then dived on the wrecked BE and fired into it before flying back across the lines.

It was 1145 and the 19-year-old Voss (he would be 20 on 13 April) secured his 23rd victory following confirmation from front-line German troops that his adversary had been successfully brought down and the machine then destroyed by shellfire. This would not be the first time that a flyer of either side had shot up a downed adversary. The war had long since left the realms of chivalry often associated with WWI war in the air, something that was more often than not a dream of the 1930s pulp fiction writers of war flying adventures.

Within minutes of this victory, the British artillery two-seaters were getting their own back. Near Arras was a BE2c of 12 Squadron, flown by Second Lieutenants Douglas Gordon and H E Baker. Jasta 3 from Guesnain, just to the south-east of Douai, flew a patrol to the front led by its Staffelführer, Leutnant Alfred Mohr, an ace with six victories. He too was flying an Albatros DII – 2012/16 – and dived on the two-seater, but the alert gunner hammered the oncoming scout, hitting the German's fuel tank. Immediately it burst into flames and engulfed the machine, which fell into the British lines at 1150. Mohr died in the inferno, the wreckage of his aeroplane being given the number G.18 by the British, who numbered all (most) enemy aircraft that fell in their territory, whether intact or a smouldering mass. Jasta 3 was taken over by Oberleutnant Hermann Kohze from Kampfgeschwader 4 (a bombing unit) the next day.

The second British aircraft lost on this quiet day occurred in the early afternoon. In an attempt to provide protection for the artillery aircraft over the front, 11 Squadron at Le Hameau, 16 km west of Arras, had sent up a patrol of their two-seat pusher

Top Captain A M Wynne of 15 Squadron, one of the first RFC airmen to be shot down as April began. Werner Voss forced him down inside British lines on the morning of the 1st, with his observer dead. It was the German's 23rd victory. **Bottom** Leutnant Werner Voss of Jasta Boelcke went on to achieve forty-eight combat victories before his own death in September 1917.

FE2b fighters at 1420. The weather was pretty bad at this time and one machine failed to make it home, last seen to the west of Boyelle. The squadron thought the crew, Corporal A Wilson and 2AM F Hadlow, may have been brought down in a storm, but the Germans claimed an FE shot down by ground fire, credit going to the gunners of Flakzug 145 and Mflak 14. Both airmen were taken prisoner, having come down north-west of Pont de Couriers.

French Front

There was little real activity along the French front on this Sunday, with no casualties recorded either. There was only one combat noted with Sergent Goux of N.67 claiming a German two-seater sent down over the enemy lines. There is no corresponding loss, although an observer with a Bavarian artillery observation unit, Flieger Abteilung (A) 288b ('b' denotes a Bavarian unit), Leutnant Werner, was severely wounded, which may have been the result of an attack by Goux's Nieuport Scout.

	A/C	KB		DES	OOC	KB
British losses	2	1	British claims	1	–	–
French losses	–	–	French claims	1	–	
German claims	2	1	German losses	1	–	

German losses in aircraft have sometimes appeared difficult to reconcile. In the German Nachrichtenblatt for 1 April there are no losses recorded but clearly Jasta 3 had a most definite loss, and although FA(A)288 had a man wounded, it could be that the aeroplane itself was not lost.

British Casualties				
Aircraft type	No.	Squadron	Crew	
BE2c	2561	15 Sqdn	Capt A M Wynne	WIA
			Lt A S Mackenzie	KIA
FE2b	4954	11 Sqdn	Cpl A Wilson	POW
			2AM F Hadlow	POW
Balloon		4-13-5	2/Lt Cochrane	Safe
			2/Lt Hadley	Safe

02 APRIL 1917
M T W T F S S

British Front

Almost all the action occurred during the morning during a day of wind, rain and low cloud. Nevertheless, reconnaissance aircraft were sent out and no fewer than 32 ground targets were given the benefit of shellfire by artillery with aeroplane observations and direction. Not unnaturally the German fighter pilots were up too, interfering with the RFC's daily incursions over the front. Among the first off from the British side were five FE2b machines of 22 Squadron airborne from Chipilly, situated on the northern bank of the Somme River, 10 km due south of Albert, at 0635. 22 shared this airfield with 24 Squadron's DH2s, 54 Squadron with Sopwith Pups and 1 Naval Squadron, which had Sopwith Triplanes.

Two of the FEs carried cameras in order to take photos of German dispositions opposite the British 4th Army front, while the other three would act as escort. The formation headed north-east, crossed the lines to the north of Péronne then flew in the direction of Gouzeaucourt, by which time one photo FE had returned home with engine trouble. Meantime Jasta 5 at Boistrancourt, 10 km to the south-east of Cambrai, took off and headed for the front, having been told of approaching British aircraft. Very often the German pilots would not take off until front-line observers reported Allied aircraft approaching or crossing the lines. This saved time patrolling up and down behind the front and stopped the problem of having to return to refuel just as enemy aircraft were finally spotted.

Jasta 5 found the FEs, which had now overflown Gouzeaucourt (south-west of Cambrai), between Beaucamp and Gouzeaucourt Wood, just before 0830 and attacked. The FE crews, now joined by some DH2s of 24 Squadron, later reported a force of 18 Albatros Scouts in two groups and in the fight which followed, the remaining photo machine was hit, began to burn, then fell in flames. The victor was Offizierstellvertreter Edmund Nathanael, who would return home having secured his 6th victory. Seeing the FE start to burn, Captain C R Cox and Second Lieutenant L C Welford (4855) tried to drive off the Albatros, but Cox was himself heavily engaged. Welford fired 60 rounds into another Albatros over the FE's left wing-tip, seeing it catch fire and go down out of control. He then saw a DH2 finish it off, the German crashing to the ground.

The five DH5s of 24 Squadron, which had taken off from Chipilly at 0730 to fly a line patrol, had seen the enemy aircraft attacking the four FEs over Havrincourt Wood and had come to engage. Lieutenant Kelvin Crawford (in 5925) fired three-quarters of a drum of Lewis ammunition at one Albatros, which caught fire, fell away and was reported as crashed near Gouzeaucourt. Lieutenant Sydney Cockerall (A2581) engaged another Albatros at close range, then during a circling manoeuvre got inside the German, fired, and sent it down out of control to crash. Another German fighter was driven down by Second Lieutenants Percy W Chambers and F O'Sullivan of 22 Squadron (A5959) and seen to land north-east of Gouzeaucourt.

In the event, there were no apparent fighter losses on the German side – certainly Jasta 5 suffered none. The Albatros Scouts did break off the action, leaving the three surviving FEs to fly home, but the crew of the one lost were both dead. The pilot had been Second Lieutenant Patrick Alfred Russell, aged 27 from Northumberland, who had seen action at Gallipoli with a Yeomanry Regiment, and his observer, a Canadian, Lieutenant H Loveland, attached to the RFC from the 78th Canadian Infantry Battalion.

Such claims became a feature of the fighting during the First War and it is difficult to reconcile the reports of the Allied airmen with the apparent lack of corresponding German losses. Crawford's burning victim was also confirmed by 22 Squadron, so why there appears to be no loss is a mystery, unless the German pilot(s) survived and only the aircraft were lost and not reported as such in the records. Over-claiming in respect of assumed out of control victories is understandable, but why so many German aircraft were seen burning and crashing, with virtually no losses admitted to is strange.

Even before this combat had taken place, the RFC had had its first loss of the day, losing an aircraft which had taken off some 45 minutes after 22 flew out. 60 Squadron based at Le Hameau (which it shared with 11 and 29 Squadrons), sent out aircraft at 0715 to fly an offensive patrol between Arras and Gommecourt. They spotted aircraft over the lines and headed towards Quéant running into Jasta 2. In the ensuing fight, Second Lieutenant C S Hall (A6766) sent an Albatros spinning down over Fontaine Notre Dame, but 60 Squadron lost Second Lieutenant Vaughan F Williams, who fell in flames following an attack by Otto Bernert at 0830. Again there is no German loss recorded.

Left Offstv Edmund Nathanael of Jasta 5 claimed his 6th victory on 2 April, a FE2 of 22 Squadron.
Right Lieutenant W V Strugnell of 54 Squadron had a fight with German two-seaters on the 2nd, forcing one down, its observer hit, but his own engine failed and he was lucky to crash-land without injury to himself, on the British side of the lines. Strugnell achieved six victories by May 1917 and received the MC and Bar for his efforts.

Meantime, the Sopwith Pups of 54 Squadron, who flew a five-man patrol which began at 0720, ran into seven enemy aircraft, five two-seaters and two single-seaters. They broke up the formation, Lieutenant Oliver Sutton (A637) claiming one shot down while Lieutenant W V Strugnell, in A639, (a pre-war air mechanic who had learned to fly in 1912 as an NCO) attacked another two-seater from close range, seeing the observer slump down hit, but then his engine began to fail forcing him to break off and head back. He just made it, crash-landing at Aizecourt-le-Haut. There are no recorded losses on the German side.

Strugnell was not yet out of the woods. Getting his engine going again he attempted a take-off only to hit a post with his propeller, which shattered. The area was covered with shell holes and he was unable to avoid a crash. The Pup was severely damaged. Men from the squadron came to the site and dismantled the machine, but that night, before they could move off, the parts were further damaged in a severe gale.

Another photo operation was mounted by 13 Squadron from Savy, 15 km to the west of Lens, the BE2d taking off at 0745. Forty-five minutes later, the pilot, Lieutenant Pat Powell, was turning for home and diving, having seen some Albatros DIIIs coming for him. Despite fire from his gunner, Air Mechanic Percy Bonner, the BE was hit from the fire of the leading Albatros and, out of control, the two-seater ploughed into a house near Farbus, north-east of Arras. The Albatros pilot had just scored his 32nd victory and his first of the month. By the end of April his score would have risen to 52; his name was Manfred von Richthofen, leader of Jasta 11. Both 'Tommies' were killed.

Their aircraft having failed to return, 13 Squadron sent off another BE at 0950, crewed by Lieutenant C F Jex and AM J H Bolton. They fared a little better than their earlier comrades in that they survived an attack by four enemy scouts, but in evading, they were driven into cloud, lost their way and finally put down at No.2 Squadron's base at Hesdigneul, south-west of Béthune – where they crashed. It would seem that the four enemy fighters were from Jasta 11, for Karl Allmenröder certainly claimed shooting down a BE at 0930, near Angres, south-west of Lens.

However, so that the reader can begin to understand how difficult it is sometimes to try and sort out who was shooting down whom, the problems with this particular combat are worth noting.

Leutnant Karl Allmenröder of Jasta 11, seated in his Albatros Scout, claimed a BE2 on the 2nd, his 6th victory. He achieved thirty by 30 June 1917, the date he fell in combat.

On the one hand we have a definite claim by Allmenröder that he brought down a BE at 0930, in the location mentioned above. However, the reader will have noted that Jex and Bolton were said to have taken off at 0950. As British and German times were the same at this period, we seem to have a time problem, unless they took off at 0850 and the records are in error! Or perhaps the German made his claim at 1030, which would fit the combat details. Added to this, Angres is right on the front line, so did Allmenröder believe his victim fell just inside German lines, in no man's land or on the British side? There is also a note that the number of the BE credited to Allmenröder was 7061; Jex was flying 2510, although 7061 is a BE number. There are no other losses reported on this day – certainly not a 7061 – and as we know, the BE was not lost in combat but crashed on landing at Hesdigneul. (Reference to the crash occurring at 23 Squadron's 'drome is wrong – 23 were at Baizieux, 60 km south of the action.)

At 0800, FE2ds of 57 Squadron took off from Fienvillers, 8 km south-west of Doullens, and no less than 50 km due west of the front lines, to fly a line patrol between Lens-Arras-Bapaume. At 0945 they were engaged by Jasta 11 just north of Douai, Richthofen's squadron being based at Douai-Brayelles. The six FEs were east of Arras when Jasta 11 came down on them, the pushers then flying south-west. However, it could be that the FEs had split up or did split, as Jasta 11 engaged part of the patrol to the north of Douai while the others headed south-west and ran into Jasta 2. The

Rittmeister Manfred von Richthofen, achieved twenty victories during April, bringing his score to fifty-two.

gunners put up a spirited return fire which hit two of the attacking Jasta 2 Albatri: Leutnant Erich König, a six-victory ace, had his machine set ablaze, crashing at Wancourt, while Leutnant Hans Wortmann (two victories) crashed at Vitry-en-Artois. If the locations are correct, Wortmann would have gone down first, south-west of Douai, and König later and further south-west. However, König was reported down at 0945 and Wortmann five minutes later. If Wortmann did go down first he would more likely have crashed at Vis-(not Vitry-)en-Artois which is just east of Wancourt.

However, what is not in question is that Jasta 2 lost two pilots. What is not certain is who got them. Lieutenant E E Pope and Lieutenant A W Naismith (A 1959) reported engaging the enemy machines but Naismith's gun jammed after one round. What is not known is if either of the 57 Squadron crews that were lost were successful before they fell, for 57 Squadron didn't get off scot-free. Two FEs were hit by Jasta 11 pilots, Leutnant Constantin Krefft (the Jasta's technical officer) and Vizefeldwebel Sebastian Festner shooting down one each. One fell at Oignies, 12 km north-west of Douai, the other south-east of Auby. The surviving four FEs began landing back at their base between 1020 and 1050. As they were doing so, 43 Squadron at Treizennes, south of Aire, were sending out six Sopwith 1½ Strutters led by Captain D C Rutter, to fly yet another photo op. Once over the lines they were in the territory of Jasta 11 and waiting for them were von Richthofen, his brother Lothar and Werner Voss.

Manfred von Richthofen, as leader, attacked first, managing to cut out one Strutter to the east of Vimy. The British pilot tried desperately to get into some nearby cloud but Richthofen's fire hit the fuel tank. With petrol spraying out and with the immediate danger of fire, Second Lieutenant A P Warren quickly put his machine down near Givenchy. Even so, his gunner, Sergeant Renel Dunn, who had been hit in the abdomen during the air attack, and undoubtedly knowing his wound was fatal, kept up a spirited return fire from his rear cockpit after the machine stopped, which hit von Richthofen's circling Albatros, he being just five metres up. Von Richthofen immediately dived on the grounded machine and shot it up. Whether he hit Dunn again is not known for certain – he certainly reported killing one of the occupants,

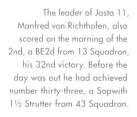

The leader of Jasta 11, Manfred von Richthofen, also scored on the morning of the 2nd, a BE2d from 13 Squadron, his 32nd victory. Before the day was out he had achieved number thirty-three, a Sopwith 1½ Strutter from 43 Squadron.

but Dunn would have died anyway, and was certainly dead when Richthofen's claim was verified. Peter Warren, a 19-year-old from Oxfordshire, was taken prisoner.

While this was going on, the others of 43 were still being engaged, Second Lieutenant C de Berigny and 2AM E Bowen claiming an Albatros Scout which they said fell in flames east of Vimy, but there is no recorded loss on the German side, and certainly not by Jasta 11.

Here the authors would like to point out again that while German personnel casualties are pretty accurate there is some doubt about aircraft losses, so it may well be that while there is no reported aircrew killed, the aircraft may well have been lost and the occupants escaped from a crash-landing. What does become apparent is the number of German aircraft seen burning and/or crashed which had no corresponding aircrew losses, which means either the pilot/crew survived, or the British pilot/crew were in fact seeing an Allied plane going down and believed it was a German.

Other German casualties that did occur this day were up on the northern part of the front, Leutnant Karl Haan of Flieger Abteilung 19 (FA19) being killed by anti-aircraft fire over Langmarck. The British flak position was around Pilkem, just to the west, which reported the two-seater falling in flames but only one crew member is reported dead. Further south, an Albatros CVII (2217/16) of FA48 was hit by flak during a sortie over the British lines and had to make a forced landing where the crew, Offizierstellvertreter F Meixner and Oberleutnant W Puckert, were taken prisoner. The two-seater – Albatros CVII 2217/16 – which was virtually intact, was given the RFC number of G.19.

Two BE2d aircraft from 2 Squadron were directing artillery west of Angres at 1030. Second Lieutenant E M Paul and Lieutenant L M Elworthy (5879) were attacked by two Halberstadt Scouts over Noeux-les-Mines, but the BE pilot rapidly dived away, as the two Germans then went for the other BE, flown by Second Lieutenants W J Stonier and H C W Strickland (6746). Again after a brief skirmish the two-seater crew escaped. BE crews were not always this lucky. Stonier, in fact, would not survive April 1917.

The German fighter pilots may not have been able to claim victories in this instant, but they had at least driven off the artillery flyers and stopped them from doing their work with the guns.

Top Second Lieutenant A P Warren piloted the 43 Squadron Strutter on 2 April. It was brought down and he became a prisoner and von Richthofen's 33rd victory. His observer was fatally wounded.
Bottom Leader of the 43 Squadron patrol on 2 April was Captain D C Rutter. He would go on to receive the Military Cross, but was killed in action on 7 June.

French Front

Again there is little to report from the French sectors apart from an observer in a Caudron being wounded by ground fire during a photo-reconnaissance sortie for VII Armée. The French ground gunners did, however, bring down an Albatros DIII of Jasta 35 (2107/16), the pilot, Vizefeldwebel Rudolf Nebel making a forced landing near Grossen Belchen where he became a prisoner. But he was not a prisoner for long. On 5 May 1917 he managed to escape and got back to Germany via Switzerland.

A Nieuport Scout pilot was lost during the day, when he force-landed inside the German lines for unknown reasons.

	A/C	KB		DES	OOC	KB
British losses	8	–	British claims	5†	2	–
French losses	–	–	French claims	1		–

| | | German claims | 7 | – | German losses | 4‡ | – |

† Three of the British claims were to AA fire.

‡ Again the Nachrichtenblatt records no losses, when four are not in dispute; two fighter pilots killed, one captured and a two-seater crew captured. In addition one two-seater crew man was killed.

British Casualties

Aircraft type	No.	Squadron	Crew	
FE2b	6953	22 Sqdn	2/Lt P A Russell	KIA
			Lt H Loveland	KIA
Nieuport XXIII	A6763	60 Sqdn	2/Lt V F Williams	KIA
Sopwith Pup	A639	54 Sqdn	Capt W V Strugnell	Safe
BE2d	5841	13 Sqdn	Lt P J G Powell	KIA
			1AM P Bonner	KIA
FE2d	A1944	57 Sqdn	Lt H P Sworder	KIA
			2/Lt A H Margoliouth	KIA
FE2d	A5151	57 Sqdn	Capt H Tomlinson MC	DOW
			Lt N C Denison	WIA/POW
BE2e	2510	13 Sqdn	2/Lt C F Jex	Safe
			2AM J H Bolton	Safe
Sop ½ Strutter	A2401	43 Sqdn	2/Lt A P Warren	POW
			Sgt R Dunn	KIA

French Casualties

Aircraft type	No.	Squadron	Crew	
Caudron G4		C.54	Lt Simonnet (O)	WIA
Nieuport XVII	2243	N.23	Adj Bertal	POW

03 APRIL 1917
M **T** W T F S S

British Front

If all the action on 2 April had occurred during the morning, then all the action of the 3rd was in the afternoon, due of course to the continuing bad weather. Heavy rain had set in during the afternoon of the 2nd, storms and low clouds lasting till noon on this Tuesday. So strong had been the winds that 29 Squadron had had two of its Nieuport Scouts overturn while taking off in gales but both pilots had been unhurt.

Activity on the ground centred around the British 7th Division's attack on Ecoust and the 4th and 5th Australian Divisions capture of Noreuil, the last positions before the Hindenburg Line itself. The cost was over 600 casualties to the Australians and 400 to the British – in what was described at the time as a 'minor skirmish'.

As soon as the weather improved, RFC machines were brought out of hangars and prepared for flight. Among the first off were FE2s of 11 Squadron to fly a recce mission, away at 1300. A808 did not get back, being reported shot down by AA fire, crashing over the enemy's side of the lines. Both crewmen were killed and anti-aircraft batteries Flakzug 28, 185 and 47 were credited with an FE shot down after scoring a direct hit on the pusher two-seater, south of Feuchy.

At 1355 hours 40 Squadron sent out seven Nieuports to escort a photo machine of 43 Squadron, both units based at Treizennes. Led by Captain Robert Gregory, some enemy aircraft were spotted east of Arras but they were out of range. However, Lieutenant E L 'Lobo' Benbow chased one which quickly disappeared while Lieutenant K Mackenzie engaged three near Arras but without result. The Germans were a patrol of Jasta 30, Leutnant Gustav Nernst claiming one of the Nieuports at 1440 over Esquerchin, east of Arras. He had picked off Second Lieutenant S A Sharpe RFA/RFC who crash-landed to be taken prisoner. It was Nernst's second victory.

More FEs were out mid-afternoon. To the south of the front 23 Squadron sent out a photo aircraft from Baizieux, while a patrol of 25 Squadron took off from Lozinghem, west of Béthune, on a photo op to Mericourt-Gavrelle at 1530. Just as they were getting airborne, the 23 Squadron machine was being engaged and brought down near Essarts. The 25 Squadron machines now flew into Jasta 11's territory and south of Lens ran into Richthofen's fighters. The Baron brought down one, Karl Emil Schäfer another, at 1615 and 1620 respectively. Sebastian Festner may have attacked another but his claim was not upheld.

Just minutes earlier five DH2s of 32 Squadron took off from Léalvillers, led by Captain William G Curphey MC. Over the front they were engaged by enemy fighters, losing one at 1630 – Lieutenant E L Heyworth – and in the subsequent fight, had another shot up. Lieutenant L W Barney struggled back to the lines, chased by an Albatros, and he eventually force-landed at 1700 hours inside British lines. So, who brought down these DH2s, and the 23 Squadron FE?

Edmund Nathanael of Jasta 5 claimed a 'Gitterrumpf' [lattice tail] north of Boursies, in front of the German lines, at 1635, while Vizefeldwebel Emil Eisenhuth of Jasta 3 claimed an FE at Hendécourt in British lines, 5 km due north of Lagnicourt, at 1655, Leutnant Adolf Schulte of Jasta 12 an FE due east of St Leger at 1710, also in British lines, and Sebastian Festner of Jasta 11, a DH2 unconfirmed at 1720 near Hendécourt.

Obviously Nathanael got Heyworth, Boursies being just to the east of Lagnicourt where the fight took place. Festner, who was either still in the air or had landed and taken off again, and Eisenhuth, probably went after Barney, so again his claim was not confirmed, but given to Eisenhuth. The 23 Squadron FE, piloted by Sergeant J A Cunniffe, had his gunner, 2AM J T Mackie, wounded, but got his machine down at Essarts, 20 km inside British lines, and well east of St Leger. Schulte said his FE went down north-east of St Leger, so in all probability he claimed this one, but there was no RFC loss, just a wounded gunner. Cunniffe had ten days to reflect on his narrow escape, before he would have a closer one!

While all this was going on, 15 Squadron at Léalvillers sent out another photo machine at 1625, which was shot down at 1730 near Croisselles by Hauptmann Paul von Osterroht, commander of Jasta 12. The Germans reported the BE down at Bullecourt, but both locations are right on the front line within a kilometre or so.

That really accounts for all the British losses, but there is one German claim outstanding, that of Unteroffizier Ludwig Weber of Jasta 3, who claimed a BE2e north-east of Brebières at 1450. There is no corresponding RFC loss for a BE, and Brebières is some 14 kilometres inside the German lines, just southwest of Douai.

The British only made one combat claim during the day, at 1435 hours. Sopwith 1½ Strutters of 43 Squadron were out and were attacked by some Albatros Scouts near Izel. Lieutenant Harold H Balfour and his gunner, Second Lieutenant A Roberts, claimed one which they reported falling in flames, but there is no reported loss of a German fighter pilot on the 3rd.

Also late in the day, Second Lieutenants G M Hopkins and 1AM Friend, 22 Squadron, who had taken off at 1620 in A5486 to fly a patrol over the 4th Army front, were forced to land near St Quentin after an attack by an enemy aircraft above the Hindenburg Line. They had been at the rear of the formation and had been hit from long range, the fuel tank being holed. They lost their engine and came down in the vicinity of Moislans, spending the night in a dug-out with front-line troops. Next morning, a party of men arrived and dismantled the FE and they all returned to their base.

The day ended with an attack upon the British balloon lines between 1910 and 1955. Once again it was Otto Bernert of Jasta 2 causing the mayhem, claiming one balloon burned at Ervillers at 1910 and a second north of Bapaume twelve minutes later, both some 10 kilometres inside British lines. The Germans did claim another just before 2000 hours but only two were lost on this evening, 13 and 18 KB Sections each losing their 'gasbag', although the observers jumped to safety.

Left Another 43 Squadron pilot was Lieutenant H H Balfour. He and his observer claimed a German Albatros on 3 April, his second of nine victories. He received the MC and post-war he became an MP and the Under-Secretary of State for Air. Later still, Lord Balfour of Inchrye.
Right Leader of Jasta 12 was Hauptmann Paul von Osterroht. He downed a BE2 on the 3rd, for his second victory, but increased this total to seven before April was out. He had learnt to fly in 1912, and in 1915 one of his observers had been Manfred von Richthofen. However, he was shot down and killed on 23 April in a fight with Sopwith Pups of 3 Naval Squadron. He is seen here with von Richthofen (left) during April 1917.

French Front

Escadrille Spa.67 had a Spad VII pilot, Caporal Bernard, wounded during the day but the exact circumstances are unclear. However, a two-seater crew of FA40, Leutnant Schumacher and Unteroffizier Scheinig, were engaged by what they said was a French Nieuport south of St Quentin and claimed they shot it down. Caporal Bernard force-landed near Noyon, south-west of this location but inside French lines, so perhaps it was him. The French made no claims.

	A/C	KB		DES	OOC	KB
British losses	6	2	British claims	1	–	–
French losses	–	–	French claims	–		–
German claims	10	3	German losses	–		–

Aircraft type	No.	Squadron	Crew	
FE2b	A808	11 Sqdn	Lt E T C Brandon	KIA
			2/Lt G Masters	KIA
Nieuport XVII	A6674	40 Sqdn	2/Lt S A Sharpe	POW
FE2d	A6371	25 Sqdn	Lt L Dodson MC	POW
			2/Lt H S Richards	DOW
FE2d	A6382	25 Sqdn	2/Lt D P MacDonald	POW
			2/Lt J I M O'Bierne	KIA
FE2b	4897	23 Sqdn	Sgt J A Cunniffe	Safe *
			2AM J T Mackie	WIA
DH2	A2536	32 Sqdn	Lt E L Heyworth	WIA/POW
DH2	A5012	32 Sqdn	Lt L W Barney	Safe *
BE2c	7236	15 Sqdn	2/Lt J H Sayer	KIA
			2/Lt V C Morris	POW
FE2b	A5486	22 Sqdn	2/Lt G M Hopkins	Safe *
			1AM H Friend	Safe

French Casualties

Spad VII		N.67†	Cpl Bernard	WIA *

† While some French fighter escadrilles were flying Spads, unit designations were not changed from N. to Spa. until the unit became fully equipped with Spads later in 1917.

04 APRIL 1917
M T **W** T F S S

British Front

The bad weather continued with low cloud and rain – 32 Squadron even reported a snow storm – which curtailed operations and only Jasta 4 at Douai saw any action. Leutnant Hans Klein gained his first of an eventual 22 victories by attacking a 12 Squadron BE2c which he shot down south of Arras at 0840, the two-seater crashing inside British lines. At 0905, Leutnant Hans Malchow brought down an 11 Squadron FE2b (his first and only victory), although the pilot of the 'Fee' managed to get over the lines before he force-landed, but German ground observers confirmed its apparent loss. 12 Squadron also had an observer wounded but his aircraft returned.

Nieuports of 40 Squadron took off for a line patrol at 0910, three aircraft patrolling the Lens-Bailleul line. Lieutenant E L Benbow had his petrol tank holed by ground fire which forced him to land at 2 Squadron's airfield at Hesdigneul at 1000.

Artillery aircraft successfully ranged guns onto several targets during the morning, before bad weather stopped virtually all flying.

There was an interesting incident up on the coast. Aircraft from the RNAS Dunkirk Seaplane base raided the sheds at Zeebrugge during the evening. Flight Sub Lieutenant Ernest John Cuckney dropped a 520-lb bomb and two 65 pounders from

2,800 ft at 2008 but he evidently knocked off his engine switch as the throttle would not answer when he tried to open it. He glided down, followed by a searchlight beam, and landed on the water a quarter of a mile from the Mole. He was on the sea for about eight minutes before tracing the cause of his trouble. By this time a large tug with a searchlight was fast approaching and came within hailing distance. He then got his engine going and took off in the nick of time. Cuckney went on to make several more raids during April.

French Front

Nothing to report.

	A/C	KB			DES	OOC	KB
British losses	2	–	British claims		–	–	–
French losses	–	–	.	French claims	–		–
German claims	2	–	German losses		–		–

British Casualties

Aircraft type	No.	Squadron	Crew		
BE2c	2563	12 Sqdn	2/Lt K C Horner	DOW	
			2/Lt A Emmerson	DOW	
FE2b	A832	11 Sqdn	Lt W Baillie	Safe	
			AM E Wood	Safe	
BE2c		12 Sqdn	Cpl A V Scholes (O)	WIA	•

05 APRIL 1917
M T W **T** F S S

British Front

The weather was misty and cloudy, but it had improved enough to bring forth aircraft from both sides to do battle as the build-up towards the Arras offensive got into its stride. Every headquarters needed photos of all sorts of things, so the observation squadrons were ordered up. With a retreat to new lines and the impending offensive against those new enemy positions – and the only maps came from photos – photo ops needed to be flown. And it was this day which can be said to have really started Bloody April.

It was also the day which saw the first operational sorties flown by the new Bristol Fighters, the BF2a machines of 48 Squadron. Great things were expected of this aircraft, and one of its flight commanders was none other than Captain W L Robinson VC (also known as Leefe Robinson) who had won his Victoria Cross for bringing down the German Schutte Lanz airship SL11 over north London on the night of 2/3 September 1916. The other two flight commanders on 48 Squadron were veteran DH2 pilots from 24 Squadron's epic battles over the Somme the previous summer – Captains Alan Wilkinson, an ace, and A T Cull. The deputy leaders of each flight were also veterans.

Designed as a two-seat fighter the BF2a went into action with entirely the wrong tactical concept. Instead of taking on enemy fighters with the pilot's front gun, leaving the observer/ gunner in the rear to ward off any attacking aircraft from behind, it had been decided, by Robinson, that if attacked, the Bristols would merely close up and let the combined fire from the rear-gunners force away the would-be attackers. Later, as the BF2b, and using more aggressive tactics, it was to become one of the most dangerous opponents for German aviators, but that was some months in the future.

However, on this April morning six Bristols of 48 Squadron, led by Robinson, took off from Bellevue at around 1000 for an offensive patrol to Douai. Their base was over 40 km from the front at Arras, and by the time they had gained height, crossed the lines and were well east of Douai, it was nearing 1100. Having been reported by the German ground observers, a telephone call to Jasta 11's base at Brayelles had von Richthofen's pilot taking off within minutes, led by the Baron himself.

Spotting the Albatros Scouts, the Bristol pilots closed up while the gunners waited for the range to decrease. Down came the five men of Jasta 11, Spandau machine guns blazing. First one then another Bristol was hit, dropping out of formation. Von Richthofen singled out one which he engaged, finally forcing it down near Lewarde, south-east of Douai. Having despatched Second Lieutenants Leckler and George, Richthofen chased after the other four, Festner already having knocked down Robinson's machine. He caught up with them over Douai and brought down Adams and Stewart near Cuincy, just west of Douai. Leutnant Georg Simon claimed the fourth, downed north of Monchecourt. The other two scraped over the lines, full of holes. The Bristol pilots, in all, claimed two of their attackers shot down but Jasta 11 were unharmed. Despite this disaster, the other two Flights set out in turn, according to orders, and claimed victories on each mission without loss.

Jasta 12 were also in the air to the south of Cambrai, engaged with FE2b pushers, but although Leutnants Röth and Otto Splitgerber were each credited with one brought down over Gouzeaucourt and Honnecourt at 1105 and 1110, both locations well inside German territory, it is difficult to know where the FEs came from. Two FEs were indeed lost this day, but one fell to Leutnant Schlenker of Jasta 3 south-west of Moeuvres at midday (and the correct number A805 is recorded by the Germans) which is 12-14 km north of Jasta 12's claims and nearly an hour later. Schlenker's FE was a machine from 23 Squadron on a photo op to Inchy and was correctly reported as lost between Inchy and Pronville.

The other FE lost was a machine from 18 Squadron, on a photo op of the 5th Army front. But it did not take off until 1105 and although attacked by enemy aircraft, the mortally wounded pilot brought it down on the British side near Bapaume. The only other pusher-types in action were a DH2 single-seater of 32 Squadron, shot up and damaged by three enemy fighters at an unknown time, and a 20 Squadron FE which force-landed at Abeele in the late morning, but that was way up on the Ypres part of the front. That was claimed by Leutnant Ernst Wiessner of Jasta 18 at 1145.

No.43 Squadron sent out a seven-man special recce mission at 1015 led by Major A S W Dore, from which Lieutenant F M Kitto and 2AM A W Cant had to return with engine trouble, Kitto crash-landing on Maison Bouche airfield just short of

Top On Thursday 5 April, 48 Squadron flew its first operations with the new BF2a two-seat fighters and ran into von Richthofen's Jasta 11. They suffered four losses, including the patrol's leader, Captain W L Robinson VC. He and his observer were shot down and taken prisoner.
Bottom Von Richthofen also brought down 2/Lt A N Leckler, who was also taken prisoner as well as wounded.

midday (A974). Seven or eight enemy fighters were spotted, which followed the formation from 1130 to 1150, finally making an attack near La Bassée. It was Jasta 30 that engaged the Strutters, Leutnant Nernst gaining his second victory of the month by bringing down one of them near Rouvroy at 1205. Lieutenants C R O'Brien and J L Dickson (A971) claimed one out of control, but Jasta 30 had no losses.

DH2s of 24 Squadron had mixed fortunes on a late morning OP, finding a two-seater doing artillery work, escorted by two, possibly three Albatros Scouts. A combat began between the five British fighters and the four German aircraft. Captain Kent was leading the DHs, attacking one enemy machine but another got on his tail and had to break off. The two-seater was seen on the tail of a DH and going down in a spinning nose-dive, which was Second Lieutenant J K Ross, brought down east of Honnecourt by Leutnant Wolluhn and Unteroffizier Mackeprang of FA(A)210. Lieutenant H W Woollett claimed to have downed this two-seater, but again there does not appear to be a loss, certainly not in personnel. Woollett reported the observer stopped firing after his attack and saw the machine crash one and a quarter miles east of Honnecourt.

FEs of 20 Squadron were in a fight over Belgium just before midday, having sent out two northern OPs at 0950 and 1047. On the first, Captain G J Mahony-Jones and Captain R M Knowles (in A1961) followed an Albatros Scout down to 700 feet in company with A29, Second Lieutenant Pike and AM Sayers. They were then attacked by nine fighters, Jones and Knowles claiming one down over Courtrai and later another over Houthulst after a running fight.

Meantime, the other three aircraft attacked two German planes over St Eloi at 10,000 feet. As already mentioned one FE (flown by 2/Lt J Lawson/Sgt Clayton – A1942) was badly shot up and landed at Abeele airfield. A second FE, equally shot up (2/Lt Hugh G White/Pvt T Allum – A6385) flopped down on Abeele, but they had just shot down an Albatros Scout and were feeling pleased with themselves.

The opposing Germans were pilots of Jasta 18; Leutnant Wiessner claimed an FE which was not credited, but the unit lost Leutnant Josef Flink, flying a DIII 1942/16. He was badly wounded in the hand by fire from Private Allum over Neuve Eglise, landed and was taken prisoner. His machine was given the number G.20.

Two Martinsyde G100s of 27 Squadron were brought down by ground fire further south on the French front around midday during a bomb raid on Hirson. Second Lieutenant W T B Tasker came down near Origny, due to engine failure, where he burnt his machine before being captured, Second Lieutenant M Johnstone crashing 12 miles east of Compiègne but inside French lines. Flakzug 407 and Flakbatts 4 and 64 claimed Tasker, while the other Martinsyde was seen to land at La Bouteille. Ground fire also accounted for two BEs of 13 Squadron on photo ops. Second Lieutenant G E Brookes and 2AM J H Bolton fell over Duissans on the British side, while Lieutenants O G F Ball and H Howell-Evans were unlucky enough to be hit by friendly fire and came down over St Catherine.

The Nieuports of 60 Squadron made a balloon attack just after midday, going for a 'drachen' near Cambrai. Lieutenant E J D Townsend, a Canadian from Vancouver, failed to return, later being reported severely wounded and a prisoner, to unknown ground fire.

The afternoon was fairly quiet, but it picked up in a last flurry in the early evening. A 29 Squadron Nieuport XXIII, part of an OP flown at 1810, was shot down. Vizefeldwebel Karl Menckhoff of Jasta 3 claimed a Nieuport just west of Athies which is in the right area. Lieutenant N A Birks was wounded and taken prisoner and he later reported that he was visited by his victor, who was of 'sergeant-major' rank – Vizefeldwebel.

The final loss of the day was from 6 Naval Squadron. Its pilots claimed one Albatros Scout in flames and two out of control by Flight Lieutenant E W Norton and Flight Sub Lieutenant A L Thorne, although Norton had to make a forced landing at Bouquemaison at 1700 hours. One of their Nieuport XVIIs was brought down between Arras and Cambrai at 1845, Flight Sub Lieutenant R K Slater being taken prisoner, by Leutnant Eberhard Voss of Jasta 20, who claimed his victim near Omissy. 6 Naval had another Nieuport shot up, Flight Sub Lieutenant M R Kingsford being injured when he crash-landed.

Twenty-nine enemy aircraft were claimed by the RFC and RNAS during this day, but again there is a lack of any evidence on the German side of losses. The Nachrichtenblatt finally acknowledged one loss which must be presumed to be that of Flink of Jasta 18. Other than a pilot of FA6 being killed in a landing accident at Courtrai, the only other personnel losses were Leutnant Karl Hummel killed at Ghent, Unteroffizier Albin Nietzold killed at St Marie and Gefreiter Simon Metzger killed at Mont d'Origny, units unknown, and they may not have been combat casualties.

While pilots of 18, 24, 25, 1 and 8 Naval Squadrons all made claims between 1200 and 1245, all eight were out of control victories over Albatros or Halberstadt Scouts. A patrol of 54 Squadron also claimed a balloon destroyed at Gouy. As the pilots flew back at low level, Captain R G H Pixley fired at a horse and rider, seeing both fall, while Captain F N Hudson opened up on 100 soldiers unloading boxes from open trucks outside a railway station. Some were seen to fall as the rest scattered in all directions.

During the evening flurry, 60 Squadron claimed an Albatros destroyed and two out of control in the Riencourt area, 29 Squadron claimed three Albatros Scouts out of control between Douai and Vitry-en-Artois, while a 12 Squadron crew claimed an Albatros DII as destroyed.

French Front

Little to report, other than a Caudron GIV lost over Sillery, south-east of Reims, shot down by Leutnant Albert Dossenbach, Staffelführer of Jasta 36. It was the Jasta's first confirmed kill. Three single-seaters were in combat, one pilot being wounded near Lure, while Lieutenant de Mortemart of N.23 was forced to land after a fight near Verdun, but was unharmed. The Frenchman may have been Caporal Alfred Guyot of N.81. He received the Médaille Militaire on this day, following a fight with five hostile scouts, during which he was badly wounded. He force-landed in the front lines but had the strength to vacate his aircraft and regain French lines.

Leutnant Hans Auer of Jasta 26 claimed a Nieuport at Sennheim at 1806 which came down inside German lines, but it is not certain who the pilot was, although Caporal Hérubel of Spa.78 was brought down at Jonchère.

	A/C	KB		DES	OOC	KB
British losses	15	–	British claims	7†	22	1
French losses	3	–	French claims	–		–
German claims	18‡	–	German losses	1		?

† Including one captured.
‡ Including two by ground fire.

British Casualties

Aircraft type	No.	Squadron	Crew	
BF2a	A3337	48 Sqdn	Capt W L Robinson VC	POW
			2/Lt E D Warburton	POW
BF2a	A3320	48 Sqdn	Lt H A Cooper	POW/WIA
			2/Lt A Boldison	POW/WIA
BF2a	A3343	48 Sqdn	Lt A T Adams	POW/WIA
			Lt D J Stewart	POW/WIA
BF2a	A3340	48 Sqdn	2/Lt A N Leckler	POW/WIA
			2/Lt H D K George	POW/DOW
Sop ½ Strutter	A1073	43 Sqdn	2/Lt C P Thornton	POW
			2/Lt H D Blackburn	KIA
DH2	A2592	24 Sqdn	2/Lt J K Ross	POW/DOW
FE2b	A805	23 Sqdn	Lt L Elsley	KIA
			2/Lt F Higginbottom	DOW
FE2b	4967	18 Sqdn	Lt H A R Boustead	DOW
			2/Lt C G R Mackintosh	KIA
Martinsyde G100	A1578	27 Sqdn	2/Lt M Johnstone	Safe
Martinsyde G100	7485	27 Sqdn	2/Lt W T B Tasker	POW
BE2d	5787	13 Sqdn	2/Lt G E Brookes	WIA
			2AM J H Bolton	KIA
BE2d	2520	13 Sqdn	2/Lt O F G Ball	KIA
			Lt H Howell-Evans	KIA
Nieuport XVII	A6693	60 Sqdn	Lt E J D Townesend	POW/WIA
Nieuport XVII	N3202	6N Sqdn	FSL R K Slater	POW
Nieuport XVII	N3187	6N Sqdn	FC E W Norton	Safe

Aircraft type	No.	Squadron	Crew		
Nieuport DVII	N3191	6N Sqdn	FSL M R Kingsford	Inj	*
Nieuport XXIII	A6791	29 Sqdn	Lt N A Birks	POW/WIA	

		French Casualties		
Caudron GIV	C.39	Lt d'Héricourt	KIA	
		Sgt Mathieu	KIA	
Nieuport Scout	N.23	Lt de Mortemart	Safe	*
Spad VII	N.81	Cpl A Guyot	WIA	
Spad VII	N.78	Cpl J Hérubel	DOW	

06 APRIL 1917
M   T   W   T   **F**   S   S

British Front

Today was Good Friday. Parties to celebrate were reported in many locations despite the obvious build-up – or even because of it. Generally these sorts of things were for civilians in Britain, not for the men facing death and destruction in holes in the ground but whenever possible a chance of normality was taken. It could be their last.

The men knew too something was in the wind. There was to be an offensive soon. All the signs were there: troops moving up, supplies being brought forward, commanders going off to briefings and sergeant-majors checking that kit and rifles were in order. Some of the senior officers knew more than they were telling; the foot soldier who would have to go over the top would be the last to know. It was not that they could not be trusted, but both sides often tried to snatch a prisoner during a trench raid when things looked as if they were about to happen, in the hope of information.

RFC Headquarters were still tasked with bringing in useful aerial photographs of the enemy's positions, while hostile batteries needed to be sighted and shelled. Over the two days 5-6 April, some 1,700 aerial photographs were taken while bombing aircraft raided German aerodromes on 17 occasions. The weather both helped a little and hindered, for the morning was fine, rain and cloud not putting a dampener on things until the afternoon. Therefore most of the aerial activity was confined to the morning – a particularly busy morning, and for many flyers their last.

The first loss of the day came at 0800, a 1 Naval Squadron Sopwith Triplane going down amid bursting AA fire south-west of Moeuvres. The OP, led by Flight Lieutenant T F N Gerrard, had left Chipilly at 0630. Flight Sub Lieutenant N D M Hewitt's machine is presumed to have been hit and was seen circling Doignies and failed to get to the lines before he was forced down and taken prisoner. He was claimed by Flakbatterie 505 at Lagnicourt, two kilometres from Doignies.

In some accounts, N D M Hewitt is supposed to have been shot down by Karl Schäfer of Jasta 11, but Schäfer (a) did not score until 1020, (b) his victim fell at Givenchy some 32 kilometres to the north-east of Doignies and (c) it was a BE2 not a Triplane. Another classic case of someone not looking at a map or taking account of the hour.

In any event, this was the first Sopwith Triplane to fall to the enemy although it had been around in limited numbers for some weeks. Indeed, the prototype, N500, was being used at the front the previous July with 1 Naval Squadron. The design so impressed the Germans that Anthony Fokker, the Dutch designer building aircraft for the Germans (his services having earlier been rejected by the British and French) produced one of the most well-known fighters of WW1 later that summer, the Fokker Dr1 Triplane.

At Le Hameau the FE2b pushers of 11 Squadron were up early, sending out a reconnaissance sortie to the Arras area at 0735. FE2s of 25 Squadron flew a protection patrol, taking off at 0743, and were involved in the same fight as 11 Squadron. Over the front a fighter was encountered which attacked FE 7025 flown by Second Lieutenants D P Walter and C Brown, slightly wounding the pilot, forcing him to crash in a forced landing near Gavrelle at 0900.

The Germans were alive to all the sudden activity of the last 24 hours and on the alert. They sent off Jasta 4 from Douai led by Wilhelm Frankl, who had already claimed his first victim of the day. Frankl had shot down a night-flying FE2b at 0230 during a night raid by 100 Squadron. His victim had fallen at Quiery le Motte, his 15th kill of the war.

Victories over night raiders were rare in WW1, this one being the first by a German fighter aircraft. The difficulties in finding a hostile aircraft in a black sky when radio and radar aids were still in the far distant future were immense. Even an experienced flyer such as Frankl would find it hard, but he had done it this night, and must have been on a 'high', for today he would add a further three day victories to his tally. He already had the Pour le Mérite, awarded when his score had reached eight in August 1916.

Now, just on 0850, he saw the FEs east of Arras and led the attack. The two-seaters closed up but already Frankl was firing at one, hitting not only the engine but also the gunner. Crippled, the FE went down, its pilot making a crash landing at Feuchy. Frankl was already firing at another which also went down, glided over the front line to crunch into the ground by the Arras-St Pol road, its crew scrambling safely from the wreckage. A third FE, shot up by either Frankl or one of his men, also headed down as it flew back over the trenches to make a forced landing at 0900, its pilot wounded. The Jasta, and Frankl, were credited with two victories.

Other FEs were in trouble just to the south of this action, 57 Squadron having sent out six from Fienvillers at 0700, led by Captain A C Wright to fly an OP between Somain, west of Valenciennes, and Beauvois, south-east of Cambrai. One FE left this formation at 0820 with engine trouble, leaving five to continue. At 0800 the FE crews spotted ten two-seaters south of Douai and attacked. Wright came in behind one of them, but the German observer put bullets into his FE and he was hit in the knee, just as the two-seater began to dive after being hit by the FE's bullets. Several single-seaters now joined in. Oberleutnant Adolf von Tutschek of Jasta Boelcke made an attack on them ten minutes later and claimed one brought down near Anneux, just to the south-west of Cambrai, while the others tried to fight their way out of trouble.

Von Tutschek was not immediately credited with this kill and it was only when Leutnant Werner Voss confirmed that von Tutschek's fire had done the initial damage that the latter was given credit. Adding to the confusion is that the FE in question

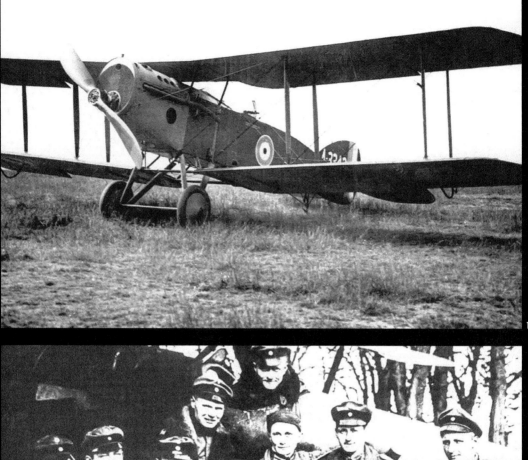

1 BF2a A3343, von Richthofen's 36th victory, in German hands.
2 The pilots of Jasta 11, with Manfred von Richthofen in the cockpit of the Albatros Scout. L to R standing: Karl Allmenröder, Hans Hinsch, Sebastian Festner, Emil Schäfer, Kurt Wolff, Georg Simon, Otto Brauneck. Front: Karl Esser, Constantin Krefft and Lothar von Richthofen in front.
3 One of von Bertrab's two Sopwith victories, a machine from 45 Squadron which crashed after colliding with another Sopwith whilst under attack from the German ace. Both crews died, the observer of this one (A2381) drowning in this water feature.
4 Leutnant Wilhelm Frankl, leader of Jasta 4, was credited with four victories on 6 April, three FE2s and a BE2c. The first was downed during the hours of darkness, and these brought his score to nineteen. Already the holder of the Orden Pour le Mérite, he was to shoot down one more British aeroplane on the 7th. However, on the 8th he fell in combat with the BF2a machines of 48 Squadron.
5 Leutnant Joachim von Bertrab of Jasta 30 downed two Martinsyde G100s on the morning of the 6th. Two hours later he shot down two Sopwith two-seaters, making four kills in one day.
6 Another German, and future 'ace' in action on the 6th was Adolf von Tutschek of Jasta Boelcke. He was credited with his second victory on this date, but would go on to score a total of twenty-seven victories by March 1918, when he was killed in action.
7 Two Albatros Scouts of Jasta 5 collided on the 6th, both their pilots falling to their death. However, one was the leader of the Jasta, Hans Berr, one of the early German aces having scored ten victories in 1916 flying Fokker Eindeckers

8

9

8 Jacobs' Albatros Scout in a line-up of Jasta 22 machines. His is the one marked 'Kobes' in the centre.

9 The wrecked 40 Squadron Nieuport XVII (A6667) flown by 2/Lt H S Pell, and brought down by flak on 6 April whilst attacking German balloons. Pell's body can be seen to the right.

10 A Spad VII from Spa.31, brought down by Heinrich Bongartz on the 6th, for his first of thirty-three victories. The pilot, Lieutenant Jean Mistarlet was taken prisoner and his Spad, shown here with his Escadrille motif, was marked with German crosses and no doubt test flown by German pilots.

11 Canadian Captain C M Clement of 22 Squadron shot down an Albatros DIII in flames on the 6th, probably a machine from Jasta 20, although it was shared with other crews of his patrol. By

mid-August his victory tally stood at fourteen, including four claims on the 14th, but he was killed in action five days later, brought down by AA fire.

12 Leutnant Walter Göttsch of Jasta 8 scored his seventh victory on the 6th, a 20 Squadron FE2b. He would down two more British machines in April and by April 1918 had achieved twenty victories. Leading Jasta 19 in 1918 he was shot down moments after gaining his twentieth kill and died in the crash.

13 Leutnant Josef Jacobs of Jasta 22, shot down a French observation balloon on the evening of the 6th, for his fourth victory, although it was unconfirmed. Jacobs would survive the war with forty-eight victories and the Pour le Mérite. He would gain two more victories during April, both confirmed.

10

11

12

13

was numbered A22 (Schreiber and Lewis), whereas somehow, von Tutschek's victim was recorded as A6. The confusion clears when one knows that A6 was the letter and number of an 'A' Flight machine from 57 Squadron, and nothing to do with the aircraft's serial number. (Even this leaves a slight question for the details of Captain Wright's fight do tally with Tutschek's combat, although perhaps there were two FEs seen going down with dead engines and being engaged by other fighters.)

Within minutes other Jasta 12 pilots were attacking the FEs again, one going down to the Staffelführer, von Osterroht, another to Leutnant Otto Splitgerber. Meantime Jasta 5 pilots had joined the fray, Edmund Nathanael claiming one at Douchy, south-west of Valenciennes, and Heinrich Gontermann another at Neuville just two kilometres further south-west. Parts of the aircraft numbers of these latter two claims were A6... for Nathanael and 1959 for Gontermann. Gontermann was later photographed in 'A4', which was A1959, so A6388 was that which Nathanael brought down.

Wright's FE was hit in the radiator, and it was not long before the FE's engine quit, the wounded Wright starting a long glide to the lines four miles away. As Wright was going down with a dead engine, two pilots of Jasta 12 spotted him and attacked. The FE crew steepened their dive, bullets being heard hitting the useless engine behind them. Finally, at low level and still gliding, Wright and Private Sibley came under small-arms fire from German soldiers, Wright being hit again, this time in the thigh, but he scraped over the trenches, force-landing 50 yards in front of some Australian outposts.

For once the Germans didn't get off without injury, for Splitgerber's fighter was hit over Thiaut and he was wounded but got back. But by far the most serious loss occurred when two pilots of Jasta 5 collided north of Noyelles. Both men fell to their death: Vizefeldwebel Paul Hoppe and the Staffelführer, Oberleutnant Hans Berr, holder of the Pour le Mérite with ten victories.

If any of the FE gunners thought they'd caused the collision, none were in a position to put in a claim as none of 57 Squadron got back except for the earlier abort, and only Captain Wright and his observer lived to fight another day, having crashed just inside British lines after their fight with von Osterroht. This would not be the only occasion during April where complete, or almost complete, formations would be annihilated by the Jasta pilots.

It would seem that German anti-aircraft guns also fired on these FEs, three being claimed over the Anneux and Lagnicourt areas but these were all the same as the fighter pilots shot down. No doubt Wright's was one such joint claim.

Even as 57 Squadron's patrol was being annihilated, four Martinsydes of 27 Squadron were being engaged up on the northern part of the front during a bombing raid on Ath in Belgium, 80 km behind the front line. Once more it was Jasta 30 that made the interception, Leutnant Joachim von Bertrab shooting down two of the G100s over Ath at 0815, and south of Leuze at 0830, both British pilots being killed.

Captain A J M Clarke, who led the raid, made out a combat report on his return, which gives a vivid description of the German tactics:

> 'Over Ath at 5,000 ft, machine guns were heard and on looking behind pilot saw one Martinsyde going down with one Halberstadt on its tail. This machine was last seen out of control in a spin close to the ground. The HA [hostile aircraft] then hovered above the formation while height was lost to 2,300 ft

to drop the bombs. Formation then rendezvoused very quickly after bombing but hostile machines – at least three and probably more – kept up above in the sun, firing bursts at intervals.

'Eventually one dived on to the formation. Pilot engaged with the rear gun. The HA shot down the rear machine of the formation which went down in flames, and then, being fired on, kept up above the formation, firing occasional shots. The hostile formation kept up above and did not attack at close range and finally left the two remaining Martinsydes at Tournai.'

It seems that all the FE units were over the front that morning, 22 Squadron operating on the southern end of the British front, escorted by the Pups of 54 Squadron. At 0730, Captain F N Hudson of 54 attacked and shot down a two-seater over Le Catelet, confirmed by three men of 22 Squadron. Half an hour later, the Pups were engaged by some fighters above St Quentin, one attacking Lieutenant S G Rome MC. Lieutenant Oliver Stewart (A6156) fired at the Albatros at close range and it went down out of control, confirmed by Captain Hudson and Lieutenant Rome to have crashed.

Then the BE2s began flying photo ops over the front, giving the Jasta pilots more target practice. First away was a machine of 8 Squadron but at 0930 it was being shot down by German fighters, credit going to Frankl of Jasta 4 whose victim fell north of Boiry at 0955. The next one was a 15 Squadron BE, driven down into British territory where it was destroyed by German shelling.

Second Lieutenants A H Vinson and E L Gwilt had been engaged by six enemy scouts over Bullecourt while taking photographs. During the combat both pilot and observer opened fire on their attackers, driving off five of the Germans but one continued the action. Vinson dived headlong earthwards, going over the vertical at which time both Lewis guns fell overboard. As the Albatros pumped bullets into the BE, three bullets grazed Vinson's face, while two more slashed through Gwilt's glove. Others pierced the petrol tank but thankfully did not ignite the fuel. The fight and pursuit lasted half an hour, until Vinson managed to scrape over the lines and put down near Lagnicourt. The Albatros had followed the BE down, firing all the time. As the two men leaped from the BE and took cover in a shell hole the German pilot came down and strafed the BE. The Albatros was finally driven off by ground fire, but then enemy artillery opened up; before the machine was hit by the falling 8" shells, Vinson ran to it and retrieved the photographic plates and camera, which later produced good pictures of Bullecourt and the Hindenburg Line.

The German pilot was Werner Voss of Jasta 2, who returned to Pronville having secured his 24th victory. Voss almost got his 25th too, for he was also in combat with a 54 Squadron Pup (A6165), flown by future ace Second Lieutenant R M Foster. Hit by the German pilot, Foster got across the lines and force-landed near Lagnicourt without injury to himself.

No. 2 Squadron had two BEs up, one on a photo op to Lieven, the other doing artillery work with the 52nd Siege Battery. The first, with Captain V J Whittaker in the pilot's seat, was shot down by a fighter over Lieven at 1015 and fell in flames, probably by Karl Schäfer of Jasta 11. The other BE was chased away by enemy fighters.

The fourth BE loss of the morning came from 16 Squadron doing artillery observation east of Neuville St Vaast. They were attacked by a fighter, their machine falling in flames near Thelus at 1030, again brought down by Karl Schäfer, whose two BE claims were made over Givenchy at 1020, and south-west of Vimy at 1037.

The air was full of aeroplanes at this time, or perhaps it is more correct to say full of falling aeroplanes. 45 Squadron had sent out a formation of Strutters at 0910 to do a recce over Lille, which were attacked by Jasta 30. The attack so upset the British formation that two of the two-seaters collided, then a third was knocked down by machine-gun fire. Hans Bethge received credit for one Strutter (7806), von Bertrab the two that had collided (A1093 and A2381), which made four victories for von Bertrab on this day.

The RE8s of 59 Squadron headed for Vitry-en-Artois at 0935 on a recce sortie, only to be intercepted by pilots of Jastas 2, 3 and 11. Kurt Wolff of Jasta 11 shot one down over Bois Bernard at 1015, Jasta 3's Karl Menckhoff sending a second down over Fampoux at the same time. Finally, Bernert of Jasta Boelcke brought down a third RE over Roux on the Scarpe River.

By this time, to the north, more FEs were out, 20 Squadron mounting a bomb raid with ten aircraft, against Ledeghem between Ypres and Courtrai. Jasta 8 intercepted them and a running fight ensued between 1000 and 1020. The Fees claimed four shot down, two destroyed and two out of control, one over Ledeghem and three south of Roulers, one being seen to crash in a field when hit by Second Lieutenant E O Perry and Private Allum (A6370). The other claims were all made by the crew of Second Lieutenants E J Smart and H N Hampson (A3). Jasta 8 had no fatalities.

Leutnant Walter Göttsch shot down A6358 north of Polygon Wood, while AM Sayers, a gunner flying in A29, was wounded. FE A3 was also hit and force-landed on the right side of the lines, while A5147 was badly shot up but the pilot got down safely on Bailleul airfield.

The second Sopwith Triplane loss of the day came shortly after noon, 1 Naval flying an OP at 0956. Late in the patrol, they ran into Jasta 12 near Hénin-Liétard, Hauptmann Paul von Osterroht claiming Flight Sub Lieutenant L M B Weil shot down, who crashed near Malakow station. While it was the second Triplane lost, it was the first brought down by a German pilot as well as the second kill of the day for the commander of Jasta 12.

British airmen were heavily engaged on this Good Friday, and although there was still a good deal of over-claiming, at least some Germans did come down. Again the number of aircraft actually lost is difficult to find but apart from the three fighter pilots already mentioned, Jasta 3 had Unteroffizier Ludwig Weber wounded in an Albatros DII (510/16), brought down near Biache on the Scarpe, possibly one of the two Albatros Scouts claimed out of control by 48 Squadron to the north-east of Arras.

The FEs of 25 Squadron also claimed two fighters shot down mid-morning, during a photo op over Farbus Wood and an assault by 14 Halberstadt and Albatros Scouts. Second Lieutenants A Roulstone and E G Green (A813) claimed an Albatros DIII in flames over Givenchy at 1030 just after it had shot down a BE in flames. Shortly afterwards Second Lieutenant B King and Corporal L Emsden claimed a Halberstadt DII destroyed east of Vimy. An FE was shot up; Second Lieutenant R G Malcolm and Lieutenant D E Holmes (4997) had to force-land by No.9 KBS at Bray.

Vizefeldwebel Reinhold Wurzmann of Jasta 20 was seen to fall in flames near Maray (or Marcy, east of St Quentin), probably the DIII claimed destroyed by

Captain C M Clement and his gunner Second Lieutenant L G Davies, in a 22 Squadron FE at 0800 by St Quentin. This squadron was on a photo-recce job southeast of Gouy when seven enemy fighters attacked and in the fight, one was sent down to land near Lesdins while a second spun away out of control. Another German casualty this day was Flieger Josef Eicholz, unit unknown, killed at Fampoux.

Two-seaters were also in evidence, 23 Squadron claiming one as early as 0730, the victor being Captain Ken McCallum, a Canadian (Spad A6709). Captain F N Hudson sent another down out of control near Le Catelet a few minutes later, while 24 Squadron claimed one out of control near Havrincourt Wood. The Germans had two-seaters come down at Lecluse (FA233, Vizefeldwebel Siegfried Thiele and Leutnant Karl Seyberth both killed) and another near Quéant (FA(A)263, Unteroffizier Rudolf Temler and Leutnant Julius Schmidt both killed). FA221 also had a machine shot up and forced to land, flown by Feldwebel Hans Donhauser and Leutnant W Wolter. Donhauser later became a fighter pilot, ending the war with 19 victories. FA(A)243 also lost a crew at Colmar, on the southern French front, near the Swiss border, although this is not believed to be a combat loss.

Curiously, 18 Squadron's FEs also claimed two Albatros Scouts, one being noted as captured at Ecoust St Mein, but there is no record of it and certainly no G-number was issued on this day, nor is it mentioned in the RFC War Diary. A 12 Squadron BE was attacked by a fighter and was reported falling in flames.

The balloon at Sallaumines, just east of Lens was ordered to be attacked and it was claimed as destroyed at 1000 by Lieutenant H C Todd of 40 Squadron (A6677) near Neuvireuil, who hit it with three Le Prieur rockets from ten yards; the observer took to his parachute. However, Second Lieutenant H S Pell was brought down by ground fire (MFlak 60) and killed during this foray. His replacement in C Flight that evening was Lieutenant Edward 'Mick' Mannock.

The Naval pilots of 1, 3 and 6 Naval Squadron were engaged during the morning claiming a number of victories but it is difficult to reconcile them with reported losses, certainly with regard to German pilot casualties.

French Front

French fighter pilots were ranged against hostile balloons in an attempt to blind the Germans' view of the build-up for the coming offensive. Adjutant Gustave Douchy of Escadrille N.38 claimed two during the day, one at Hauvine, and a second at Montchâlons at 1800 hours. Sous Lieutenant Emile Régnier of N.112 flamed one at Époye. The other two were shot down by Brigadier Pierre Leroy de Boiseaumarie of N.78 at Ardeuil and Lieutenant Mistarlet of N.31 at Lavannes.

The Jasta pilots were alive to the sudden increase in activity and shot down a number of French aeroplanes. Caudrons were brought down by Oberleutnant Rudolf Berthold of Jasta 14, Vizefeldwebel Georg Strasser of Jasta 17 and Leutnant Walter Böning of Jasta 19. Four Caudrons were in fact lost during the day, with the observer of a fifth wounded. Farmans were also claimed by Leutnant Dieter Collin of Jasta 22 near Terny-Sorny and Leutnant Kreuzner of Jasta 13 (Collin's not being confirmed), the French losing at least one, with another hit by ground fire, its pilot being wounded. A Sopwith two-seater was also lost, the machine making a forced landing north of Laon. Berthold's victim was numbered 1559, which corresponds to a Caudron R4 lost by Escadrille F.35 near Malvel.

Two Spads were also claimed, one by Leutnant Bongartz of Jasta 36 and one (a delayed confirmation) by Leutnant Baldamus of Jasta 9, although no Spads are recorded as lost in surviving records. A Nieuport and another Caudron were claimed by two-seater crews from FA228 and FA212.

Leutnant Josef Jacobs of Jasta 22 shot down a French balloon of 21 Cié at Blanzy-Vailly at 1930 for his fourth victory of an eventual 48. Jasta 22 had taken off at 1905 because French fighters had burned a balloon right over their own airfield at Laon, and they wanted revenge. Jacobs found his balloon amid rain clouds, attacked and watched it erupt in flames as he flew off while the observer parachuted down.

	A/C	KB		DES	OOC	KB
British losses	24	–	British Claims	13	15	1
French losses	6	1	French Claims	–		5
German claims	40†	1	German losses	6‡		2

† Includes six by ground fire. ‡ Nachrichtenblatt admits five.

British Casualties

Aircraft type	No.	Squadron	Crew		
FE2b	7714	100 Sqdn	2/Lt A R M Rickards	POW	
			2AM E W Barnes	POW	
FE2b	A811	11 Sqdn	Sgt F H Evans	POW	
			2AM E Wood	KIA	
FE2b	A5000	11 Sqdn	2/Lt D S Kennedy	Safe	
			2AM J F Carr	Safe	
FE2b	7025	25 Sqdn	2/Lt D P Walter	WIA	*
			2/Lt C Brown	Safe	
Sop Triplane	N5457	1N Sqdn	FSL N D M Hewitt	POW	
BE2c	A2879	8 Sqdn	Lt G J Hatch	KIA	
			Cpl E Langridge	KIA	
BE2c	A3157	15 Sqdn	2/Lt A H Vinson	Safe	
			2/Lt E L Gwilt	Safe	
Martinsyde G100	7465	27 Sqdn	2/Lt J R S Proud	POW/DOW	
Martinsyde G100	7478	27 Sqdn	Lt J H B Wedderspoon	KIA	
FE2d	A1959	57 Sqdn	Lt T F Burrill	POW	
			Pvt F Smith	POW/WIA	
FE2d	A22	57 Sqdn	Lt T B Schreiber	POW	
			2/Lt M Lewis	POW	
FEbd	A21	57 Sqdn	Lt D C Birch	POW	
			Lt J K Bousfield MC	POW	
FE2d	A6388	57 Sqdn	2/Lt H D Hamilton	POW/WIA	
			Pvt E Snelling	POW/WIA	
FE2d	A1952	57 Sqdn	Capt A C Wright	WIA	
			Pvt R Sibley	Safe	
FE2d	A6358	20 Sqdn	2/Lt R Smith	KIA	
			Lt R Hume	KIA	
Sop 1½ Strutter	A1093	45 Sqdn	Lt J A Marshall	KIA	
			2/Lt F G Truscott MC	KIA	

Aircraft type	No.	Squadron	Crew	
Sop 1½ Strutter	A2381	45 Sqdn	2/Lt C StG Campbell	KIA
			Capt D W Edwards MC	KIA
Sop 1½ Strutter	7806	45 Sqdn	2/Lt J E Blake	KIA
			Capt W S Brayshay	KIA
RE8	A3206	59 Sqdn	Lt C F Bailey	KIA
			2AM V N Barrie	KIA
RE8	A3421	59 Sqdn	2/Lt A C Pepper	POW
			Lt W L Day	KIA
RE8	A112	59 Sqdn	2/Lt R W M Davies	KIA
			2/Lt J C D Wordsworth	KIA
BE2d	5834	2 Sqdn	Capt V J Whittaker	KIA
			2/Lt A R Brown	KIA
BE2c	6823	16 Sqdn	Lt O R Knight	KIA
			2/Lt U H Seguin	KIA
Nieuport XVII	A6667	40 Sqdn	2/Lt H S Pell	KIA
BEC2		7 Sqdn	2AM C G Mitchinson (O)	KIA (shellfire) *
Triplane	N5448	1N Sqdn	FSL L M B Weil	KIA

French Casualties

Caudron R4		R.210	Sgt Gauron	WIA
			S/Lt Cazier (O)	KIA
			Pvt Brasseur (AG)	KIA
Caudron G4		C.227	Sgt Lafaille	WIA
			S/Lt Vrolyck	KIA
Caudron G4		C.224	S/Lt E Sommier	KIA
			S/Lt R Jouvenot	KIA
Sopwith two-seater		N.62	MdL A Clerisse (O)	MIA
Caudron G4		C.220	Lt Berquet (O)	WIA *
Farman 60		F.208	Capt P Grimault	WIA
			S/Lt C Feltin	WIA
Caudron G4	1559	F35	S/Lt P Desbordes	MIA
			Lt J Borgoltz (O)	MIA
			Sol A Lebleu (AG)	MIA
Farman 61		F.211	Sgt Valence (P)	WIA *
Spad VII		N.31	Lt J Mistarlet	POW

07 APRIL 1917

British Front

After the blood-letting of the previous day, the 7th was quieter, despite the nearness of the offensive, but due no doubt to the low cloud and rain which persisted throughout much of the day.

Reconnaissance aircraft still went out, one machine of 16 Squadron making a valuable recce from 500 feet, facilitated by an effective shrapnel barrage by Canadian artillery. German batteries were still subjected to artillery fire with observations from Corps aeroplanes, 57 targets being dealt with.

Offensive patrols were flown between the showers, 1 Squadron losing a Nieuport on the 0842 special mission to attack a balloon, with Lieutenant Robert J Bevington brought down by marauding fighters of Jasta 8, Hauptmann Hans von Hünerbein gaining his one and only victory. The Nieuport went down over Becelaere, east of Ypres. Von Hünerbein would take command of Jasta 5 before April was out, only to be killed the following month.

Air combat was very much restricted until clearer weather came to the Western Front in the late afternoon, the next losses not occurring until 1745 hours. 60 Squadron's Nieuports flew an OP at 1640 and were engaged by von Richthofen's Jasta 11 at 1745 north of Mercatel, right over the front. In fact the fight drifted over the British side, but near enough to the trenches for the German ground observers to confirm three Nieuports had gone down, as indeed they had. Two of the British pilots died, the third being wounded. Despite recording that the formation had been attacked by a superior force, von Richthofen only had three of his men with him, and he, Schäfer and Wolff secured the kills. One Albatros had been seen to fall too, credited to the two dead pilots, but Jasta 11 had no losses.

The British unit lost Second Lieutenants Hall and Smart, with D Norman Robertson wounded and forced down. Lieutenant J M Elliott's Nieuport – A6771 – was badly shot up too, while Lieutenant H E Hervey MC – B1517 – got a bullet in the engine but got back. Several of the Nieuport's guns had become frozen before the fight, which did not help while trying to defend themselves against the German pilots.

Shortly before this action, another pilot of 60, Lieutenant W A Bishop, had attacked the German balloon lines and claimed a balloon destroyed at Vis-en-Artois, as well as an Albatros DIII out of control.

Half an hour after 60 Squadron had been mauled, FE2s of 20 Squadron, flying a bomb raid south of Ploegsteert Wood, right on the lines in the northern part of the front (15 km south of Ypres) were attacked by German fighters. On this day, 20 Squadron had been assigned to bomb the aerodrome at Mouvaux, just north of Lille. They had bombed it that morning, having one aircraft crash on the way back through engine trouble, although its crew were safe and on the right side of the lines.

West of Arras, the British lost a balloon at 1645 hrs, to Leutnant Hans Klein of Jasta 4. In the basket of FM32, 9th KB Coy, was the unit CO, Captain G S Samson. He and Second Lieutenant W G Dreshfield were at 3,200 feet, 300 feet below the cloud layer. Samson heard machine-gun fire and turned to see a German fighter 200 feet away, diving straight at them. He immediately ordered Dreshfield to jump, and out he went. As soon as he was clear, Samson went over the side too. By the time his parachute opened, the enemy fighter had gone back into the cloud, but flame was now coming from the stern of the balloon, so Klein had got his first balloon and his second confirmed victory. He would claim 22 by the end of November 1917, but a wound the following February put him out of the flying war.

Interestingly, the War Diary notes that the enemy aeroplanes looked so much like a Nieuport Scout that a nearby aeroplane did not think to interfere until the attack proved the machine to be hostile, by which time Klein was on his way back home.

At 1712 eight FEs went back, bombed the base again then headed for home. After recrossing the lines, Captain George Mahony-Jones looked back and saw one of his crews being engaged by nine German fighters and he immediately turned to assist. The pilot of the other FE was then wounded and force-landed just inside British lines, but by now Mahony-Jones and his gunner, Second Lieutenant W B Moyes, a former 6th Royal Scots officer, were fighting for their lives in the midst of the enemy fighters. At first they seemed to succeed in driving off some of the fighters but finally a burst set their machine on fire and the FE fell in flames, both men being killed. Shortly afterwards, 20 Squadron received a letter from the Headquarters of the 34th Battalion, AIF:

> To the Commandant, RFC Bailleul, 8 April 1917.
>
> 'The CO 34th Battn AIF has asked me to express a deep sense of admiration which was inspired by the gallant flying of an airman, apparently belonging to a squadron under your command. About 6 pm on the evening of the 7th instant, two of our planes were engaged with nine of the enemy's. One plane was damaged and the other, although retreat looked possible, turned and fought. Several of the enemy's planes scattered but unfortunately our plane was hit and immediately burst into flames.
>
> 'The scene was witnessed by the men of the Battalion from the trenches and the conspired bravery was much spoken of by them and the gallantry is sure to foster a spirit of emulation for our men to strive hard on their parts, to act in the same heroic and self-sacrificing manner as this gallant airman. The true bravery of your fine Corps was thus strikingly brought home to our men.'
>
> Adj, 34th Battn.

Mahony-Jones was brought down by Vizefeldwebel Max Müller of Jasta 28, his 6th victory, but the first for the Jasta, seen to fall in flames into the British lines. The other FE, with its pilot wounded, crash-landed south of Ploegsteert, with a dead gunner, claimed by Leutnant Walter von Bülow-Bothkamp of Jasta 18, his 10th victory.

More Nieuport patrols were out at this time, 29 Squadron meeting German fighters and losing two pilots, one falling to Leutnant Bernert of Jasta 2, south of Roeux, the other to Vizefeldwebel Linus Patermann of Jasta 4, north-west of Biache.

Two hours later, at 1910, Wilhelm Frankl, CO of Jasta 4, would bring down yet another Nieuport, and yet another from 60 Squadron. This was Captain M B

Knowles, from Ashford, Middlesex, who came down south of Fampaux where he was captured. It was Frankl's last victory.

Jasta 11 scored one final victory on this day, a Bristol Fighter of 48 Squadron. A patrol of 48 had flown out at 1802 to fly an OP north-east of Arras. In a brief skirmish with Jasta 11, Sebastian Festner had attacked what he identified as a two-seater Sopwith, which went down over the British lines to crash north-west of Maroeuil. The Bristol in fact force-landed at Saulty, with a dead gunner.

Lieutenant H C Todd of 40 Squadron claimed a balloon destroyed on this evening (his second in two days), while pilots of 8 Naval were in a fight with German fighters, claiming one destroyed and one out of control. 20 Squadron also reported a scrap, and also claimed one Albatros destroyed with another out of control.

Up on the coast, 5 Naval Squadron had bombed a destroyer alongside the Mole at Zeebrugge in the early hours, Flight Lieutenant I N C Clarke (Australian) dropping 12 LePecq bombs from 11,000 ft.

French Front

On the Châlons front one enemy aircraft was forced to land near Hourges, where it caught fire on the ground. Whether this had anything to do with Vizefeldwebel Ludwig Müller, of FA46, who was killed near St Mihiel, is uncertain. More likely it was the Rumpler CI (2605/ 16) of Schutzstaffel 7 flown by Gefreiter Schoop and Leutnant Hupe that was lost at this time.

Top Vizefeldwebel Max Müller of Jasta 28, shot down a 20 Squadron FE2 on the 7th, for his sixth victory. He would achieve thirty-six victories by the end of 1917 but was killed in action with Jasta 2 (Boelcke) on 9 January 1918.
Bottom Nieuport XVII of 29 Squadron (A6692), flown by Captain A Jennings, shot down by Vfw Linus Patermann of Jasta 4, for his first victory, 7 April 1917. Patermann was killed in July 1917.

	A/C	KB		DES	OOC	KB
British losses	8	1	British claims	3	3	2
French losses	–	–	French claims	1		–
German claims	10	1	German losses	1		?

Aircraft type	No.	Squadron	Crew		
Nieuport XVII	A6605	1 Sqdn	Lt R J Bevington	POW	
Nieuport XXIII	A6766	60 Sqdn	2/Lt C S Hall	KIA	
Nieuport XVII	A6645	60 Sqdn	2/Lt G O Smart	KIA	
Nieuport XVII	A311	60 Sqdn	2/Lt D N Robertson	WIA	*
Nieuport XVII	A6671	60 Sqdn	Lt J M Elliott	Safe	*
Nieuport XVII	A6692	29 Sqdn	Capt A Jennings	KIA	
Nieuport XVII	A6775	29 Sqdn	2/Lt J H Muir	KIA	
FE2d	A1961	20 Sqdn	Capt G J Mahony-Jones	KIA	
			2/Lt W B Moyes	KIA	
FE2d	A6400	20 Sqdn	2/Lt J Lawson	WIA	
			2/Lt H N Hampson	DOW	
Nieuport XVII	A6773	60 Sqdn	Capt M B Knowles	POW	
BF2a	A3317	48 Sqdn	2/Lt J W Warren	Safe	*
			2/Lt G C Burnard	KIA	
BE2c		15 Sqdn	2AM A O Dilley (O)	WIA	*

Spad VII		N.48	Lt Lorillard	MIA	
Spad VII		N.48	S/Lt de Larminat	MIA	

08 APRIL 1917
M T W T F S **S**

British Front

Easter Sunday; a fine day but cloudy. In preparation for the offensive, British ground troops pushed forward in the vicinity of the Bapaume-Cambrai road on a front of 3,000 yards north of Louverval.

While people in Britain and France were celebrating communion services, 60 Squadron were taking off for an 0835 offensive patrol, among whom was Major J A Milot, a Canadian from Quebec, who despite his rank was a relatively inexperienced pilot and former infantry officer. After a few days with 13 Squadron, he had joined 60 on 15 March. East of Vimy they spotted German fighters ahead and within moments were in a dog-fight. It was Jasta 11 again, and Festner turned in behind one Nieuport and opened fire, sending Major Joseph Milot down on fire. In the scrap, Second Lieutenant Hamilton Hervey had his gun jam, so he pulled off to one side and headed for the lines. Later he wrote from a prison camp:

'In the first fight we had, my gun jammed and by the time I had got it going again I had lost the other machines. I waited about for a bit and then, as more of them had turned up, started for home. I had already got over our lines when I saw four enemy machines scrapping with some others and so went back to join in. On the way, when I had got some distance over and rather low, I think something or other to do with my engine was hit by a bit of "archie"; anyway, several shots burst very close to my machine and then my engine started to run very badly and finally stopped altogether. I turned back at once but could not reach our lines and landed about two miles behind the German front line. I broke the petrol glass as soon as I landed and let all the petrol out of my tank but some soldiers came up and got me away from the machine before I could set light to it.'

Left One of the early flight commanders with 48 Squadron, Captain D M Tidmarsh MC. He had flown DH2s with 24 Squadron in 1916, and on 8 April 1917, downed an Albatros for his fourth victory. Within the next three days he brought his score to seven before being shot down and captured by Kurt Wolff of Jasta 11 on the 11th.
Right Edwin Cole flew Nieuport Scouts with 1 Squadron at this time and in April shot down two aircraft and two balloons, bringing his overall score to seven, plus one more in May.

Hervey had most probably been hit by fire from KFlak 43, who claimed a Nieuport Scout east of Arras. But these were not the first losses of the day. Night victories might have been rare, but the German Air Service claimed its second of the month at 0440. FEs of 100 Squadron had flown a bomb raid against Douai airfield, home of Jasta 4, soon after midnight and Jasta 4's Hans Klein had taken off to try an interception. He was lucky and brought down 7669 south-east of the town.

Artillery observation and reconnaissance missions were flown throughout the day, with offensive patrols flown by British scouts to ward off hostile attacks. For the most part this worked, for it was not until late morning that another British machine was lost.

Sopwiths of 43 Squadron were flying a line patrol when Manfred von Richthofen and two of his Staffel attacked the three 1½ Strutters over Farbus, bringing down A2406 with a wounded pilot and a dead gunner at 1140.

Noon saw FE2s of 57 Squadron taking off for an OP with six aircraft, and these got into a fight near Arras with an equal number of enemy fighters. Three of the FEs were shot about but all got back over the lines before having to put down. Thus no German pilots made any claim, but one pilot and two gunners had been wounded and one FE lost. The third crew, Lieutenants Erlebach and Trotter, who force-landed near Arras, later flew back with their aircraft after temporary repairs, three days later.

Jasta 4 took off after lunch when more enemy machines were reported heading for Étaing. These were RE8s of 59 Squadron, out on a photo op. Like some other two-seater observation units, 59 tended to escort its own photo machine with its own aircraft, rather than hope that fighter patrols would be in the area to protect them against the nimble Albatros Scouts. This was fine in theory but in practice, a slow two-seater was no real help to an equally slow two-seater. This squadron had already found this out on 6 April, and were about to learn the lesson again.

Jasta 4 swept down on them, one RE8 almost immediately falling away while the others were harried as they sped for the lines. A second RE8 was shot up, both crewmen being wounded while the gunner in a third was also hit. There seems little doubt that Wilhelm Frankl shot down the one which failed to get back, but as we shall see, he did not have the opportunity to claim this victory.

Frankl's RE8 went down at 1330, but he still had fuel enough to continue to patrol behind the front. At 1400, 48 Squadron were taking off to fly an OP between Arras, Lens and Vitry and they were intercepted by Frankl's Jasta 4 pilots as soon as they crossed the lines. In the brief fight which followed, 48's gunners claimed two Albatros Scouts as shot down, one by Captain D M Tidmarsh/Second Lieutenant C B Holland, the other by the combined fire from three other crews, both over Rémy-Éterpigny. Frankl's Albatros, 2158/16, fell between Vitry and Sailly, breaking up as it did so. Continuing with their patrol, 48 Squadron were later intercepted by Jasta 2. Otto Bernert quickly despatched one near Rémy at 1510, at the same time claiming an RE8. The Bristol was A3330, of that there is no question, but the RE8 is a bit of a mystery. The Bristol was timed at 1510, the RE8 five minutes later. There are no known RE8s lost at this time, only the 59 Squadron machines being in combat and that was at 1330, one hour and twenty minutes earlier. It is possible that once the other RE8s were driven off they may have returned and at least one had run into Bernert – 48 Squadron may even have seen the two-seater and tried to give it some protection. The Bristol went down south of Éterpigny, where the Bristols would have been, but the 'RE8' five minutes later is reported as being brought down north of Bailleul-Sir-Berthoult, just west of Gavrelle, about 12 km to the north-west (not to be confused with the more famous Bailleul, 56 km to the north-west). While this was going on, de Havilland 4 bombers of 55 Squadron were raiding a château at

Hardenpont, up near Mons. This squadron was based at Fienvillers, south-west of Doullens, and was the first DH4 squadron to operate in France, having come out from England in March. Their first operation was flown on 3 April. Today it would suffer its first losses.

The château housed the Headquarters of Crown Prince Rupprecht's 6th Army Group although the raid did not cause him any personal problems. On the return journey, Jasta 11 were waiting for the bombers, and met them north of Cambrai at 1425. In the fight which ensued, two 'Fours' were brought down, one by Schäfer (A2140), the other by Wolff (A2141), one at Épinoy, one at Blécourt, while a third (A2160) was hit by flak, coming down south-west of Amiens. This was probably the 'grosskampf aircraft' claimed by Flakzug 17, seen to go down over Amigny.

On the northern, Ypres sector, a 46 Squadron Nieuport XII two-seater ran into trouble on a photo op, coming up against three Albatros Scouts of Jasta 18. The two-seater was hit by Leutnant Walter von Bülow-Bothkamp, wounding both of the crew, but the pilot struggled over the lines to crash to the east of Ypres. From there the aeroplane was in full view of the Germans who promptly shelled it.

Manfred von Richthofen gained another victory for himself and his Jasta 11 by shooting down a 16 Squadron BE2g west of Vimy at 1640, both British airmen being killed. It was the Baron's 39th kill. The day ended in a flurry of late afternoon activity, six aircraft of 25 Squadron flying a bomb raid on Pont-à-Vendin, led by Captain C H C Woolven (A782), losing an FE2b to flak – claimed by several flak units north of La Bassée at 1900. Ten minutes later, Leutnant Georg Schlenker of Jasta 3, picked off a Nieuport of 29 Squadron flying an evening OP, the Scout coming down north-east of Croisselles, for the German's 7th victory.

An untimed German victory was one by Offizierstellvertreter Walter Göttsch of Jasta 8 who shot down a Belgian BE2c from the 6me Escadrille, east of Dixmuide. They were on a recce to Bruges and came down south of Couckelaere. Another was a balloon claimed by Heinrich Gontermann of Jasta 5, west of St Quentin.

The RFC had been in amongst the balloons during the morning, 1 Squadron's Nieuports flaming two. One was at Quesnoy at 0830 by Lieutenant E S T Cole (A6668), the second by Captain C J Quintin Brand at Moorslede around 1130. Also during the

This DH4 of 55 Squadron was brought down on 8 April by Ltn Emil Schäfer of Jasta 11, for his 13th victory. The British crew, Lts R A Logan and F R Henry are standing by their machine, in their 'fug-boots'. Note too that they wore their service head-gear in case they diverted to another airfield, or in this event, came down inside enemy lines.

morning, 60 Squadron had been in some air fights, Major A J L Scott and Lieutenant W A Bishop claiming an Albatros two-seater destroyed near Douai at 0930, Bishop also claiming two Albatros Scouts out of control. In the afternoon 66 Squadron's Pups claimed three more out of control, and 3 Naval Squadron two more north-east of Pronville. 22 Squadron's FEs, led by the six-foot-four-inch Canadian, Lieutenant Carlton M Clement, had been helped out by the Pups. They had been on an OP between Mont-d'Origny, Fonsomme and Homblières, east of St Quentin.

Just on 1700 they had been approached by two Albatros Scouts. As the two Germans attacked, the FEs' return fire appeared to hit one Albatros whose pilot promptly went down and landed on the airfield at Mont d'Origny, while the Sopwiths drove off the other. The FEs then spotted four two-seaters (they recorded them as Halberstadt types) which were between them and St Quentin. The Fees attacked, firing at close range. The leading two-seater went down vertically, losing part of a wing before hitting the ground near Regny. A second two-seater was driven down and seen to land heavily in a field just north of Marcy.

No.29 Squadron claimed one destroyed south-east of Arras, in the fight in which Second Lieutenant Owen was lost.

Other than Frankl, the only German pilot listed as a casualty this day on the British front was Leutnant Alfred Träger of Jasta 8, who was wounded by an exploding bullet. The Nachrichtenblatt noted three aircraft lost in all. Sebastian Festner force-landed his Albatros DII (223/16) due to a wing cracking, and may have been one of the enemy scouts claimed by 60 Squadron.

Second Lieutenant Walter B Wood, who had just reached France and 29 Squadron, but who would win the MC and bar in 1917 and gain several victories, wrote home on this day:

> 'It does make me wild to see articles in the papers running down our Flying Corps on account of the casualties. If you only knew the work we do compared to the Hun, you would realise how ridiculous it all is. Very rarely do we see a Hun machine over our lines, and, regularly, our patrols go, perhaps three times a day, 15 or 20 miles over their lines and wait over their aerodromes for the Huns going up. We have them beaten.'

However, the casualties were real and the truth is that neither the British nor the French were inflicting anywhere near the hurt on the Germans they thought they were.

French Front

On the Châlons front Caudrons were active against front-line targets, both G4s and R4 escort gunships. The R4 was the French answer to the problem of escorting their bombing/reconnaissance aircraft by having a more powerfully armed machine of the same general type, rather than relying on Spad or Nieuport Scout single-seat escorts. Two Caudron crews claimed German aircraft shot down, one north of Berry-au-Bac, and a second at 1615 over Aguilcourt.

On the Chauny sector, Lieutenant de Laage de Meux, flight commander of N.124 – the famous Lafayette Escadrille, manned mostly by American volunteers – shot down a single-seater north of St Quentin at 1330, which force-landed inside French territory. The pilot, Leutnant Roland Nauck of Jasta 6, was flying

Albatros DIII 2234/16, actually coming down at Villevecque, but either died in his aircraft or very soon afterwards. His aircraft was given the RFC number G.21. De Laage also claimed a two-seater north of Moy – possibly a FA61 aircraft – receiving the Légion d'Honneur for this day's work. A Vizefeldwebel Josef Schreiner was killed at Amifontaine/Prouvais this day, unit unknown.

However, French losses were quite severe. On the Chauny front no fewer than ten Caudrons were either brought down in combat, or flew home with wounded crewmen plus one Farman shot up. Escadrille C.46 were involved in a fight with four enemy fighters, losing one aircraft, probably to Oberleutnant Erich Hahn, leader of Jasta 19 based at Le Thour, 30 km north of Reims, who claimed a Caudron down north of Loivre. Another Caudron was claimed by a two-seater crew of FA23, at Effigny.

	A/C	KB		DES	OOC	KB
British losses	14	1	British claims	4	11	2
French losses	1	–	French claims	4		–
German claims	18†	1	German losses	3		?

† Includes one Belgian aircraft.

British Casualties

Aircraft type	No.	Squadron	Crew		
FE2b	7669	100 Sqdn	2/Lt L Butler	POW	
			2AM R Robb	POW	
Nieuport XXIII	A6764	60 Sqdn	Maj J A Milot	KIA	
Nieuport XXIII	A311	60 Sqdn	2/Lt H E Hervey MC	POW	
RE8	A4178	59 Sqdn	Lt K B Cooksey	KIA	
			2AM R H Jones	KIA	
RE8	A4185	59 Sqdn	Lt E L Hyde	WIA	*
			Lt R M Grant	WIA	
RE8	A3418	59 Sqdn	Lt E G Leake	Safe	*
			2/Lt P L Hogan	WIA	
Sop 1½ Strutter	A2406	43 Sqdn	2/Lt J S Heagerty	WIA/POW	
			Lt L H Cantle	KIA	
DH4	A2140	55 Sqdn	Lt R A Logan	POW	
			Lt F R Henry	POW	
DH4	A2141	55 Sqdn	Lt B Evans	KIA	
			2/Lt B W White	KIA	
DH4	A2160	55 Sqdn	Lt A J Hamer	KIA	
			2/Lt J A Myburgh	DOW	
FE2d	A1955	57 Sqdn	Lt A D Pryor	WIA	
			AM C Goffe	WIA	
FE2d	A1957	57 Sqdn	Lt T Grosvenor	Safe	*
			2/Lt W W Glen	WIA	
BF2a	A3330	48 Sqdn	2/Lt O W Berry	KIA	
			2/Lt F B Goodison	DOW	
BE2g	A2815	16 Sqdn	2/Lt K MacKenzie	KIA	
			2/Lt G Everingham	KIA	
Nieuport XII	A156	46 Sqdn	2/Lt J E de Watteville	WIA	
			Lt R A Manby	WIA	
Nieuport XXIII	A6765	29 Sqdn	2/Lt T J Owen	KIA	

Aircraft type	No.	Squadron	Crew		
FE2b	A813	25 Sqdn	2/Lt E V A Bell	WIA/POW	
			Lt A H K McCallum	WIA/POW	
DH2		24 Sqdn	2/Lt E Kent	DOW	*
BE2c		4 Sqdn	2/Lt A C Finlayson	DOW	*

French Casualties

Caudron R4		C.46	MdL Theron (G)	KIA	
Caudron R4		C.46	S/Lt Wilmes (O)	KIA	
			Adj de Cuyper (G)	WIA	
Caudron G4		C.219	Adj de Saint Pierre (P)	WIA	*
Caudron R4		R.209	Sol Pichot (G)	DOW	*
Caudron R4		R.209	Cpl Picquot (G)	WIA	*
Caudron R4		R.209	Lt Charpiot	WIA	*
Caudron R4		R.209	Lt Conby (O)	WIA	*
Caudron G4		C.212	S/Lt Villemy (O)	KIA	*
Caudron G4		C.212	Cpl Debrie (P)	WIA	
Caudron G4		C.30	Sgt Munier (P)	WIA	*
Farman 40		F.201	Lt Martin (O)	WIA	*

Belgian Casualties

BE2c		6me Esc	Adj A Glibert	KIA
			Lt J Callant	KIA

09 APRIL 1917
M T W T F S S

British Front

At around midnight the shelling began. It was always so before a battle. It was a prerequisite that artillery fire would pound the enemy trenches and wire to demoralise, if not kill, maim and bury, the opposing soldiers and cut the barbed-wire entanglements so that the troops who would storm the enemy's positions at dawn would have a reasonable chance of getting across no man's land and into the German trenches before they were mown down by machine-gun and rifle fire. Sometimes it worked, often it didn't. The Germans replied in kind but with less ferocity.

Soldiers on both sides easily read the signs and kept themselves deep inside their bunkers, hoping a direct hit would not cave in their otherwise fairly strong shelters. Both knew that they would have to sit and bear it as the rain of steel and explosives fell on them. It was no easier for the old hands as it was for the new. What was a shock for the new was anxiety for the old. The shelling went on all night. It gave some small comfort to the men who would be 'going over the top' on the morrow, and discomfort to the recipients – so the attackers hoped.

Dawn, when it came, was cold, with low clouds and a strong wind that persisted most of the day. But as light filtered across the barren but smoke-filled landscape, the men in the Allied trenches stood ready, each with his own thoughts and fears. Had the wire been cut? Had the enemy been pounded and destroyed? Would today be a walkover? Could they at last break through to open countryside? Would they all be dead five minutes from zero hour!?

The order to fix bayonets was given. This was it. Dawn. A last dawn? Officers moved among their troops, occasionally checking a watch, looking up at the grey sky. The last minutes ticked by and still the shells whistled and screeched overhead and into the German trench systems. Was this really Easter Monday; peace on earth, good will to all men? 0530 hours; whistles blew. It was time.

Scrambling up ladders, or steps made in the side of the trench-works, the kha-ki-clad soldiers, encouraged by their officers and cursed by their NCOs, went 'over the top'. Ahead lay the shattered dead ground between them and their enemy. Smoke blew across this pulverized moon-like landscape, the noise of explosions got nearer but would soon stop, then move on as the artillery gunners upped the range. Where was the wire? When would the first rattle of machine-gun fire come to their ears, quickly followed by scything metal and death? Breathing became difficult; feet and legs felt like lead. There were some snow flurries. God be with us all.

The front stretched from Lens to St Quentin. South of Arras and west of Cambrai British troops stormed Hermies and Boursies. West of St Quentin, Fresnoy-le-Petit was captured. North of Arras the prize of Vimy Ridge was under assault by the Canadians.

Despite the wind and snow showers, the BE crews were out soon after 0600 to support this Battle of Arras. Their job was to make contact with forward elements of the soldiers, to see how far they had progressed, then report back. Contact patrols they were called. Make contact and report.

Unlike the dreadful carnage of the Somme the previous July, the soldiers of the British 1st and 3rd Armies reached their initial objectives, had got through the wire and into the shattered German trenches. From behind the British lines the balloons went up despite the strong wind, eager eyes also seeking information through the smoke via powerful binoculars.

A 16 Squadron BE2 skimmed over the battle front, seeking signs of both friend and enemy. Machine-gun fire greeted them, so the enemy was not totally knocked out. Bullets zipped through the wood and fabric of the BE, finding flesh. With both men wounded, the pilot headed back and they were lucky to survive. Another BE, this time from 13 Squadron, was also met by guns and shell fire, but this only found wood and fabric. The pilot crash-landed inside British lines, both men safe. A machine from the 1st Brigade located a German gun battery moving to the rear and the pilot dived, firing with his machine gun. The guns were abandoned, temporarily.

Triplanes of 1 Naval Squadron flew an early OP to Cambrai at 0640, one machine flown by Flight Commander C A Eyre (N5478) having to return with a dud engine, crash-landing at Dancourt.

As the morning progressed targets observed behind the enemy front were engaged by shell fire, the fall of shot being registered and corrected by both aeroplane and balloon observers by radio, while fighter patrols were flown behind the battle front to protect the artillery machines and balloon lines from attack. It succeeded pretty well, but the weather helped too. Despite the fact that this was the opening day of the new offensive, enemy air opposition was almost nil.

By 0815, the advance was starting to falter. German artillery had begun to pound the front lines despite the work of the artillery flyers. A 12 Squadron BE came back with a wounded observer. However, by noon it could be reported that Highland troops had reached Roclincourt; Canadian troops, after a struggle, took Les Tillenes. As the day progressed St Martin-sur-Cojeul and the chapel at Feuchy village were captured. Further Contact Patrols spotted British troops in St Laurent Blagny and Athies, then Fampoux and Point du Jour, mostly to the north of the Scarpe River. To the south of the river, the German resistance was stronger. Another 13 Squadron BE (5875) with Lieutenant D H Ball and Captain W W Boyd was hit by machine-gun fire from the ground, forcing them to make a landing near Arras, but they were safe.

When weather permitted, some fighters attempted to shoot up German troops and positions, much to the delight and satisfaction of the Allied soldiers. A Spad from 19 Squadron (A263) was hit in turn by ground fire, Lieutenant F L Harding safely getting down on Lille-Villers airfield.

The Bristol Fighters of 48 Squadron got into a scrap with some Albatros two-seaters late morning claiming two destroyed and another out of control. FA202 had Unteroffizier Eugen Reuter killed and Leutnant Schröder wounded over Vitry on the 6 Armee front and were probably the victims of 48 Squadron. There was also a Offizierstellvertreter Franz Hermann and Gefreiter Oskar Weller killed on this day, unit unknown. Pilots of Naval 6 and Naval 8 were also involved in air fights in the Cambrai-Arras-Noyelles area around noon, claiming three fighters out of control. Upon returning from this action, the 6 Naval pilots were caught in a storm and two of its Nieuports crashed, having Flight Sub Lieutenant A L Thorne killed and Flight Sub Lieutenant J deC Paynter (a future ace) injured.

There was less reported action during the afternoon and it was not until evening that fresh fighting occurred in the air. At 1835, a 2 Squadron BE2d (6253), crewed by Captain F Fernihough and Second Lieutenant R Hamilton MC, was attacked while on an artillery patrol at 5,000 feet. Their aggressor flew an all-black Albatros with a white cross on the rudder but Hamilton's fire appeared to hit the German, who turned away and went east, losing height.

48 Squadron again got into a fight and claimed two DIIIs out of control at around 1800, although Lieutenant Jack Letts had his gunner mortally wounded and 25 Squadron got an out of control near Lieven at 1905. Captain A M Wilkinson of 48 Squadron shared in all five of 48's claims, and in his subsequent DSO citation it records his help in gaining these four victories on this day.

It fell to Jasta 11's Karl Schäfer to make the German Air Service's only confirmed kill of the day. Over the front he spotted a 4 Squadron BE2d and, with four other Jasta pilots, dived to the attack. It was 1900 hours, and the BE went down to crash at Aix Noulette, seven kilometres west of Lens, but inside British lines. Lieutenants J H Brink and R E Heath had taken off at 1850 to recce the Quéant area. They came under AA fire which in turn attracted Schäfer and his men who dived to the attack. Heath saw the five Halberstadts coming down and began to fire the rear gun which jammed after a few rounds. As he began to clear it he was hit in the foot.

Getting his gun going again, he fired back once more but then Johannas Brink received a bullet in the back and slumped forward, the BE beginning a spiral downwards. Heath attempted to take control but Brink signalled that he could land it, and did so, but the BE turned over and Heath was thrown out. Heath, despite his wound and being winded, dragged his pilot from the wreck and laid him on the ground.

Two of the German fighters then came down to strafe them. Heath grabbed a Lewis gun from his cockpit and called to a nearby soldier – an Australian private – hoisted the gun onto the man's shoulder and began firing at the two Halberstadts, driving them off. Brink died of his wound two days later, but it is not recorded if the Australian soldier was temporarily deafened by the Lewis gun being fired next to his ear!

By the end of the day's fighting, the British front had moved east by some 6,000 yards along a 15,000-yard stretch, the most important victory being the capture by the Canadians of Vimy Ridge. In this predominantly flat landscape, any high ground was an important and strategic feature. It had been in German hands since October 1914, but now the Allied forces could look down on the Douai plain from its 200-feet heights, while it also became the defensive flank for the British 3rd Army along the Scarpe.

French Front

With everything concentrated up on the British front, and Nivelle still planning his part of the overall strategy, there was little activity in the south. There were no losses and no claims. The Germans, however, lost a two-seater crew of FA(A)276 at Manningen, near Metz, probably an accident at Manningen Bar aerodrome. Leutnants Rudolf Müller and Max Trautmann were killed.

	A/C	KB		DES	OOC	KB
British losses	3	–	British claims	3	6	–
French losses	–	–	French claims	–		–
German claims	1	–	German losses	–		–

British Casualties

Aircraft type	No.	Squadron	Crew		
BE2g	6818	16 Sqdn	2/Lt E B Smythe 2/Lt S Cooper	WIA WIA	
BE2e	A2878	13 Sqdn	Lt J H Norton Capt T L Tibbs	Safe Safe	
BE2d	5742	4 Sqdn	Lt J H Brink Lt R E Heath	DOW WIA	
BE2c		12 Sqdn	2/Lt O D Norwood (O)	WIA	*
BF2a	A3315	48 Sqdn	Lt J H T Letts Lt H G Collins	Unhurt DOW	*

10 APRIL 1917
M **T** W T F S S

British Front

On the Arras front British troops reached the outskirts of Monchy-le-Preux while further south the British line advanced to the north of Louverval. In spite of the land battle raging along these sectors, continued strong winds and snow kept aeroplanes of both sides on the ground through much of the day. Certainly the Germans made no fighter claims and the RFC only made one out of control claim at 1900 hours that evening, by two 48 Squadron crews over Rémy.

Two BE2 pilots were wounded during the day by ground fire while on either contact patrol or artillery observation work, and an AWFK8 – 'Big Ack' – of 35 Squadron had to force-land at Monchy-le-Preux at 1600 after being hit by flak, and was written off. Major W S Douglas (later Sir W Sholto Douglas) and his observer 2AM A W Cant in a 43 Squadron Strutter (A7804) had their petrol tank shot through by AA fire and force-landed north-west of Arras at 1710. In the above-mentioned fight of 48 Squadron, one Bristol Fighter (A3334) was damaged by the fire from an Albatros Scout, Captain A T Cull and his gunner Corporal Edwards making a forced landing near Quéant, fortunately on the right side of the lines.

French Front

Just one Nieuport Scout was lost, piloted by Brigadier Chautard of N.31, and he came down inside German lines, due to becoming lost in bad weather, and is presumed to have been taken prisoner. An observer in a Salmson two-seater was wounded by ground fire. There were no claims.

	A/C	KB		DES	OOC	KB
British losses	1	–	British claims	–	1	–
French losses	1	–	French claims	–		–
German claims	–	–	German losses	–		–

British Casualties

Aircraft type	No.	Squadron	Crew		
AWFK8	A2683	35 Sqdn	2/Lt H S Lees-Smith	Safe	
			2/Lt H L Storrs	Safe	
BE2c	A2829	12 Sqdn	Lt J H Cooper	WIA	*
			2/Lt W A Winter	Safe	
BE2e	A2839	8 Sqdn	2/Lt P B Pattison	WIA	*
			2/Lt E M Harwood	Safe	

French Casualties

Nieuport XVII	1930	N.31	Brig Chautard	POW	
Salmson-Moineau		F.41	– Lefrancois (O)	WIA	*

11 APRIL 1917
M T **W** T F S S

British Front

A very slight improvement in the weather during the morning brought renewed activity in the air-war, but more high wind, low clouds and snow storms restricted afternoon sorties. On the ground, Monchy was taken and La Bergère. The 4th Australian Division attacked – without any artillery support – and broke into the Hindenburg Line, but were thrown back with enormous losses. The 4th Brigade lost 2,339 out of 3,000 men, with 1,000 captured, the single biggest prisoner loss of Australians in the war. This 'experiment' was a totally useless blunder by General Gough.

No.4 Squadron sent out machines to bomb targets at Cambrai at 0708, while 40 minutes later, 23 Squadron were sending out Spads to provide some form of escort. 23 had only recently become a single-seat unit, having previously flown FE2s, with the arrival of Spad VIIs from the French.

Most of the early German combats over the front came on or after 0845, but between 0800 and 0820, 48 Squadron were in combat with some Albatros Scouts over Fampoux, claiming one destroyed and two out of control. They then continued with their patrol, eager for more action. They were to get it in an hour's time.

Just on 0845, Jasta 12 intercepted the 4 Squadron BEs that were turning for home. The BEs had sacrificed a gunner/observer for extra bomb weight, so only carried pilots. Leutnant Georg Röth came down on Second Lieutenant F Matthews, hitting his BE and sending him down to crash-land north of Abancourt, just a few kilometres east of the Jasta's base at Épinoy. It was Röth's first confirmed victory which would, like all pilots, bring him the coveted Ehrenbecher – the silver Victory Cup.

The running fight continued, the BEs being harried slightly to the north-west, so when Lieutenant F L Kitchen went down to Leutnant Adolf Schulte, ten minutes after Matthews, at 0855, he fell near Tilloy right on the line. Another pilot, Second Lieutenant A F T Ord was wounded but brought his BE back to base.

Meantime, Jasta 2 had become airborne and spotted the Spads, Leutnant Hermann Frommherz shooting down one at Cuvillers, north-east of Cambrai at 0900, for his first victory – the BEs having long gone. Sopwith Pup pilots from 3 Naval Squadron were also in the air over Cambrai at this period, Flight Commander Lloyd Breadner claiming an Albatros in flames and another crashed, while Flight Lieutenant Joe Fall claimed three out of control, Flight Sub Lieutenant P G McNeil a fourth. Neither Jasta 2 nor 12 suffered any personnel losses, but 3 Naval did. Towards the end of the scrap, Joe Fall's Pup (N6158) was hit, he lost his engine and had to land in German territory west of Neuvireuil, being legitimately claimed by Leutnant Adolf Schulte, his second victory of the morning, and his 7th overall. However, Fall managed to get his engine going again, and before anyone arrived to take him prisoner, he took off and flew home, his machine riddled with bullet holes! Flight Sub Lieutenant S Bennett's Pup (N5199) was also shot up but he got it home, but it was so badly damaged it was later scrapped.

Also in the air was Jasta 11, led by Manfred von Richthofen. At just on 0900, Sebastian Festner spotted a BE (5848), attacked and shot it down into the British lines near Monchy with a wounded pilot. Within minutes the Jasta pilots saw more aircraft, this time the patrol formation of 48's Bristol Fighters. Jasta 11 dived upon them, inflicting a second defeat on the new two-seater and taking another flight commander, Captain Tidmarsh, leaving Alan Wilkinson as the only one left. Lothar von Richthofen, Kurt Wolff and Schäfer each blasted one from the sky, the machines falling around Fresnes.

No sooner had this victory been achieved than the Baron himself spotted another BE on artillery work. Going down on it in company with Wolff, von Richthofen shot it down into the British lines at 0925, by Willerval – another 13 Squadron machine. That made five kills for the Jasta and they were not finished yet, but first they flew back to Douai to refuel and rearm.

Almost an hour later, Jasta 4 were on patrol, Hans Klein seeing more BEs working over the front. He singled out yet another 13 Squadron machine (5851) and shot it down at Biache, on the Scarpe, well inside German lines. Forty minutes later, at 1100, he was after another BE, which he put into the ground at Feuchy, inside the British lines. This was probably the 12 Squadron machine (7242) which was on a contact patrol, and which was wrecked when forced down by a German fighter – having made contact of the wrong sort!

The Germans had not finished with the poor Corps machines yet. Jasta 11 were back on the hunt at midday, Lothar von Richthofen spotting a British 'Tommy' just after 1230. Attacking it he watched it fall into the British lines north of Fampoux, noting it as a Sopwith. However, no Sopwiths appear to have been brought down this day, so it was either an RE8 of 59 Squadron, on a lone Line Patrol having taken off at 1215, or one of two 8 Squadron BEs lost at this time. The two 8 Squadron aeroplanes had taken off after midday, one being claimed by Schäfer who went down on a BE at 1250, shooting it down east of Arras.

The pilot of one of these BEs got his damaged machine down at Neuville, inside British lines, where it turned over, but both men scrambled clear. The other crew were seen to be attacked by four German fighters whilst on a 'shoot' south-east of Arras and shot down, apparently on the right side of the front line. Their BE was wrecked and both men wounded. The only other loss at this time was a 52 Squadron BE2e which had begun a front-line patrol at 1205. However, this was lost on the German side of the lines, so could not have been either Schäfer's or Lothar's victim.

While Jasta 11 was causing all this mayhem around Arras, Otto Bernert was doing his best to curb the British Corps aircraft further south, nearer Bapaume. At 1230 he is reported to have downed a Morane north-west of Lagnicourt. This was a 3 Squadron machine, operating out of Laviéville, to the west of Albert, who lost a Parasol at exactly 1230 between Vaux and Morchies while on artillery observation. It fell into British lines, both crewmen being killed. Then Bernert went after a 23 Squadron Spad (A6696), although it has been reported in the past as an FE2. However, 23 Squadron having recently been a FE unit, some past historian may have noted the 23 Squadron loss, assumed it to have been an FE and thus recorded the incorrect type. The Spad, piloted by Lieutenant F C Troup, had taken off at 1140 and force-landed in the Hendécourt-Ecoust area, in the British lines, Troup reporting that he had been shot down by a DIII that had just shot down a Parasol.

1 An RE8 of 10 Squadron, brought down by Hermann Frommherz on 14 April, his second victory.

2 Another future ace, Hermann Frommherz of Jasta 2, opened his account in April, with victories on the 11th and 14th. Injured in a crash on 1 May 1917, he did not see active duty again until his return to Jasta 2 in March 1918. At the end of the war his score had risen to thirty-two. Seen here with some trophies from his victories, the serial E2514 refers to a BF2b of 22 Squadron he shot down on 27 August 1918. Nominated for the Pour le Mérite the end of the war meant it was not awarded.

3 The Royal Naval Air Service fighter pilots aided the RFC squadrons during the Arras Battle, including the Sopwith Pups of 3 Naval Squadron. Lloyd Breadner, from Canada, is seen here by his Pup (N6181, named 'HMA Happy'), in which he claimed five of his six April victories, including a Gotha bomber on the 23rd. (Presumably the HMS stood for His Majesty's Aircraft.)

4 Canadian and 3 Naval pilot, J S T 'Joe' Fall in front of Breadner's Pup. Fall achieved thirteen victories with 3 Naval, and a further twenty-five with 9 Naval by the year's end, on Camels. He claimed his first six victories during April 1917.

5 On 11 April Armand Pinsard of Escadrille N.78 caused Jasta 29's first loss by downing Vfw Karl Möwe. It was the Frenchman's sixth victory and he would claim four more before the month ended. By August 1918 his score had risen to twenty-seven as commander of Spa.23.

6 Also on the French front during the 11th, Albert Dossenbach of Jasta 36 shot down a Farman of Escadrille F.215 for his eleventh victory. He went on to score fifteen victories before his own death on 3 July having taken command of Jasta 10 in June

This ended the day's air fighting of any note, as the weather worsened. During the day the artillery flyers had directed shell fire onto several targets, helping to knock out gun positions and troop concentrations all along the front. Captain Bird of 16 Squadron, observing for the 5th Canadian Siege Battery, had seen four pits of a five-gun battery completely destroyed. Aircraft, especially those of 43 and 25 Squadrons, had again attacked ground troops with machine-gun fire, an activity that was very much on the increase.

French Front

The main emphasis of action was still in the northern sectors, but along the French front more activity took place than had been the case the previous day. On the Châlons front Lieutenant Armand Pinsard of N.78 brought down an Albatros Scout south-east of St Souplet, which had been flown by Vizefeldwebel Karl Möwe of Jasta 29, who was dead when ground troops got to the scene – the Jastas' first pilot loss.

A Farman of F215 was brought down north of Berry-au-Bac by Leutnant Albert Dossenbach of Jasta 36, while the observer of another Farman was wounded by ground fire. A Caudron of R.214 force-landed at Harmonville with a wounded crew.

On the Chauny front, Adjutant Jeronnez of N.26 also claimed a victory over Cerny-le-Laonnois, for his third kill. This was probably Leutnant Heinrich Karbe of Jasta 22 on a balloon hunt around noon. He was engaged by three Spads and was hit a grazing shot above the right eye, but it was enough to knock him unconscious. His next recollection is of being on the ground and running, luckily on the right side of the lines.

Escadrille N.73 were in a fight with Jasta 14, near Berry-au-Bac, losing two Spad VIIs, with one pilot missing and one wounded. This was at 1145, the victors being Rudolf Berthold, his 11th, and Offizierstellvertreter Hüttner, his second. N.62 had one of their Nieuport two-seaters forced down inside their own lines, although it is not certain if the crew were casualties. Another Caudron returned with a wounded observer after being hit by ground fire.

Leutnant Gebhardt Salzwedel of Jasta 24 got his first victory by downing a Nieuport Scout at Xures, in the French lines way down on the Nancy sector, which was Maréchal-des-Logis Preher of N.68, who failed to return.

	A/C	KB		DES	OOC	KB
British losses	15†	–	British claims	3	6	–
French losses	4	–	French claims	2		–
German claims	19	–	German losses	1‡		

† Including one finally written off on 27 April. ‡ Nachrichtenblatt admits to one aeroplane loss.

British Casualties					
Aircraft Type	No.	Squadron	Crew		
BE2c	2769	4 Sqdn	2/Lt F Matthews	POW/WIA	
BE2d	5849	4 Sqdn	Lt F L Kitchin	KIA	
BE2		4 Sqdn	2/Lt A F T Ord	WIA	*
Spad VII	A6690	23 Sqdn	2/Lt S Roche	POW	

Aircraft Type	No.	Squadron	Crew		
Pup	N5199	3N Sqdn	FSL S Bennett	Safe	SOC
BE2d	5848	13 Sqdn	2/Lt E R Gunner	WIA	
			Lt C Curtis	WIA	
BF2a	A3323	48 Sqdn	2/Lt G N Brockhurst	POW/WIA	
			2/Lt C B Boughton	POW	
BF2a	A3338	48 Sqdn	Capt D M Tidmarsh	POW	
			2/Lt C B Holland	POW	
BF2a	A3318	48 Sqdn	2/Lt R E Adeney	KIA	
			2/Lt L G Lovell	KIA	
BE2e	2501	13 Sqdn	Lt E C E Derwin	WIA	
			2AM H Pierson	WIA	
BE2d	5851	13 Sqdn	2/Lt E T Dunford	POW/DOW	
			Cpl G Stewart	Safe	
BE2e	7242	12 Sqdn	2/Lt G H Jacobs	WIA	
			2/Lt P L Goudie	WIA	
Morane Parasol	A6722	3 Sqdn	Lt M M A Lillis	KIA	
			2AM A Fyffe	KIA	
Spad	A6696	23 Sqdn	Lt F C Troup	Safe	*
FE2b		18 Sqdn	2/Lt J R Smith	WIA	*
RE8	A4190	59 Sqdn	Lt G T Morris	KIA	
			Lt J M Souter	KIA	
BE2c	A2838	52 Sqdn	Capt A F Baker	KIA	
			2/Lt A J Etches	KIA	
BE2c	A2813	8 Sqdn	2/Lt F J E Stafford	WIA	*
			Lt G E Gibbons	Safe	
BE2e	5811	8 Sqdn	Sgt V J Bell	WIA	
			2/Lt H Q Campbell	WIA	

French Casualties

Nieuport XVII	1955	N.68	MdL Preher	POW	
Farman 61		F.71	Lt Grabes (O)	WIA	*
Farman 61		F.215	Sgt Perseyger	KIA	
			Asp Nardon	KIA	
Caudron R4		R.214	Sgt Bodin	WIA	
			S/Lt Grignon (O)	WIA	
			Sol Dermirgian	WIA	
Spad VII		N.73	Sgt Paris	WIA	
Spad VII		N.73	Adj Barioz	MIA	
Caudron G4		C.42	Lt Clerc(O)	WIA	*
Nieuport XII		N.62	Cpl Mougeot	Safe	
			Lt Lemaignen	Safe	

12 APRIL 1917

M T W **T** F S S

British Front

A clear morning, followed by cloud and snow storms for the rest of the day, reflected the reduced activity in the air. Ground fighting secured the capture of Wancourt, Heninel, Gauche Wood, Gouzeaucourt Village and its woods.

What combat there was only took place in the morning, beginning with a photo and escort job by FEs of 18 Squadron over the 5th Army front, taking off just before to just after 0900. The FEs were intercepted by aircraft of Jasta 12 near Éterpigny at 1035, Sopwith Pups of 3 Naval Squadron also joining in.

Hauptmann von Osterroht engaged one of the Pups near Bourlon Wood, as the formation headed north-west for the lines. Acting Flight Commander R G Mack, flying a Pup named 'Black Tulip' and with the letter 'M' on its side, was hit and Mack wounded. He came down at Marquin on the Arras-Cambrai road where he was taken prisoner.

Meanwhile, Vizefeldwebel Arthur Schorisch attacked and brought down FE 4984, which force-landed at Éterpigny, but Leutnant Adolf Schulte, in Albatros DIII 1996/16, collided with FE 4995, and all three men fell to their deaths between Rumaucourt and Baralle at 1040. This would have been Schulte's 9th victory.

The other Pups dog-fought the Albatros Scouts above Jasta 2's base at Pronville, claiming three down out of control, but Schulte was the only reported casualty. 18 Squadron's gunners also claimed two Scouts out of control over Cagnicourt, one possibly being Schulte, although his Albatros, seen falling with wings smashed, was the one credited – in his absence – to Mack.

A 34 Squadron RE8, crewed by Captain F L J Shirley and Lieutenant L T Smith, took off on a photo sortie at 1000, and were engaged by Kurt Schneider of Jasta 5, in his all-black Albatros DIII. Shirley was wounded, being hit in the pit of his stomach and force-landed in British lines at Ascension Farm, near Herbécourt. Smith got Shirley clear before their machine was destroyed by German shelling. That ended the main activities, although 48 Squadron crews also reported shooting down an Albatros DIII out of control during the morning.

French Front

There was considerably more action along the French sectors despite the snow storms. A Nieuport two-seater was brought down south of Nauroy at 1100, by Unteroffizier Eduard Horn of Jasta 21, his first and only victory. This machine was from N.38, engaged on a photo mission. In the evening three fighters were shot down inside German lines; one, a Spad VII of N.112 was brought down by Leutnant Helmut Baldamus of Jasta 9 for his 17th victory, Adjutant-Chef Chemet being taken prisoner. The Frenchman came down near Attigny north of Pont Faverger, north-east of Reims, at 1900 hours.

Perhaps it should be pointed out again that while some French fighter squadrons were operating with Spads, their main equipment was still the Nieuport. Squadron designations of, say, N.38, would not become Spa.38 until later in the year once the whole unit had re-equipped with Spads.

Some of the other French losses came down through unknown causes, but the Germans knew the causes. Two pilots got themselves lost. One from N.26 landed on the wrong side of the lines. Another, from N.112, equally lost, actually landed on Leffincourt airfield, the home of Jasta 9.

In combat, a Salmson-Moineau of SM.106 brought down at Orainville was the victim of Oberleutnant Erich Hahn, Staffelführer of Jasta 19, despite Hahn's claim for a Caudron. A Caudron from R.214 that was brought down, fell to Flakzug 54 at Le Beau Château.

In turn, French pilots claimed two German aircraft, an Albatros Scout south of Époye by Lieutenant Armand Pinsard of N.78, his 7th victory, and an aircraft by Maréchal-des-Logis Marcel Nogues of N.12 over the Bois de Cheval, for his second of an eventual 13 victories.

The Germans did lose personnel from Flieger Abteilungen on this day: Gefreiter Arno Rebentisch and Leutnant Ernst Beltzig of FA (A) 272 were killed at Alincourt, and Flieger Max Vogl of FA46 was also killed. Gefreiter Richard Streubel was thought to be another casualty on the French front, unit unknown.

	A/C	KB		DES	OOC	KB
British losses	4	–	British claims	1	6	–
French losses	6	–	French claims	2		–
German claims	8†	–	German losses	1		–

† Including one to flak; plus two forced to land inside their lines.

British Casualties

Aircraft type	No.	Squadron	Crew	
FE2b	4984	18 Sqdn	Lt O D Maxted	POW
			Lt A Todd MC	DOW
FE2b	4995	18 Sqdn	Lt O T Walton	KIA
			2AM J C Walker	KIA
Sopwith Pup	N6172	3N Sqdn	FC R G Mack	POW/WIA
RE8	A104	34 Sqdn	Capt F L J Shirley	WIA
			Lt L T Smith	Safe

French Casualties

Nieuport XVII	2779	N.112	Cpl Carre	POW
Nieuport XII		N.38	MdL Richard	MIA
			Lt Hallier	MIA
Spad VII	184	N.26	MdL de Tascher	POW
Spad VII	2507	N.112	Adj-Chef Chemet	POW
Salmson-Moineau		SM.106	Lt de Montfort	MIA
			Sol Portolieu (O)	MIA
			Brig Robillard (G)	POW

Aircraft type	No.	Squadron	Crew		
Caudron G4		R.214	Brig Brunet	MIA	
			S/Lt Hembrat (O)	MIA	
			Sgt Levy (G)	MIA	
Caudron G4		C.222	Lt Guimberteau (O)	WIA	*

13 APRIL 1917
M T W T **F** S S

British Front

Fine weather brought out the aviators on this Friday the Thirteenth which was to prove unlucky for a good number of young British airmen. The ground fighting still raged around Vimy and near the Drocourt-Quéant switch line, so the various Army HQs still called for contact patrols and photographs.

British infantry took Givenchy-en-Gohelle, Angres and Wancourt tower, while Fayet to the north-west of St Quentin was also taken. Since the offensive had started, 13,000 German prisoners had been captured as well as 166 pieces of artillery.

Six FEs of 57 Squadron lifted off from Fienvillers at 0700 to fly an OP, led by Captain Jones, but Jones and Lieutenant Cullen had to return home with engine troubles, the latter having to make an emergency landing west of Arras, so that left four.

Just over an hour later, RE8s of 59 Squadron, assigned the task of bringing back photos of the rear areas around Étaing, also took off. It was only a week since 59 had taken a drubbing at the hands of Jasta 11, and now they were flying into von Richthofen's area again. They once more provided their own escort – RE8s escorting RE8s. There were fighter patrols in the general area of the front, but direct escort operations had not yet become a normal occurrence.

Of course, there were some valid reasons why direct escort had its problems. One has to remember that there was no radio communication between aircraft in WWI, so it was difficult to make a rendezvous, and other than hand signals and wing-waggling, no means of making contact with other aircraft when in sight of one another. Different speeds made it necessary for the single-seater pilots to throttle down and therefore become more vulnerable to sudden attacks. Official thinking, by commanders who had never flown a fighter aircraft, preferred their fighters to patrol the area of activity and intercept enemy fighters – and any hostile two-seaters they found – leaving the British two-seater machines to get on with their work unmolested. All very fine, but it didn't work. The sky is a big place and what is more, the Germans were well aware of the tactic and the more experienced would choose the most favourable moment to pick out a British two-seater.

Generally at this time, German fighters patrolled only in Jasta strength, usually no more than five or six aeroplanes. 59 Squadron may have thought that with a sortie of six aircraft they were more or less equal to any hostile patrol they might encounter. Undoubtedly 59 Squadron were trying to overcome a difficult problem but this wasn't the answer as they were about to find out yet again.

Nieuport two-seaters of 46 Squadron were operating, flying as escort to artillery machines over Polygon Wood, taking off at 0800. The Nieuports were attacked by two German scouts from the rear. Lieutenant K W Macdonald in one machine heard his gunner begin to fire but then the gun jammed after three-quarters of a drum. Whilst trying to clear it, the observer, Second Lieutenant C P Long, was hit in the neck and collapsed. Seeing he was seriously wounded, Macdonald dived straight for the lines and landed at Abeele airfield, but Long had bled to death.

The FEs of 57 Squadron were not too far to the north as the big hands on clocks and watches ticked towards 0900, but then the pushers were engaged by Jasta 5 just east of Gavrelle, between there and Vitry-en-Artois. They were suddenly busy having taken on a hostile patrol, and it let Jasta 11 have an open sky to engage 59 Squadron who were then alone.

Heinrich Gontermann, more remembered for his attacks on Allied balloons, and Kurt Schneider, both of Jasta 5, each shot down an FE2, claimed – as most pusher-types were – as a Vickers. Gontermann shot down A5150, Schneider A1950. In fact Schneider claimed two FEs, but the other two returned home safely. One of his victories was reported as having gone down on the British side, so either one had flown back very low which deceived ground observers into thinking it had crashed, or perhaps someone had seen Cullen going down earlier and it had been confused with Schneider's claim.

Meantime, six pilots of Jasta 11, led by the Baron himself, with at least one fighter from Jasta 4, fell upon the six RE8s minutes before 0900. The two Scotsmen aboard the photo machine – A3203 – headed for the lines while the other five tried to protect it. There was no contest. First to go down was A3199 to Festner, the RE8 falling north of Dury at 0854. Lothar von Richthofen knocked out two within seconds at 0855, A4191 hitting the ground north of Biache, A3126 at Pelves. Then the photo machine fell to Hans Klein of Jasta 4, and A3225 to Kurt Wolff, both at 0856. Klein's kill fell south-west of Biache, Wolff's north of Vitry. Oddly enough, the Baron's victim was the last to fall, at 0858, A3190 falling in flames between Vitry and Brebières.

As if in deference to the men who had just died, there was more than two hours of respite in the air on the Arras front. Jasta 11 went back to Douai victorious to refuel and rearm their Albatros fighters. The 'sharks' had tasted blood and the day might not yet be over.

At 1125, 11 Squadron sent out FEs for an OP, into Jasta 11's area. The signal came for the pilots to get back into the air and they needed no second bidding. With Manfred von Richthofen leading, they found 11 Squadron east of the lines, west of Douai. Wolff went in as the FEs headed west, pursued one and, after a chase across the lines north of La Bassée, the pusher (A827) force-landed near Bailleul at 1235. This was credited to the German as his 11th victory. This, of course, was Bailleul-Sir-Berthoult, just north-east of Arras. (This should not be confused with Bailleul town, which lies south of Poperinghe and Ypres, way up on the more northern part of the front. Germans working on the Arras front generally recorded this southern town plain Bailleul, which has led to much confusion over the years with the more famous northern location.)

Von Richthofen, in company with Leutnant Georg Simon, chased another southwest, his fire wounding both men in the two-seater which went down and crash-landed inside British lines between Feuchy and Monchy at 1245.

Once more Jasta 11 went home victorious, and why not. As the morning ended, Jasta 11 had been credited with seven kills thus far, with 39 British aircraft brought down so far in April, and the day was far from over, let alone the month.

The Bristols of 48 Squadron operated a line patrol at 1450 to the east of Arras and had a scrap with some Albatros Scouts, Captain A M Wilkinson and his gunner claiming one destroyed, Lieutenant J W Warren and his back-seater another out of control. However, the squadron lost one machine which was hit by ground fire, claimed by Flakzug units near Courcelles.

Again there was a lull in the air fighting, and it wasn't until 1630 that Spandau machine guns were again stitching a line of bullets into a RFC machine. No. 29 Squadron flew a defensive patrol at five minutes to four, only to be engaged by Jasta 11, Kurt Wolff gaining another kill by forcing Second Lieutenant B Scott-Foxwell to land inside British lines south of Monchy. The British flyer scooted for cover as artillery shells began to rain down, blasting the Nieuport into scrap.

Two hours later Jasta 11 were once more east of the lines. More FEs were out as well as the Martinsydes of 27 Squadron which were to bomb Hénin-Liétard. 11 Squadron's 'Fees' were on another OP and so were six machines of 22 Squadron, and as 22 were to report: '... enemy aircraft very active.' The FEs were engaged by Jasta 11 and Jasta 3, but it is not clear who was engaged with whom. No.22 Squadron had an engagement with four enemy aircraft near Itancourt, which is five kilometres south-east of St Quentin, reporting one crashed by Second Lieutenant J V Aspinall and Lieutenant M K Parlee (4983) at 1830. No. 11 Squadron had their fight much further north. Karl Schäfer of Jasta 11 claimed his victim down in British lines south-west of Monchy at 1830, which is more than 50 km north-west of Itancourt, and in any event they only had an FE shot up and a crewman wounded, although it is possible it force- landed and was recorded as a kill.

No. 11 Squadron also had one of their machines shot up, the pilot being forced to crash-land in British lines. Leutnant Karl Bauer of Jasta 3 was credited with a FE2b on the British side of the lines at 1915 south of La Bassée, well north of Lens. It would be Bauer's only victory and he would die in combat a month later.

If one tries to determine what other Jasta 3 and 11 pilots were doing at around this time, one finds that Wolff was shooting down the 27 Squadron Martinsyde at

The BF2a of 48 Squadron (A3322), forced down after action with a German two-seater on 13 April. Both of the crew were captured.

1852 near Rouvroy, south-east of Lens, while Leutnant Karl Stobel of Jasta 3 was gaining his one and only victory, over a BE2, south-west of Oppy, inside British lines. The only BE lost this day was a 5 Squadron machine on a line recce over Oppy, which came down inside its own lines, so this one is beyond doubt.

This 5 Squadron machine was attacked by two fighters, described as Halberstadts, and had its elevator controls shot away. Being unable to level out, the pilot made a rapid landing into what he later reported to be the enemy's lines, but most probably it was right in the middle of the battle area. The crew of Second Lieutenants N C Buckton and G L Barritt clambered out of their wrecked machine and decided to take the Lewis gun and make for a nearby sunken road. As they were doing so, a patrol of German soldiers appeared – they counted eight – so they opened up with the Lewis and the soldiers retreated. A few minutes later an advanced Canadian patrol came up and the two airmen were able to give them valuable information as to the whereabouts of the enemy. They also saw an FE2b brought down in flames near Farbus by the 'same hostile aircraft' almost immediately after they had come down. The two men also found a wrecked RE8, No. A112, with a dead pilot and observer. The only identity found was that the pilot was a former Northumberland Fusilier and the observer had been in a light infantry regiment.

What is interesting is that one must assume that the FE was brought down by Jasta 3 as well, and as fire is mentioned, must presumably be the 11 Squadron machine; thus it seems more likely that it was Bauer's victim. The RE8 wreck – A112 – was one of the 59 Squadron machines brought down not on this day, but the previous Good Friday, the crew being Second Lieutenants Davies and Wordsworth, Robert Davies having indeed been in the 16th Northumberland Fusiliers and Joe Wordsworth having served with the 8th Durham Light Infantry.

Second Lieutenant Buckton in fact had quite an eventful Friday the 13th. Quite apart from being shot down into no man's land and rescued by Canadian soldiers, he had flown two test flights that morning. After lunch he had flown with Lieutenant Steele on a recce sortie, attacking a party of 30 enemy troops, and then another group they had found near Bailleul – who had not unnaturally scattered in all directions. All flights had been in the machine now lying wrecked – 7156.

An interesting note in 5 Squadron's records states that aircraft wanting to cross the lines should fire off a red Very light to attract the attention of patrolling fighters. However, it also notes that one of its machines had in fact fired red flares twice at a couple of FEs which had ignored them – twice! So much for help and co-operation, and one supposes that if there are no obvious friendly aircraft about, the two-seater crew must continue on alone!

At Douai Jasta 11 were congratulating Schäfer on what appeared to be his 17th victory, when once more the call to become airborne came. Nine 25 Squadron FE2s had taken off at 1840 on a bomb raid against Hénin-Liétard. Taking the air, the Jasta pilots were too late to stop the attack, and the air battle began while the FEs were still dropping their bombs. The clash came over Hénin at 1930, the FE crews claiming no fewer than four Albatros DIIIs destroyed as the running fight ensued. Klein of Jasta 4 also showed up again so the two units were obviously flying together, attacking the FEs at the front of the stream that were now heading for home.

The first FE to go down went under the guns of Klein, A6372 falling near Vimy, having almost made it. Sebastian Festner shot down A784 near Harnes at 1915, while Manfred von Richthofen got 4997 at 1935 over Hénin itself, the pusher falling into a house at Noyelles Godault. Klein's victim was Captain L L Richardson, an Australian who had achieved seven victories with his gunners since mid-1916 and was about to receive the MC. He and his observer were both killed.

The RFC had two other losses during the day, but they appear not to have been claimed by any German pilots. At 1815 a Morane Parasol of 3 Squadron on a photo op crashed near the front lines at Quéant after being attacked by three fighters, both RFC men being wounded. And a Nieuport XII two-seater from 46 Squadron was also brought down inside British lines, the dead observer being buried at Lijssenthoek, having been killed in combat with a German aircraft. This machine had almost got back to its base at Droglandt and was 16 kilometres from the front line, thus was not seen to go down and land by German front-line observers.

Claims by German anti-aircraft units amounted to three, including a BE and an FE at Willerval, Brebières and Quiery-la-Motte – the latter being a type unknown. Willerval is just north of Oppy and this may be the same 5 Squadron machine claimed by Jasta 3.

During the day the RFC pilots had made several claims in addition to those already mentioned. 66 Squadron drove down a two-seater and a scout on an early morning patrol, while Lieutenant G S Buck of 19 Squadron, claimed a DIII out of control over Brebières. At 1130, Lieutenant H E O Ellis of 40 Squadron claimed a C-type Albatros as destroyed over Courrières. He put just 20 rounds into it but must have hit the pilot, for the two-seater cartwheeled, turned over, went down in a spin and crashed.

Two German airmen are reported casualties. Unteroffizier Binder of Schusta 24, severely wounded on the 6 Armee front, and a Jasta 37 pilot wounded on the French front (see opposite). The Nachrichtenblatt records no aircraft lost and one Unteroffizier pilot wounded.

In the evening, Jasta 5 made an attack on the balloon lines west and south of St Quentin and claimed two destroyed, although it seems only one British balloon, that of the 34th Section of 4 Wing, was actually lost, the observers making a safe parachute descent. Nathanael and Gontermann were the claimants, their attacks timed at 1935 and 1940, Gontermann's being the French balloon of 55 Cié.

During the ground battle, troops of the 4th Canadian Division entered a recently abandoned German dugout, finding two wounded RFC officers, Second Lieutenants Smythe and Cooper of 16 Squadron, who had been missing since the 9th. They had been brought down by machine-gun fire during one of the first Contact Patrols upon the opening of the Arras Battle.

Although non-combat casualties are not being specifically covered in this work, the RNAS did lose one of its squadron commanders on this day, Squadron Commander J J Petrie DSC, CO of 6 Naval, killed in a flying accident. He was flying Nieuport XVII N3206.

French Front

Combat on the French sectors was confined to just three claimed successes. A Farman crew from F.41 claimed a victory over Mont Sapigneul on the Châlons front, while Adjutant Bertrand of N.57 claimed another near Guignicourt. In fact the pilot of the Farman was Louis Gros, later to become an ace flying with Spa.154. Adjutant Raoul Lufbery, the ace of the Lafayette Escadrille – N.124 – claimed a two-seater north-west of St Quentin for his 8th victory.

The French lost a Spad VII at 1400 hours in combat with Jasta 36 near Sapigneul. The German, Leutnant Albert Dossenbach, holder of the Pour le Mérite, downed Sous Lieutenant Marcel Nogues of Spa.12, who was captured. Nogues had two victories at this time, but he was to escape his captors five weeks later and return to active duty, and by the war's end he had increased his score to 13.

A Salmson two-seater of F.72 on the Châlons front was downed near Châlons-sur-Vesle by Leutnant Heinrich Bongartz of Jasta 36 at 1700, the second victory for this future ace, who would eventually gain 33 successes. In the heat of combat, Bongartz had claimed a Caudron. In other actions, a Letord, a Sopwith and a Farman had returned with dead or wounded aircrew, mostly following combats with enemy fighters.

Balloons were attacked, Gontermann of Jasta 5 as already mentioned shooting down one of 55 Cié, while Jastas 34 and 37 made assaults against the 'drachens'. Oberleutnant Eduard Dostler of Jasta 34 made a claim at Genicourt but this was not confirmed, while Unteroffizier Simon Ruckser of Jasta 37, based at Montingen, by Metz, flamed one but was severely wounded by ground fire. It also happened to be Jasta 37's first success and first casualty.

At 1955, Leutnant Josef Jacobs of Jasta 22 spotted a Farman over the French side of the lines, flying in and out of cloud. Despite French AA fire, Jacobs attacked and watched as the Farman went down 'end-over-end' over Barisis, 20 kilometres west of Laon. Confirmation came from German gunners that the Farman had gone down although it may not have crashed.

	A/C	KB		DES	OOC	KB
British losses	18	1	British claims	5	3	–
French losses	2	2?	French claims	3		–
German claims	27	3	German losses	?†		

† No losses recorded in the Nachrichtenblatt, just one NCO pilot wounded.

British Casualties

Aircraft type	No.	Squadron	Crew		
FE2d	A5150	57 Sqdn	Capt L S Platt	KIA	
			2/Lt T Margerison	KIA	
FE2d	A1950	57 Sqdn	2/Lt G W Gillespie	KIA	
			Pvt R Sibley	MIA	
RE8	A3225	59 Sqdn	Lt A H Tanfield	KIA	
			Lt A Ormerod	KIA	
RE8	A3190	59 Sqdn	Capt J Stuart	KIA	
			Lt M H Wood	KIA	
RE8	A4191	59 Sqdn	Lt H G Mc Home	KIA	
			Lt W J Chalk	KIA	
RE8	A3199	59 Sqdn	Lt A Watson	POW	
			Lt E R Law	POW	
RE8	A3216	59 Sqdn	Capt G B Hodgson	KIA	
			Lt C H Morris	KIA	
RE8	A3203	59 Sqdn	Lt P B Boyd	KIA	
			2/Lt P O Ray	KIA	
Nieuport XII	A258	46 Sqdn	Lt K W Macdonald	Safe	*
			2/Lt C P Long	KIA	
FE2b	A827	11 Sqdn	Lt C E Robertson	Safe	*
			2/Lt H D Duncan	Safe	
FE2b	A831	11 Sqdn	Sgt J A Cunniffe	WIA	
			2AM W J Batten	WIA	
FE2b		22 Sqdn	Lt E A Thomas	WIA	*
BF2a	A3322	48 Sqdn	2/Lt H D Davies	POW	
			2/Lt R S Worsley	POW	
Nieuport XXIII	A6768	29 Sqdn	2/Lt B Scott-Foxwell	Safe	
BE2f	7156	5 Sqdn	2/Lt N C Buckton	Safe	
			2/Lt G L Barritt	Safe	
Martinsyde G100	A1564	27 Sqdn	2/Lt M Topham	KIA	
FE2b	4997	25 Sqdn	2/Lt A H Bates	KIA	
			Sgt W A Barnes	KIA	
FE2b	A784	25 Sqdn	Sgt J Dempsey	POW	
			2/Lt W H Green	WIA/POW	
FE2b	A6372	25 Sqdn	Capt L L Richardson	KIA	
			2/Lt D C Wollen	KIA	
Morane Parasol	A6760	3 Sqdn	Lt L F Beynon	WIA	
			Lt A C Lutyens MC	WIA	
FE2b	A819	11 Sqdn	Lt E T Curling	WIA	
			2/Lt J Rothwell	Safe	

French Casualties

Aircraft type	No.	Squadron	Crew		
Salmson-Moineau		F.72	S/Lt Fequand	KIA	
			Lt Locquin (O)	KIA	
			Sol Hutreau (AG)	KIA	
Spad VII	1057	N.12	MdL M J M Nogues	POW	
Letord L J		R.210	Ens de la Tullaye (O)	WIA	*
			Sgt Lentrain (AG)	KIA	
Sopwith 2		F.2	S/Lt Paulli-Krause	WIA	*
			S/Lt Clave	WIA	
Farman 40		F.41	MdL Gros	Safe	*
			S/Lt de Dreux	WIA	

14 APRIL 1917
M T W T F **S** S

British Front

With Vimy Ridge firmly in Allied hands and the line dented if not smashed, Field Marshal Haig now awaited General Nivelle's promised attack along the French front to the south. Not that Haig trusted the Frenchman to carry out what he had promised. Nobody knew more than Haig that to effect a breakthrough was almost impossible. Not totally impossible, or no general would even try, but Haig had his doubts that Nivelle would do it now.

Nevertheless, for five days the British forces had taken the battle to the enemy, hoping to take any pressure off the French sectors before the French launched their attack. Haig, having halted his attacks on Vimy and at the Scarpe now awaited Nivelle's mighty thrust, but it was delayed. Pressure along the 25-mile British front would need to be maintained – but for how long? Meantime, this Saturday saw Lieven and Lens taken as well as Gricourt to the south.

German troops were coming up from the rear, which is why the railhead at Hénin-Liétard had been attacked the previous day. At 0420, 10 Squadron sent out some 'pilot-only' BE2s for a late night raid on Hénin. They made their attack but machine-gun fire brought down one aeroplane and its pilot was put into a prison camp.

With the dawn came the Corps machines, and up went the fighters to fly their offensive patrols. The morning looked fine enough but the forecast was for a more cloudy afternoon. Pups of 54 Squadron flew a dawn patrol and had one pilot wounded in a fight, but the pilot got back so there was no victory for the German pilot. However, Leutnant Schöll of Jasta 30 did claim a Sopwith over Douai at 0810. In fact he claimed a two-seater Sopwith, but in all probability it was a Pup of 54 Squadron. A Pup pilot, Lieutenant M B Cole, encountered a two-seater over Gonnelieu at 0810 (in A6168) and claimed it out of control, reporting the observer hit by his fire and seen hanging over the side of the rear cockpit.

No.29 Squadron sent out machines to escort the two-seaters at 0840, and got tangled up with Jasta 4 south-east of Fresnoy and lost Second Lieutenant E J Pascoe to Oberleutnant Kurt von Döring at 0934, his first of an eventual 11 victories.

At the same moment, Hermann Frommherz of Jasta 2 was savouring his second victory, a 9 Squadron BE2c which he had just forced down at Ribécourt, south-east of Cambrai. He would end the war with 32 kills.

The Corps machines hopeful of some protection over the Arras battle area found, nevertheless, that the Albatros Scouts were getting to them. An 11 Squadron FE on a photo mission was attacked by an Albatros and its gunner was killed. The pilot scooted back over the lines, heading down, still being chased by the German who finally had to let him go, but not before he saw him hedge-hopping low over the ground. Vizefeldwebel Menckhoff's claim for the FE was not upheld. He hadn't seen it crash, only reported it close to the ground near Ecoust St Mein, but the FE pilot got his shot-up pusher down at his base of Le Hameau at 1010. As men watched the shot-up FE land, the chaps of 60 Squadron, which shared the airfield with 11 and 29 Squadron, were anxiously awaiting the return of their 0830 OP to Douai.

Douai! One might have guessed; Richthofen country! The patrol, with a mixture of Nieuport XVIIs and XXIIIs ran into Jasta 11 at 0915 and in just eight minutes four were shot down. Captain Alan Binnie MC, leader, was hit in the upper left arm as he reached for his wing-mounted Lewis gun, shattering the bone. The Australian, from New South Wales, saw his blood spurting all over his instruments, then passed out and came to amid wreckage and German soldiers. He'd been hit by Lothar von Richthofen's fire. Cock, a New Zealander, went down under Wolff's, while Festner hit and mortally wounded Chapman from south London. The other Londoner fell to the Baron over Bois Bernard and he too was taken prisoner. Alan Binnie later had his left arm amputated at the shoulder and was repatriated in January 1918 but flew again despite his disability. (He died in an accident during WW2.) So Le Hameau had had five of its Nieuports lost (four from 60 and one from 29) and had an FE return shot about and with a dead gunner on board.

The Nieuports had been engaging a German two-seater recce plane when Jasta 11 intervened, and one wonders if this had been the FA(A)224 aircraft flown by Vizefeldwebel Karl Meckes and Leutnant Paul Otto, engaged on reconnoitring railway movements, spotting numerous rail-cars at Grenay Station, six kilometres north-west of Lens. They were attacked by three British fighters and hit in the propeller, wings and observer's seat, Otto being slightly wounded. Meckes received the Württemburg Golden Military Merit Medal on 2 August as a result of this day's action.

Another BE went down to Jasta 5's Gontermann over Metz-en-Couture during a front-line photo job, and although it came down inside British lines both RFC men – from 52 Squadron – were killed.

An RE8 of 34 Squadron failed to return from a photo op, having taken off at 0920 from its base at Foucaucourt. No German pilot seems to have claimed it (although reference has been made to Schäfer of Jasta 11, but the time is wrong). Perhaps it was the aircraft claimed by Flakzug 50.

In the late afternoon, Captain L C Coates with Second Lieutenant J C Cotton, of 5 Squadron, were engaged on a Line Recce and artillery patrol, and at 1830 were west of Willerval. Here they were attacked by half a dozen German fighters, and a running fight ensued. Returning fire, Cotton thought he'd sent one fighter down – confirmed later by Canadian troops on Vimy Ridge as going down out of control – and despite being wounded in seven places, he still continued to fire back until his gun finally jammed with a broken cartridge guide spring. Coates was also wounded but kept the BE under control and, despite having his aileron controls shot away, landed the BE without further injury to either himself or his observer.

Schäfer and Jasta 11 were in action at 1700 to 1730, Schäfer attacking a lone 25 Squadron FE2b (4877) during a patrol between Lens and Arras, that went down in flames near Lieven at 1705 inside British lines just west of Lens. Schäfer then chased after a BE2 of 2 Squadron, on artillery duty over the Bois de l'Hirondelle, seen to be shot down by two enemy fighters at 1720.

Wolff shot up another BE of 2 Squadron (2525), but its crew, Second Lieutenant W P M Brettell and Lieutenant C E Leggett, escaped despite having to make a forced landing inside British lines, thanks to another BE crew.

Brettell and Leggett had also been on an artillery patrol near the Cité St Theodore at 3,500 feet. At 1910, over Lens, they were attacked by two German fighters, Brettell diving away rapidly. One German – Wolff – followed them down, the observer firing back at him, with several rounds appearing to hit Wolff's machine. Another 2 Squadron BE flying nearby, with Captain H Fowler and Lieutenant F E Brown (2521), an experienced couple who had had several encounters with German fighters and survived (Fowler had already had a fight with Jasta 11 during the afternoon), saw the action and came to assist their comrades. They attacked Wolff, drawing him away from Brettell, only to have Wolff turn on them, but Brown fired another drum of Lewis ammunition at him and saw the fighter spiral down towards Maroc, before flying off, helped on its way by gunfire from Maroc and Grenay. Brettell's BE had been hit in several places, and eight bullets had pierced the petrol tank.

An hour later Jasta 11 were on the prowl again, this time finding Spads of 19 Squadron on an OP along the line Bailleul-Vitry-Sains-Bullecourt. Lothar von Richthofen claimed one in British lines south of Vimy, Wolff another near Bailleul. However, 19 only lost one machine and its pilot, Lieutenant E W Capper, although it had Lieutenant J W Baker wounded. Edward Capper very nearly shot down Wolff before the German got on his tail and brought him down.

French Front

Most of the air combat took place around noon. Two Caudrons were claimed by Jasta 14 at Craonelle and Juvigny, north of Soissons, while Rudolf Berthold claimed a Spad two-seater over the Bois de Marais. However, this latter victory was more probably a Sopwith two-seater of N.15 that came down near Pontavert, west of Berry-au-Bac, after a combat with three enemy fighters. Josef Veltjens was also credited with a Spad at this same time, his first victory. The Jasta lost Leutnant Otto Weigel who was killed at 1215 over Craonelle, probably by the crew of a C.46 Caudron whose 'ace' crew (Capt Didier Lecour Grandmaison, Adj Marie Vitalis and MdL Achille Rousseau) claimed a German fighter south of Craonne at 1210.

The French made several claims on the 14th. On the Belfort sector, Maréchal-des-Logis de Belleville of N.49 brought down a fighter in flames at Elsbach. The German pilot was Leutnant Fritz Grünzweig of Jasta 16, who was engaged in a balloon attack when shot down. N.93 claimed three enemy planes and a balloon, Adjutant Gustave Daladier and MdL Vieljeux claiming the aircraft, Adjutant Hamel the balloon. For Daladier, who claimed a two-seater, it was his first of an eventual 12 victories, and he received the Médaille Militaire for this combat.

During a mission on the Nancy sector, Adjutant Grelat and Lieutenant Cavinet of GB4 claimed an aircraft over Brisbach, the Germans also losing Unteroffizier Hermann Jopp of Jasta 37 on this front, brought down by the 71st Balloon Section near Mont Toulon, when Jopp attacked it.

Also on the Soissons front, Sous Lieutenant Languedoc of N.12 claimed an enemy plane over the Bois de Noyelles at 0600 hours. Capitaine Georges Guynemer of N.3 claimed an Albatros in flames by La Neuville at 1030 (the Frenchman's 36th victory), while Lieutenant Thiriez of N.15 got one over Corbeny.

On the Châlons front Lieutenant Armand Pinsard of N.78 shot down a two-seater north of Somme-Py – his 8th victory – while a Farman and a Caudron crew each claimed one EA shot down during the day.

The Germans had several losses: Vizefeldwebel Ludwig Demmel and Unteroffizier Simon Stebel of Schutzstaffel 26 were both killed near Neubriesach; Leutnant August Schlorf and Oberleutnant Erich Schwidder of FA(A)251 were brought down near Wibeah Ferme, Pauvres, north-east of Reims; Leutnant Otto Druck and Unteroffizier Erich Hartmann of FA(A)243 were shot down near Diebolshausen, Alsace; and Leutnant Friedrich Bierling of FA(A)253, was killed just west of Anizy le Château. Another two-seater observer, Leutnant Theodor Aichele of FA14 was killed at Rusach in Alsace. KG4 also lost Leutnant Kurt Matthias, who was brought down with his pilot – Ruger – at Clermont les Fermes. The losses from SS26 and FA(A)251 were probably caused by N.93.

By far the most serious loss to the Germans this day was that of Helmut Baldamus of Jasta 9 shortly before midday. The unit was in combat with Nieuport Scouts of N.37 near St Marie-à-Py, Baldamus colliding with Caporal Simon, both German and Frenchman falling to their deaths. The Germans gave credit to Baldamus for the Nieuport, his 18th and final victory.

Another victory this day went to Eduard Dostler of Jasta 34, south-west of St Mihiel, while Flakzug 79, 171 and 413 claimed another Spad south-east of Moyenmoutier. For once, the Germans seemed to have claimed more aircraft than actually lost.

However, on the French front, the British 3 Naval Wing mounted a raid upon Freiburg, Germany, just across the Rhine south of Strasbourg. It was planned as the Wing's last bomb raid before reorganisation and supposedly as a reprisal for the recent sinking of hospital ships. The bombing force comprised Sopwith two-seaters and they were intercepted by Jasta 35, who shot down two of the Strutters, Vize-feldwebel Gustav Schindler claiming N5171 down at Schlettstadt, and Vizefeldwebel Rudolf Rath N5117 down at Scherweiler. A third Sopwith (9667) was brought down by ground fire. In one of the downed aircraft was Wing Commander C E H Rath-borne, and although he was taken prisoner, he was later to escape. In the 1930s he would command the RAF in the Mediterranean as an air commodore CB DSO and bar. Harold 'Gus' Edwards, one of the other pilots brought down, would become an air marshal in the RCAF in WW2. One of the victorious observers, the Australian Bert Hinkler, would gain immortality as a pioneer aviator in the 1920s, flying from Britain to Australia.

The Navy flyers claimed three Albatros Scouts shot down during the raid and Jasta 35 did indeed have three pilots brought down. Leutnant Gerhard Anders was wounded, and so was Leutnant Margraf. The third was the Staffelführer, Oberleutnant Herbert Theurich, flying a DIII 2097/16, who was mortally wounded.

The Germans also claimed two French balloons, one to Leutnant Fritz Pütter of Jasta 9, 48 Cié east of Suippes and another to Leutnant Hans Adam of Jasta 24, a balloon of 57 Cié west of St Mihiel.

	A/C	KB		DES	OOC	KB
British losses	15	–	British claims	4	9	–
French losses	3	2	French claims	12		1
German claims	27 †	2	German losses	9		1‡

† 7 to flak and ground fire. ‡ The Nachrichtenblatt notes 9 aircraft lost (4 in combat, 4 missing, 1 by flak) with 2 pilots and 3 observers killed, 4 pilots and 1 observer wounded, plus 1 balloon lost.

British Casualties

Aircraft type	No.	Squadron	Crew		
BE2f	2567	10 Sqdn	2/Lt C W D Holmes	POW	
Sopwith Pup	A661	54 Sqdn	Lt R N Smith	WIA	*
FE2b	7702	11 Sqdn	2/Lt A W Gardner	Unhurt	*
			Cpl W Hodgson	KIA	
Nieuport XXIII	A6794	29 Sqdn	2/Lt E J Pascoe	KIA	
RE8	A78	34 Sqdn	Lt H R Davies	POW	
			Lt J R Samuel	POW	
BE2c	7241	52 Sqdn	2/Lt C T L Donaldson	KIA	
			2/Lt S R Carter	KIA	
BE2c	2562	9 Sqdn	Lt W Harle	POW/WIA	
			2/Lt W B E Cramb	KIA	
Nieuport XXIII	A6772	60 Sqdn	Capt A Binnie MC	POW/WIA	
Nieuport XVII	B1511	60 Sqdn	2/Lt J H Cock	KIA	
Nieuport XVII	B1523	60 Sqdn	2/Lt L C Chapman	DOW	
Nieuport XVII	A6796	60 Sqdn	Lt W O Russell	POW	
Spad VII	A6746	19 Sqdn	Lt E W Capper	KIA	
Spad VII	A6683	19 Sqdn	Lt J W Baker	WIA	*
FE2b	4877	25 Sqdn	Lt H E Davies	WIA	
			2/Lt N W Morrison	KIA	
BE2g	6814	5 Sqdn	Capt L C Coates	WIA	*
			2/Lt J C Cotton	WIA	
BE2c	2527	2 Sqdn	Capt G B Lockhart	KIA	
			Lt A P Wilson	KIA	
Sop 1½ Strutter	N5117	3N Wing	WC C E H Rathborne	POW	
			GL/AM1 V Turner	KIA	
Sop 1½ Strutter	N5171	3N Wing	FSL H Edwards	POW	
			1AAM.GL J L Coghlan	KIA	
Sop 1½ Strutter	9667	3N Wing	Lt G R S Fleming	DOW	
			GL/AM1 A G Lockyer	KIA	
BE2c		42 Sqdn	Lt G C Walker (O)	WIA	*
BE2c		13 Sqdn	2AM W S Boon (O)	WIA	*

French Casualties

Aircraft type	No.	Squadron	Crew		
Nieuport XVII	2539	N.37	Cpl Simon	KIA	
Sopwith 2		N.15	S/Lt de Maison Rouge	DOW	
			S/Lt Revi	WIA	
Caudron G4		C.225	Lt Floret	Unhurt	
			S/Lt Piquet	Unhurt	

15 APRIL 1917
M T W T F S **S**

British Front

Low cloud and rain which persisted throughout the day precluded any air combat at all on the northern sectors, although Corps aircraft did operate a few recce sorties and a few guns were ranged; otherwise all was quiet. On the ground the Germans made a counter-attack at Lagnicourt, south-east of Arras, opposite Cambrai, breaking into the Australian lines, but were then thrown back from almost all their initial gains during the day. The Australians suffered 1,010 casualties; the Germans 2,313.

Effective co-operation between the RFC and the artillery helped blunt the attack, and there was no interference from Germany's airmen evident. The guns fired over 43,000 shells! As at this date, RFC HQ listed the following aircraft states:

9th Wing	19 Sqdn	16 Spads	
	27 Sqdn	18 G100s	
	55 Sqdn	18 DH4s	
	56 Sqdn	13 SE5s	
		1 Nieuport Scout	
	57 Sqdn	17 FE2ds	
	66 Sqdn	19 Sopwith Pups	
	70 Sqdn	19 Sopwith 1½ Strutters	
	SD Flt	5 BE12/2cs	
I Brigade		69 BE2s	(2,5,10 and 16 Sqdns)
		11 FE2bs	(25 Sqdn)
		3 FE2ds	"
		17 Nieuports	(40 Sqdn)
		15 Sopwith 1½ Strutters	(43 Sqdn)
		17 Sopwith Triplanes	(8N Sqdn)
II Brigade		24 BE2s	(6 and 53 Sqdns)
		44 RE8s	(21 and 42 Sqdns)
		17 Nieuport XIIs	(46 Sqdn)
		18 Nieuport Scouts	(1 Sqdn)
		17 FE2ds	(20 Sqdn)
		18 FE8s	(41 Sqdn)
		16 Sopwith 1½ Strutters	(45 Sqdn)
III Brigade		70 BE2s	(8, 12 and 13 Sqdns)
		18 RE8s	(59 Sqdn)
		18 AWFK8s	(35 Sqdn)
		26 FE2bs	(11 and 100 Sqdns)
		36 Nieuport Scouts	(29 and 60 Sqdns)
		11 BF2as	(48 Sqdn)
		18 Sopwith Triplanes	(1N Sqdn)
IV Brigade		56 BE2s	(7, 9 and 52 Sqdns)
		16 RE8s	(34 Sqdn)
		17 FE2bs	(22 Sqdn)
		18 DH2s	(24 Sqdn)
		18 Sopwith Pups	(54 Sqdn)
		13 Nieuports	(6N Sqdn)

V Brigade	17 Morane Parasols	(3 Sqdn)
	35 BEs	(4 and 15 Sqdns)
	18 Spads	(19 and 23 Sqdns)
	18 DH2s	(32 Sqdn)
	17 FE2bs	(23 Sqdn)
	17 Nieuports/Pups	(3N Sqdn)

In the general Order of Battle there had been only a few subtle changes since the start of the month, although one or two squadrons had changed equipment and bases. One squadron (No.42) had now been equipped with RE8s, so with the other two units, there were now 78 on the front. But still the main Corps machine was the various BE2s – numbering 259 – taking the brunt of the artillery and contact patrol work.

Fighters – that is Pups, Triplanes, Spads and Nieuports – only totalled 143. The DH2s and FE8s were hardly being used, the units which had them awaiting new equipment. The single unit of Bristol Fighters was now down to just 11 machines, and the main long-distance fighting was being handled by the FE2 squadrons which had 90 aircraft on strength (the other FEs were used by 100 Squadron for night bombing). Long-distance recce missions were in the main being flown by the three RFC 1½ Strutter units. The new AWFK8 would soon prove itself as a front-line recce and contact patrol machine that also took to bombing, ground attack and artillery work.

The one glimmer of hope in Trenchard's arsenal was the arrival of the first of the promised 'new types' from England – the single-seat SE5. No.56 Squadron had arrived from England on 7 April, although its pilots were still working-up at their base at Vert Galant, north of Amiens, on the Amiens-Doullens road. Its 13 machines were the forerunners of several thousand of the type – mainly the improved SE5a – to be built and see action over France for the remainder of the war and which, with the Sopwith Camel that began to arrive later in the year, would bear the brunt of the fighter air war. But for April 1917, 56 would be the only SE5 squadron in front-line service.

The reason why 56 had a single Nieuport on charge was due to its senior flight commander, the famous and well-respected Captain Albert Ball DSO MC, who had scored over 30 victories (of the period) during 1916 while still only 20 years old. In deference to his ability with and liking of the Nieuport, he was allowed to have a personal one for his own use – B1522 – a type XVII. Ball made two lone flights across the lines on the 14th although 56 itself would not make its first war patrols until the 18th.

French Front

Still Nivelle was not ready to start his offensive. At 1040, Lieutenant Albert Deullin of Spa.73 claimed a German aircraft shot down over Festieux – the only positive encounter of the day. The only German loss admitted to was a two-seater of FA(A)242, lost to ground fire. A pilot, Unteroffizier Franz Kassel of FA2, was killed, while Leutnant Paul Dörr of FA45 was wounded, and died on 17 April.

However, the German fighter pilots were more successful. In a fight with N.15, Leutnant Dossenbach of Jasta 36, having already forced a Nieuport Scout of N.83 down into French lines at Bétheny near Reims with a wounded pilot, shot down Adjutant Epitalon at St Fergeux. Two more N.15 pilots fell, one over Thugny to

Vizefeldwebel Hans Mitkeit, also of Jasta 36, and Lieutenant Bergeron to Unteroffizier Max Zachmann of Jasta 21, falling near Sery at 1030. Leutnant Werner Albert, Staffelführer of Jasta 31 downed another Spad of N.3 – the Storks Group – over Nauroy, north of Reims.

A Spad of N.102 which fell near Prouvais was the 4th victory of Vizefeldwebel Julius Buckler, a future leading ace who would end the war with 35 victories and the Pour le Mérite.

Two Nieuports failed to get back, Dossenbach's and a machine of N.519 on the Nancy front. The only claim for a second Nieuport was that made by Leutnant Dotzel of Jasta 19, his one and only victory, which fell into the French lines at La Neuvillette.

The crew of Schusta 10 claimed a Farman over Oulcher Wald, although there are no Farmans listed as lost, but a Salmson-Moineau of F.71 was hit and its pilot wounded, although this is believed to have been caused by AA fire.

	A/C	KB		DES	OOC	KB
British losses	–	–	British claims	–	–	–
French losses	6	–	French claims	1		–
German claims	8	–	German losses	1		–

British Casualties

Nil

French Casualties

Aircraft type	No.	Squadron	Crew		
Nieuport XXIII	2539	N.519	Adj Sirieys	MIA	
Nieuport XXIII		N.83	S/Lt Sénéchal	WIA	*
Spad VII	1059	N.15	Lt Bergeron	POW	
Spad VII	1234	N.15	Adj Epitalon	POW	
Spad VII	373	N.15	Sgt Buisson	POW	
Spad VII	117	N.3	Sgt Papeil	MIA	
Spad VII	1056	N.102	Cpl Quaissaron	MIA	
Salmson-Moineau		F.71	MdL Wang (P)	WIA	*

16 APRIL 1917

M T W T F S S

THE READER MUST NOTE that on this day the times changed on the Western Front. From now until 9 April 1918 German time was one hour ahead of Allied time, and any historians or enthusiasts trying to match events should remember to take account of the time difference.

British Front

There seemed little let-up in the poor weather, rain and low clouds persisting all day although there were a few bright intervals. Despite this there was more activity along the Arras front, with contact patrols, artillery observation and recce missions all being flown. This naturally brought up the German fighters with the consequential casualties. Men died in those few bright intervals.

A line patrol and recce sortie was flown by 43 Squadron, starting out at 0630, to La Bassée and Bailleul. They encountered a two-seater of Schutzstaffel 4 over Douai, Leutnant Figulla and Unteroffizier Steudel making a fight of it at 0810 which resulted in the Strutter falling with a dead gunner and a wounded pilot. Further south, FEs of 18 Squadron were flying a photo op and escort sortie and had a fight with German single-seaters. One of the observers was Lieutenant O J Partington, formally of the Queen's Royal West Sussex Regiment. He recorded in his logbook:

'16.4.17. FE 4898 pilot [2/Lt E W A] Hunt. 6.55–9.10 am.
11,000 ft, visibility poor owing to clouds; archies good. Formation attacked by six HA, one shot down. Combat north-east of Cagnicourt. Followed HA down to 4,000 ft when he disappeared into clouds; we then went home. Steam tractor seen moving NW on road Cambrai-Arras.'

Raoul Lufbery's Nieuport Scout in 1917, N1615, with the first and last letters of his name on its fuselage. Note the roundels painted beneath the top wing.

Whether 60 Squadron had got over its defeat of two days earlier cannot be known, but the pilots must have had it on their minds this day when they took off at 0805 to fly a patrol to the Vitry area. Jasta 11 rose to meet them. At 0930 (1030 German time) the two formations met. In a running fight between Biache and Roeux, Lothar von Richthofen, Wolff and Festner each shot down one Nieuport. In fact four Nieuports went down, three of the British pilots being killed while the fourth died at Douai the next day. Lieutenant Pidcock drove down two enemy aircraft but made no substantial claim. Nobody seems to have claimed or been credited with the fourth Nieuport.

The next action came during an artillery observation sortie by a BE2d of 7 Squadron. It attracted anti-aircraft fire in the early afternoon, and was hit and shot down near Savy, accounted for by KFlak 93, falling just inside British lines with a wounded crew. A Morane from 3 Squadron also returned from a sortie with a wounded observer, probably the 'BE' claimed by KFlak 63 north-west of St Quentin. A pilot of 9 Squadron was also wounded during the day.

The final loss came in mid-afternoon: another artillery crew, this one ranging for guns on 17 Corps' front. Manfred von Richthofen, having missed out on the morning show, was out hunting, spotting the BE two-seater belonging to 13 Squadron north of Gavrelle. He attacked unseen, his fire causing the BE to smoke as it fell. The wounded pilot just managed to scrape over the lines, landed and turned over. The machine was smashed up and then shelled, so the Baron had his 45th victory, and Jasta 11 its 56th of the month.

At 1650 German time, Heinrich Gontermann attacked the British balloon lines at Manancourt, north of Péronne. He flamed a balloon of the 6th Company (6-15-4), and then went for one of the 29th Company. Ground observers saw and reported the Albatros flying round and round the balloon as it was pulled down, firing at it from well below 2,000 feet but it did not catch fire. Gontermann must have believed he'd damaged it sufficiently to claim a kill, although it may be significant that while the first balloon was his 10th official victory, he had been credited with six more kills before the second balloon was made official, to become his 17th victory. However, it seems that his second balloon was a 14th Company one (14-14-4), lost this day.

French Front

General Nivelle finally launched his attack, named the Second Battle of the Aisne. Aerial activity, therefore, was great along the Aisne sector with casualties high.

Fighter squadrons flew in support of their bombing and recce machines, three German aircraft being claimed as shot down, one each by N.12 (S/Lt Henri Languedoc) at 0600 east of Cauroy, and N.73 (Brig Rigault) at 1025 over Cormicy, and the third by N.26 (Brig Thomassin) west of Juvincourt. In addition, balloons were claimed as destroyed by N.73 (also Brig Rigault) at Bruyères at 1510 and another by N.67 (Cpl Cordelier) at Gros Usage. Another aircraft was claimed by gunners of F.72 and C.222 during a bomb raid north of Hermonville.

On the French front the Germans lost Leutnant Hans-Olaf Esser of Jasta 15, killed near Winterberge; the two-seater Abteilungen lost Leutnant Karl Helbig (O) of FA278 on the Aisne sector; Leutnant Hans-Jurgen Kalmus (O) of FA208 over Liesse; and Leutnant Walter Utermann (O) of FA(A)248 over Juvincourt (possibly Thomassin's victim). The crew of Unteroffizier Walter Köppen and Leutnant Heinrich Wecke of FA(A)248 fell over Villers Franqueux. Another single-seat pilot shot down

Top Rudolf Berthold gained his twelfth victory on 16 April, a French Spad during the Battle of the Aisne (the Nivelle Offensive). He would eventually achieve forty-four victories despite several serious wounds during the war, by which time he was commanding a fighter wing.

Bottom Raoul Lufbery flew with the Lafayette Escadrille during 1916-17, being the unit's top scorer with sixteen victories. Although born in France, his father was an American, hence his association with the American volunteers that made up this famous escadrille. He scored three times during April, two of which were confirmed. He would be killed flying with the American 94th Aero Squadron in May 1918.

was Vizefeldwebel Rieger of Jasta 17. His controls were damaged and in crash-landing he was severely injured.

The French, however, paid a heavy price. A Caudron G4 was attacked by five enemy fighters and crashed north of Sapigneul – probably the victim of Emil Thuy of Jasta 21 who downed a Caudron near Berry-au-Bac at 1505. Four fighters were lost, three Nieuports and a Spad. Three Nieuports were claimed by Leutnant H Wendel of Jasta 15 over Prouvais, Vizefeldwebel Buckler of Jasta 17 over Berry-au-Bac, and Unteroffizier Janning and Gefreiter Reimers of Schusta 5, north-west of Reims. The Spad was claimed by another two-seater crew, Gefreiter May and Unteroffizier Wiehle of Schusta 3, over Corbeny.

The fourth Nieuport was brought down by AA fire and flown by an American volunteer with the Lafayette Escadrille, Caporal Edmund Genet of N.124. Raoul Lufbery was leading a patrol between St Quentin and La Fère when they came under AA fire, shells bursting close to Genet's machine. The American turned for home, presumably wounded or his aircraft damaged, but then went into a spin, the wings of the Nieuport coming off, and it finally ploughed into the ground near Ham.

Another Caudron failed to return – from C.47, probably the one attacked by Leutnants Rose and Parlow of FA22, east of Cernay. Several other two-seaters were hit by ground fire and a number of airmen were brought back wounded.

French balloons were once more a target, Josef Jacobs of Jasta 22 claiming one during the afternoon despite interference from several Caudrons. Jasta 22 had in fact taken a leaf from the RFC's book on this day, Jacobs and Vizefeldwebel Graf Biessel strafing French trenches and forward observation posts.

Forced down after an encounter with a two-seater of Schutzstaffel 4 over Douai on 16 April, 2/Lt J G H Frew became a prisoner, his observer, 1AM F Russell being mortally wounded. Their 1½ Strutter (7804) appears to be beyond repair.

	A/C	KB		DES	OOC	KB
British losses	7	2	British claims	–	2	–
French losses	6	–	French claims	4		2
German claims	16†	3	German losses	6		2‡

† Three by flak. ‡ The Nachrichtenblatt states four of the losses were Schusta aircraft of the 7 Armee; five pilots/observers killed or wounded, one observer missing. Two balloons lost with their observers killed.

British Casualties

Aircraft type	No.	Squadron	Crew		
Sop 1½ Strutter	A7804	43 Sqdn	2/Lt J G Frew	POW/WIA	
			1AM F Russell	KIA	
Nieuport XVII	B1501	60 Sqdn	2/Lt D N Robertson	KIA	
Nieuport XVII	B1509	60 Sqdn	Lt J M Elliott	KIA	
Nieuport XVII	B1507	60 Sqdn	Lt T Langwill	DOW	
Nieuport XXIII	A6769	60 Sqdn	2/Lt R E Kimbell	KIA	
BE2d	5869	7 Sqdn	2/Lt W Green	WIA	
			2/Lt C E Wilson	KIA	
BE2e	3156	13 Sqdn	2/Lt A Pascoe	WIA	
			2/Lt F S Andrews	DOW	
BE2c	7163	9 Sqdn	2/Lt W R Baldwin (P)	WIA	*
Morane Parasol		3 Sqdn	1AM H Copstake (O)	WIA	*
			2/Lt H H Riekie	Safe	

French Casualties

Aircraft type	No.	Squadron	Crew		
Caudron G4		C.228	Sgt Pissavi	KIA	
			S/Lt Bekkers	KIA	
Farman 40		F.41	Lt Clavier (O)	KIA	*
Nieuport XXIII	2827	N.75	Lt Moreau	KIA	
Nieuport XVII		N.124	Cpl E C C Genet	KIA	
Nieuport XXIII		N.65	Cpl Cavinet-Lagrange	MIA	
Spad VII		Spa.48	S/Lt P de Larminat	MIA	
Caudron G4		C.47	S/Lt Houmens	MIA	
Nieuport XXIV		N.83	Brig Thomassin	WIA	*
Nieuport XXIII		N.83	MdL Dagonnet	WIA	*
Farman 40		F.226	S/Lt Desmyttere (O)	WIA	*
Farman 40		F.8	Lt Leloup (O)	WIA	*
Salmson-Moineau		SM.106	Lt Crosnier (O)	WIA	*
Caudron G4		C.47	Lt Caudillot (O)	WIA	*
Caudron G4		C.39	Lt Petit (O)	WIA	*
Caudron G4		C.104	Asp Humbert (O)	WIA	*
Farman 40		F.206	S/Lt Cote (O)	WIA	*
Sopwith 2		F.16	Lt Goisbaualt (O)	WIA	*
Farman 40		F.201	Lt Touard-Riolle (O)	WIA	*

17 APRIL 1917
M **T** W T F S S

British Front

With rain almost non-stop throughout the day there was very little aerial activity over the front. A few Corps aircraft registered for some artillery fire and some recce work was achieved but that was all. Lieutenant F Wessel, a Danish volunteer with 15 Squadron, successfully ranged guns of the 152nd Siege Battery on some new wire, five direct hits being achieved. During the night of 17/18th, FE2 of 100 Squadron flew bombing raids to a transport park at Cantin and some MT columns near Brebières. There were no losses.

French Front

A similar story here, with just one casualty, a Farman pilot being wounded by AA fire.

On the ground the French ground assault was already starting to falter. The attack against Laffaux which began the previous day, despite strong artillery support and barrage of the previous ten days, was not going well. It appears that the French commanders had not taken fully into account the natural obstacles their troops would encounter. The French V and VI Armées trying to go forward in the Chemin des Dames area – the buttress of the Champagne front – faced prepared defenders holding higher ground. These inflicted crippling casualties on the French troops. In just over a month this would lead to many desertions followed by the famous French army mutinies.

French Casualties

Aircraft type	No.	Squadron	Crew	
Farman 42		F.54	Adj Gealagas (P)	WIA
Caudron		C.46	Sgt L Joussen	WIA

18 APRIL 1917
M T **W** T F S S

British Front

Low clouds and rain prevented all work. One German two-seater of FA17 was shot down by infantry fire. On the ground, however, the British moved on Épehy and captured Villers-Guislan.

French Front

Despite the casualties, the French troops managed to drive into German positions to take Chavonne and Chivy, advancing as far as Braye-en-Laonnais, reporting several thousands of prisoners and 75 guns. There were no claims in the air but a Spad VII of N.78 was lost, claimed by MFlak 54 near Donnrein. At 0800 Leutnant Joens of Jasta 31 reported downing a Voisin at Auberive for his first victory.

	A/C	KB		DES	OOC	KB
British losses	–	–	British claims	–	–	–
French losses	1	–	French claims	–	–	–
German claims	2†	–	German losses	1‡	–	–

† One to flak. ‡ Infantry fire.

French Casualties				
Aircraft type	No.	Squadron	Crew	
Spad VII		N.78	S/Lt de Pasquier	MIA

19 APRIL 1917
M T **W** **T** F S S

British Front

The wet weather continued all day, and practically no work was possible. A balloon of the 14th Section was attacked by a German aircraft and damaged but there was no claim made. The only casualty of the day was the balloon company commander of the 17th Company, Major A C B Geddes MC, killed by shellfire.

French Front

Some slight activity resulted in five combat claims, although only two are recorded in any detail: an LVG two-seater was brought down by Sous Lieutenant Paul Tarascon of N.62 east of Trucy for his 10th victory, and Sous Lieutenant René Dorme of N.3 scored his 19th kill by downing a single-seater north-east of Brimont at 1450.

The Germans admitted one aircraft lost in combat and one officer wounded by ground fire, but at least two men were killed. Schutzstaffel 28 lost an aircraft in combat with a Caudron (possibly one of the three French claims where no details have been found), Gefreiter Hermann Brauer landing unhurt, but his observer, Unteroffizier Friedrich Schneider, was hit in the head and killed, the machine being forced down at Warmoville, near Prosnes. Brauer survived until his own death over Zonnebeke in July. Leutnant Paul Herrmann of Jasta 31 was killed in action in combat with a Spad over Bois Malvel – probably the victim of René Dorme.

Escadrille N.38 lost a Morane Parasol, and N.69 had a pilot wounded. The Morane was brought down at Prosnes, south-east of Reims, by Leutnant Willi Daugs of Jasta 36 for his first victory. Other claims by the Jasta pilots comprised a Spad by Leutnant Werner Marwitz of Jasta 9 south-west of Auberive at 1000; Leutnant Adolf Frey of the same unit downed a Farman south of Moronvilliers; and Leutnant Richard Wenzl of Jasta 31 also claimed a Spad in the same area, all three locations being within the French lines.

New fighters for the RFC were about to appear over France, Camels replacing the Sopwith Pups, while SE5s would gradually replace Nieuport Scouts. No. 56 Squadron was the first SE5 unit, which moved to the Western Front during April. Its senior flight commander was Captain Albert Ball DSO MC, already a legend despite his age – twenty. With 11 and 60 Squadrons during 1916 he had achieved thirty-one victories, and so loved the Nieuport that he was allowed one of his own with 56 Squadron. Ball would score five more victories in April, although only one with his Nieuport. With a score of forty-four he was to die in May, becoming disorientated in low cloud. He later received a posthumous VC.

	A/C	KB			DES	OOC	KB
British losses	–	–	British claims		1	–	–
French losses	1	–	French claims		5		–
German claims	4	–	German losses		1		–

French Casualties

Aircraft type	No.	Squadron	Crew	
Spad VII		N.69	Lt Conneau	WIA *
Morane Parasol		C.228	Capt Fevre	KIA
			Lt de Broglie-Revel	KIA
Farman		F.205	S/Lt A Reynaud	KIA
			S/Lt H Marche	KIA

20 APRIL 1917
M T W T **F** S S

British Front

British troops took Gonnelieu. After three days of wet weather the rain eased but left a pall of mist and low cloud over the battle front, making the work of the RFC very difficult. But the aeroplanes were out in small packages, 15 Squadron operating a BE over the 5th Corps area on artillery observation duties until attacked by five aircraft of Jasta 12. The BE had flown out at 0620 and was intercepted at 0735, Jasta 12's Vizefeldwebel Arthur Schorisch claiming his victim at 0940(G) near Ecoust St Mein, inside the British lines. The pilot was the same Danish volunteer, Lieutenant Wessel, who had ranged so successfully three days earlier.

Another BE, from 8 Squadron, took off at 0745, and was attacked by a German aircraft, damaged and forced to land, probably by the crew of Leutnant Peters and Vizefeldwebel Schopf of FA235 who forced down an aircraft near Vimy, although they claimed it was a 'Vickers'.

In the afternoon Sopwith 1½ Strutters of 43 Squadron flew a line patrol over the Loos Salient and seeing troops, descended to 200 feet to fire at small parties on the Gavrelle-Fresnes road. Second Lieutenant the Hon. S H D'Arcy and Lieutenant A E Pickering dispersed several of these as well as troops in some trenches, but Second Lieutenants Crisp and Newenham were not so fortunate and were brought down by ground fire from Flakzug 46. Newenham had only joined the Squadron on 8 April.

AA fire also accounted for the other loss of the day, a 16 Squadron BE2f which started its patrol at 1610 between Avion and Willerval and was shot down by Flak-batterie 503 between Fresnoy and Oppy.

Lieutenant W A Bishop of 60 Squadron claimed an Aviatik two-seater in flames over Biache-St-Vaast at 1458. The Germans only record an observer killed near Péronne, 40 km to the south of Bishop's claim.

French Front

French troops occupied Sancy on the Vregny plateau, while areas near Moronvilliers in the Champagne region were taken. In air actions no claims were made in the south. Two Farmans were attacked, one being brought down by Leutnant Schurz of Jasta 13 at Landricourt. The Germans had a Jasta 10 pilot wounded, Vizefeldwebel Viktor Hebben, but the cause is uncertain.

	A/C	KB		DES	OOC	KB
British losses	3	–	British claims	1	–	–
French losses	1	–	French claims	–		–
German claims	6†	–	German losses	–		–

† Three by flak.

British Casualties

Aircraft type	No.	Squadron	Crew		
BE2c	A2868	15 Sqdn	Lt F F Wessel	WIA	
			2/Lt S E Toomer	Unhurt	
BE2e	A2823	8 Sqdn	Lt J D McCall	Unhurt	*
			2/Lt F J Martin	Unhurt	
Sop ½ Strutter	A1098	43 Sqdn	2/Lt A E Crisp	POW/WIA	
			2/Lt G A Newenham	POW/WIA	
BE2f	2553	16 Sqdn	Sgt J Dangerfield	POW	
			2AM E D Harvey	POW	

French Casualties

Farman 42		F.1	Adj Bondaire	KIA	
Nieuport		N.73	Lt J Verdié	WIA	
			Lt Blanchi	DOW	
Farman 60		F.44	Lt le Barbu (O)	WIA	*

21 APRIL 1917
M T W T F **S** S

British Front

Low cloud and mist prevailed most of the day, not clearing until 1700 hours. Some recce and artillery observation work was carried out on the Arras front and 9 Squadron scored a particular success. Captain Lowcock and Lieutenant Macartney spotted a motor convoy moving along a road and sent out a zone call to the guns. Artillery fire destroyed the road ahead of the trucks and lorries then blasted them to destruction.

In the land fighting, British troops gained ground along the northern banks of the Scarpe River, east of Fampoux.

Evidence of the mist and cloud came as a 32 Squadron DH2 crashed into trees in the early afternoon at the unit's forward landing ground, killing the pilot. Captain

Billinge had led a sortie to the enemy balloon lines between Bapaume and Cambrai but three enemy fighters were seen patrolling above them so they came back.

Of the many artillery squadrons operating, it was to prove a rough day for 16 Squadron's BEs. At 1345, Second Lieutenants Bishop and Milligan took off to operate over Vimy and they were brought down by AA fire inside British lines where their machine was wrecked – probably the BE claimed by KFlak 105 north of Vimy. Shortly after 1500 the squadron sent out aircraft to fly a photo op over Vimy and were met by Jasta 11. Kurt Wolff despatched a BE, which went down in flames between Vimy and Maricourt. In some records, Lothar von Richthofen also shot down a BE, and a second 16 Squadron machine was brought down at about this time, although other records only note him with one kill on the 21st (see next paragraph) and another unconfirmed.

Just as this fight was going on, a six-man flight of 29 Squadron, led by Captain E F Elderton was taking off on an OP of the front now that the Corps aircraft were out. They too fell victim to Jasta 11 as soon as they reached the lines. Coming down on the Nieuports from the broken cloud, three went down under the guns of Lothar, Wolff and Schäfer. It brought Jasta 11's victories for the month so far to a devastating 60 – for no loss! (Other than Festner's forced landing on the 16th.) Or was it no loss? Karl Schäfer in fact crash-landed near the front line after another combat – chasing a BE2 at low level – having then been hit by ground fire, but he got back to Douai that night, so at least one of the Jasta's Albatros Scouts may have been lost or certainly badly damaged.

Further south, at 1730, between Quéant and Cagnicourt, the Pups of 3 Naval had a fight with some Albatros DIIIs, claiming three out of control and one destroyed. J J Malone (N6208) also claimed a two-seater Albatros out of control at 1740, five miles north of Quéant.

An aircraft the Germans did not apparently claim was a 25 Squadron FE2 on a photo op in the late afternoon. The crew of Captain J L Leith and Lieutenant G M A Hobart-Hampden were engaged by enemy aircraft and badly shot up but the pilot got them back over the lines where they later crashed at 1845, but flyers themselves were safe. However, the crew did claim an Albatros shot down, while the other crew claimed one driven down which was then finished off by a RNAS pilot. Pilots of 8 Naval Squadron who were patrolling nearby came to the two pushers' assistance and were quickly in the fight. Flight Sub Lieutenant R A Little and Flight Lieutenant A R Arnold each claimed Scouts brought down, Rex Arnold's coming down inside British lines. It was given the RFC number G.22.

It was a fine effort by Rex Arnold, for his gun had jammed soon after attacking the first Albatros but he continued to harass the other Germans, trying to frighten them off. After a few moments of this, he looked down but could not see the FE although he did see a German aircraft falling towards the ground with two of its planes floating down slowly after it.

Bob Little, meantime, had engaged three Albatros Scouts claiming one out of control, but then the FE stalled and Little almost flew into it, the fighting being so close. His gun shoot then broke and he had to break off but saw the FE gliding west and went down towards it. He followed it until it hit the ground near Bouvigny Wood. Little then landed beside the FE to see if he could be of help but both crew members were all right. Little would make a similar landing on the 24th but with an embarrassing ending.

It was Jasta 30 pilots who were in the fight with 25 and 8 Naval and they lost Leutnant Gustav Nernst who fell into the British lines near Arras. He had attacked the FE flown by Lieutenant R G Malcolm and Second Lieutenant J B Weir (A8373), was hit by their fire, then finished off by Rex Arnold, in Triplane N5458. Flying Albatros DIII 2147/16, Leutnant Oskar Seitz, who had been with the Jasta just five days, was brought down by Bob Little (N5449, after presumably crippling Leith's FE) but got away with a crash landing. However, there is some suggestion that Nernst and Seitz in fact collided first.

Among two-seater losses this day, Unteroffizier Brosius and Leutnant Koehler of Schusta 11 were brought down on the Arras front, while Flieger Julius Oettinger of FA275 died of wounds. Lieutenant R H Stocken of 23 Squadron, flying a Spad (A6697), claimed a two-seater out of control over Souchy-Lestrée, north-west of Cambrai at 1810. This and Malone's C-type at 1740 were the only German two-seaters claimed this date.

French Front

On the ground Nivelle's offensive was becoming bogged down while the casualties amongst his troops became nothing less than appalling. The battle area was littered with dead and wounded, lives thrown away for a few yards of dirt. Sadly a feature of the war on the Western Front.

For once, on a day seeing some air action, the French recorded no combat losses but did achieve some victories. Sous Lieutenant Henri Languedoc of N.12 gained his 7th victory by bringing down an enemy aircraft over Somme-Suippes, but the day went to Armand Pinsard of Spa.78.

His first victory of the day was over Leutnant Wichard of Jasta 24, flying Albatros DIII 2096/16, who came down between Nauroy and Moronvilliers where he was taken prisoner. His machine became well known due to a number of photographs of it appearing in several magazines and books, with the large-lettered name VERA painted on the fuselage. It was later sent to America where it was photographed even more.

Pinsard's second victory came that evening. This time he shot down Leutnant Günther von der Heyde of Jasta 9, whose comrades last saw him in action with three Spads over Nauroy at 2000 hours.

	A/C	KB		DES	OOC	KB
British losses	7	–	British claims	5	7	–
French losses	–	–	French claims	3		–
German claims	6†	–	German losses	4 ‡		–

† Includes two by flak. ‡ The Nachrichtenblatt notes one two-seater and three scouts missing.

British Casualties				
Aircraft type	No.	Squadron	Crew	
BE2g	A2888	16 Sqdn	2/Lt E L Bishop	Unhurt
			2/Lt C N Milligan	WIA
BE2g	A2766	16 Sqdn	Capt E J D Routh	WIA
			2/Lt K MacKenzie	Unhurt

Aircraft type	No.	Squadron	Crew	
BE2g	A2915	16 Sqdn	2/Lt J P C Mitchell	KIA
			Lt G R Rogers	KIA
Nieuport XXIII	A6797	29 Sqdn	2/Lt F Sadler	KIA
Nieuport XVII	A6755	29 Sqdn	2/Lt C V deB Rogers	KIA
Nieuport XVII	B1568	29 Sqdn	2/Lt A B Morgan	DOW
FE2d	A6383	25 Sqdn	Capt J L Leith	Unhurt
			Lt G M A Hobart-Hampden	Unhurt

French Casualties

Nil

22 APRIL 1917
M T W T F S **S**

British Front

Today the aviators of both sides awoke to fine but cloudy weather. With the ground fighting still going on around Havrincourt Wood and Trescault village, as well as south-east of Loos, although on a reduced scale, Haig was anxiously waiting on the break-out from Nivelle's offensive. Still trying to exert pressure on the British sectors, the flyers needed to be up for artillery shoots and contact patrols.

Three Triplanes of 1 Naval were out early: Flight Commander R S Dallas, with Flight Sub Lieutenants T G Culling and Carr, taking off at 0430. Carr became separated but the other two found and engaged 14 enemy aircraft – unsupported – making 20 individual attacks and claiming three Scouts shot down, two destroyed and one out of control.

The RFC's 1 Squadron was also out early, nine Nieuports taking off at 0555 to patrol Lille-Seclin-Carvin-La Bassée, led by Captain E D Atkinson. Two aircraft returned home with engine troubles, escorted by a third. This third man was Second Lieutenant E S T Cole and having seen them safely across the lines he headed back, spotting a balloon up over Wervicq. He attacked and shot it down in flames at 0640. The rest of the patrol were engaged by eight fighters, Atkinson and Second Lieutenant E M Wright claiming two down out of control at 0705(A) but one British pilot failed to make it back. They had fought Jasta 28, Leutnant August Hanko bringing the Nieuport down over Wavrin for his first victory. Lieutenant Walter Wood was taken prisoner.

Nieuports of 60 Squadron were also after balloons, Lieutenants H G Ross and G L Lloyd each burning one north of Drury and Boiry Notre Dame at just after 0700, Lieutenant W E Molesworth claiming a third smoking. At 0730 Lieutenant A R Penny flamed another at Vis-en-Artois.

Spads of 19 Squadron, led by Lieutenant W E Reed, took off at 0608 to patrol Bailleul-Vitry-Sains-Bullecourt on the north, along with Lieutenants Applin and Hamilton. Applin became separated so when a German two-seater was located, it was just Reed and Hamilton who attacked. Hamilton's gun jammed, forcing him to break off. Reed continued the attack (in B1563) and claimed the Albatros C-type as brought down at Quiery, as well as driving down two others over Courcelles before his gun too jammed. On the way home he was hit by ground fire and slightly wounded.

In this scrap there were also a couple of Naval Triplanes involved but it is uncertain who other than Dallas and Culling were around, although Flight Sub Lieutenant A R Knight popped up from somewhere and claimed an Albatros out of control east of Oppy at 0730, but only Reed claimed a two-seater at this time. It seems apparent that the two-seater was from FA(A)211 flown by Leutnant Martin Möbius (who was wounded) and his observer Leutnant Goldhammer. They came down at 0830(G), so the time is approximately right, although they reported being brought down by two Sopwiths. They may have mis-identified the Spads, and one might assume they would have said Triplanes rather than Sopwiths if Triplanes had been involved. Möbius had only joined FA(A)211 on 10 April but the wound to his leg was not serious and he got their burning machine down without further injury. He was a recipient of the Knight's Cross of the Military St Henry Order in June but was later killed as a fighter pilot with Jasta 7.

The Germans made a determined effort to blind the British with Jasta 5 attacking their balloon lines during the morning. Heinrich Gontermann claimed one at Arras at 0935(G), while Kurt Schneider flamed two, one at Épehy, the other at Essigny-le-Grand, at 1130 and 1145. These latter two were 28 km apart, so he certainly worked hard for his kills.

The British lost balloons of No.3 and 14 Sections. Gontermann got the 3rd Section's (a second claim was disallowed), Schneider getting the 14th, then a French balloon of 55 Cié. (In the afternoon, Nathanael of Jasta 5 attacked and was credited with another balloon at Bus – perhaps Section 13.) At No.16 Section at Ficheaux, Arras, Captain E A Twidale (Canadian) was killed due to his parachute failing to deploy when he jumped during an attack – probably Gontermann's second effort. Major R L Farley, No. 10 Balloon Company commander, and 2/Lt C W Berry of the 28th Section were also wounded.

With one exception (see later) this ended the morning action (apart from a single Albatros Scout claimed out of control by Bishop of 60 Squadron east of Vimy at 1120) and it was not until the early afternoon that aircraft clashed once more. 11 Squadron flew a photo operation and ran into the exuberant Jasta 11 at 1610.

Manfred von Richthofen led his staffel down onto the pushers, shooting one down at Lagnicourt, just inside the British lines, Kurt Wolff getting his to fall at Hendécourt. A third FE was badly shot about and caught fire in the air, the pilot finding most of his controls shot away. His observer fell mortally wounded, slumping over the side of his front cockpit. Lieutenant C A Parker grabbed onto him as he brought the FE down for a forced landing, then got him out of the burning aeroplane, carrying him to cover despite falling shell fire. Unfortunately the man succumbed to his wounds. Four other FEs returned with wounded observers, one making a forced landing, another a crash landing. However, despite the losses, Jasta 11 were only credited with two kills, even though Parker's FE must have been seen to land on fire as well as being subsequently shelled.

Meantime, Spads of 23 Squadron were escorting more FEs, this time those of 18 Squadron. At 1900 they came under attack from Jasta 12 and 5 between Marcoing and Havrincourt Wood. Two of the Spads were quickly shot down, one by von

Osterroht the Jasta 12 Staffelführer, the other by Nathanael of Jasta 5, whose victim fell at Ribécourt. Vizefeldwebel Reinhold Jörke was credited with another Spad seen to go down over the British lines but although the British pilot was wounded he got down safely. Leutnant Röth also received credit for an aeroplane shot down over Marcoing, but it is unclear who or what this might have been, as all the known British losses have been accounted for. One of 18 Squadron's FEs was hit by ground fire, its pilot wounded.

Jasta 11's Kurt Wolff ended the day's scoring by downing a 3 Squadron Morane at 2005(G), also near Havrincourt. Karl Schäfer was also credited with a BE at 2020(G) west of Monchy in the British lines. There is no corresponding British loss; the only BE coming down during the day was a 13 Squadron machine which had taken off that morning at 0644. It came down just north of Fampoux. If there has been a mistake with the time, and the claim was at 0820 (0720 Allied time), then time and approximate location might fit. Suggestions that this was another of the downed FEs do not stand up as regards time, being more than an hour after the FE action of the afternoon.

French Front

Three hostile aircraft were brought down on the Soissons front by French fighter pilots, two at least being two-seaters. Lieutenant Albert Deullin gained his 14th victory with a kill at 1750 west of Craonne, then N.3's Sous Lieutenant René Dorme and Capitaine Alfred Auger scored their 20th and 4th victories respectively with two-seaters at 1835 and 1910, over Beaurieux and Lierval.

Lierval is 4 km from Chevrigny where FA212 lost the crew of Unteroffizier Gustav Richter and Leutnant Erich Bersu. Another crew, Flieger Albert Karzmarek and Unteroffizier Karl Schulz, came down at Oulcherswald and Oulchers is just to the west of Craonne. All four men died.

Losses amounted to just one Caudron G4 of C.42, claimed by Leutnant Gerlt of Jasta 19 and his first and only victory, over St Etienne.

	A/C	KB		DES	OOC	KB
British losses	7	2	British claims	2	15	5
French losses	1	1	French claims	3		–
German claims	10	4	German losses	3		1†

† According to the Nachrichtenblatt, which also records one pilot and two observers wounded.

British Casualties

Aircraft type	No.	Squadron	Crew		
Nieuport XVII	A313	1 Sqdn	Lt A W Wood	POW/WIA	
BE2e	7089	13 Sqdn	2/Lt H S Robertson	Safe	*
			Lt G J Farmer	Safe	
FE2b	A5501	11 Sqdn	Sgt T K Hollis	POW	
			Lt B J Tolhurst	KIA	
FE2b	A5500	11 Sqdn	2/Lt J J Paine	Injured	
			2/Lt J Rothwell	Injured	
FE2b	A820	11 Sqdn	Lt C A Parker	Safe	
			Lt J E B Hesketh	DOW	
FE2b	A810	11 Sqdn	Capt E R Manning	Safe	*
			Cpl R Tollerfield	WIA	
FE2b	7020	11 Sqdn	Lt W F Fletcher	WIA	*
			Lt W Franklin	WIA	
FE2b		11 Sqdn	2AM J F Carr (O)	WIA	*
FE2b		11 Sqdn	2/Lt P A de Escofet (O)	WIA	*
Spad VII	A6695	23 Sqdn	2/Lt K R Furniss	POW/DOW	
Spad VII	A6682	23 Sqdn	2/Lt F C Craig	POW	
Spad VII		23 Sqdn	Capt K C McCallum	WIA	*
FE2b		18 Sqdn	Capt H L H Owen (P)	WIA	*
Morane Parasol	A6727	3 Sqdn	2/Lt F L Carter	KIA	
			2/Lt A S Morgan	KIA	

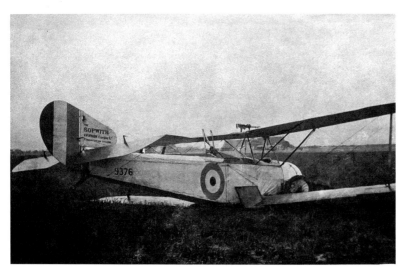

This Sopwith two-seater, 9376, was flown by No. 5 Naval Wing, and force-landed in Holland on 22 April, following engine failure, while engaged in a bomb raid. It had a sole occupant, FSL D A H Nelles DSC (Canadian), who was interned by the Dutch.

Aircraft type	No.	Squadron	Crew		
BE2c		13 Sqdn	2/Lt L A Davis	WIA	*
			2/Lt G G Fairbairn	WIA	
Nieuport Scout		29 Sqdn	2/Lt W P T Watts	WIA	*
Spad VII	B1563	19 Sqdn	Lt W E Reed	WIA	*
Sop 1½ Strutter	9376	5 Wing	FSL D A H Nelles	Int	

French Casualties

Caudron G4		C.42	MdL Le Clerc	MIA	
			Lt Mercier	MIA	

23 APRIL 1917
M T W T F S S

British Front

Today was St George's Day, and with it came fine weather – and death. With the French offensive crumbling Haig launched a new offensive, with the main attack commencing at 0445 along the nine-mile front from Croisilles to Gavrelle covering both sides of the Scarpe River. At the same moment another, smaller attack went towards the south-west of Lens. The British 3rd Army pushed forward to Pelves, Chérisy and Fontaine. All met heavy opposition.

The Army, as usual, were soon calling for information as to where their troops were in the battle area, HQ RFC sending out aircraft to make contact. Not only visual contact, for the soldiers were supposed to signal the aeroplanes with flares, but in the heat of battle, it was not always possible or perhaps advisable to start lighting flares so that some aviator could spot them, so it was difficult. Other aircraft went out to shoot up ground targets, especially troops who might be either holding up the advance, massing for a counter-attack, or reinforcements moving up to the line.

Some early air-fights took place between 0630 and 0800(A), the pilots of 1 and 3 Naval mainly involved. 3 Naval claimed one Albatros Scout destroyed and four out of control between Croisilles and Havrincourt, while further north Dallas and Culling each claimed a DFW two-seater out of control west of Douai.

Captain Albert Ball of 56 Squadron opened the squadron's account by shooting down an Albatros two-seater over Abancourt at 0645, in his personal Nieuport. He chased another two-seater but its gunner put several bullets through the Nieuport's wings, so Ball broke off.

A BE of 13 Squadron was the RFC's first casualty, flying a contact patrol over the 17th Corps area. It was hit by ground fire 500 yards north of Fampoux and while the pilot got it down safely it was soon wrecked by gunfire. RE8s were also out attacking ground troops, taking a leaf from the Schutzstaffeln book. Sopwith 1½ Strutters and Martinsyde G100s were also sent into the fight, while DH4s took bombs to the rear areas. The bombers were given an escort of Pups from 66 Squadron while Spads would patrol the area too.

Captain C M Clement of 22 Squadron led a six-machine OP and photo sortie, seeing numerous enemy fighters between Cambrai and St Quentin. Over Le Verguier at 0710 they were attacked by six scouts, FE 7681 at the rear of the formation spiralling down in flames. However, the pilot got it down inside British lines where it overturned, although he and his observer were badly burned and the FE destroyed. A 15 Squadron BE was also hit by ground fire near the Hindenburg Line, and returned with a wounded observer.

Offensive patrols were meant to saturate the battle area, but the sky is a big place and the Germans were expert at dodging the fighters and picking off the two-seaters. AWFK8s – Big Acks – of 35 Squadron entered the arena sending out aircraft at 0900. Two hours later they ran into Jasta 12. It is not clear what happened in this fight. 35 Squadron lost one aircraft which came down at Wancourt on the British side, and Arthur Schorisch claimed one down at this location at 1200(G). Another Big Ack returned home with a wounded gunner. However, Jasta 12 claimed and was credited with four 'Sopwiths' (the AWFK8 being a newish type to the front), which seems rather excessive. Possibly 66 Squadron's Pups may have been involved, although they did not lose anyone.

At 0925 16 Squadron sent out aircraft on a photo op, which were met by the two von Richthofen brothers just after midday German time, 1105 Allied time. Two BEs went down, both falling inside British lines but close enough for them to be reported by German ground observers. Manfred's score rose to 47, Lothar's to ten. Lothar's victims were Second Lieutenants Crow and Turner. In making for the lines, Crow was hit in the head and chest and died instantly, Turner being fortunate to survive the subsequent crash although he was wounded.

One spectacular event of the morning was an encounter by Flight Sub Lieutenant L S Breadner, a Canadian, with a huge Gotha GIV (610/16) bomber over Vron at 1030(A). The machine, of Kagohl III/16, came over in daylight – the first many had ever seen. Lloyd Breadner was on his way to the airfield from his billet when he heard anti-aircraft fire and looking up saw the large twin-engined aeroplane right overhead at around 10,000 feet. Rushing to his Pup he took off, chased the bomber and from directly behind it, fired 190 rounds at both engines. Crippled, the bomber came down near Vron inside British lines where it became G.23.

Its crew, Leutnants K Schweren, O Wirsch and Offizierstellvertreter A Hecher were taken prisoner. It was the first Gotha brought down by a British fighter aircraft.*

* The French ace Georges Guynemer claimed a Gotha on 8 February 1917.

The RFC pilots put in more claims late morning, Captain Ball reporting a DIII in flames at 1145 over Cambrai, 40 Squadron claiming a Halberstadt Scout out of control over Lens.

Artillery flyers were in trouble after lunch, 12 Squadron losing a machine in flames but with no German claim. Then at 1530(A) 55 Squadron with the Martinsydes of 27 Squadron flew a bomb raid on Boue and a factory at Lechelle, escorted by four Nieuports of 29 Squadron. After bombing, they returned via St Quentin and 12 miles south of Boue they were engaged by a reported seven Albatros Scouts from the northwest (Jastas 12 and 26). A big fight developed during which several British planes were shot up, with men wounded, but all staggered back across the lines, denying the German pilots any definite successes. Second Lieutenant A D Taylor, observer to Second Lieutenant I V Pyott DSO, opened fire at one attacker from 300 yards and it dived steeply. Ian Pyott (he had won his DSO in 1916 for shooting down Zeppelin L36 over England) saw a red enemy fighter go down out of control, but then Taylor was hit in the arm by a fighter which dived underneath and then across them.

Second Lieutenant F L Oliver in another 'Four' had his gun jam after two shots and he was then hit in the foot, while another bullet smashed his Lewis gun. 1AM W Bond fired two bursts at a fighter on his tail and it went down in a spinning nose dive. However, the Four's engine was damaged and they began to lose height but they crossed the lines to crash-land at Buire. A7408 crash-landed at Ervillers and was wrecked, its pilot dead and gunner wounded.

Despite the lack of sure kills, Unteroffizier Jörke and Vizefeldwebel Grigo of Jasta 12 were credited with DH4s brought down. Lt M H Coote in a G100 was engaged by Offizierstellvertreter Rudolf Weckbrodt (although he claimed a DH4) south-west of Itancourt. Coote was wounded in the leg but he got back.

Two of the four Nieuports were brought down, both making forced landings at Rochincourt at 1645 where they came under German artillery fire and were destroyed. Only one pilot had been wounded and all came down inside British lines.

The FE2s of 22 Squadron were out again this afternoon, and were once again engaged by Jasta 5 over the same locality as they had been that morning – Bellenglise. And it was Kurt Schneider who did the damage. He engaged a DH2 escort, of 24 Squadron, and in trying to evade the Albatros, the luckless pilot collided with one of the Fees, all three men falling to their deaths. Schneider was credited with two more kills, bringing his score to ten.

A Spad VII of 23 Squadron RFC, brought down by Paul Osterroht, leader of Jasta 12, on 23 April – his sixth victory. The pilot, Lieutenant F C Craig, was taken prisoner.

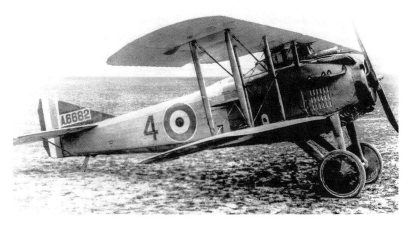

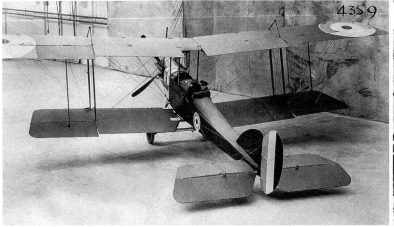

Another FE2b claimed at this time was a machine of 18 Squadron on a bomb raid which was engaged over Barelle by Leutnant Hermann Göring of Jasta 26. The FE pilot was wounded and came down north-east of Arras, on the British side. The FE gunners claimed four Albatros Scouts out of control. The Pups of 3 Naval were also involved in this fight as were Jastas 12 and 33. The Naval pilots claimed several enemy fighters shot down and among those who did fall was Jasta 12's leader, Paul von Osterroht, who came down west of Cambrai at 1800 hours. A Jasta 33 pilot was also brought down, Unteroffizier Nauczak being severely wounded over Quéant.

Heinrich Gontermann of Jasta 5 brought down an RE8 of 34 Squadron south-east of Arras at 1925(G), making the final claim of the day. No.29 Squadron flew a ground attack sortie in the late afternoon, led by Major Hugh Champion de Crespigny, Captain E F Elderton being wounded by small arms fire, but he got home.

The afternoon fighting had seen several more claims by RFC units, Lieutenant Bishop reporting downing a two-seater and a scout in flames east of Vitry while Lieutenant J M Child of 19 Squadron claimed an Albatros two-seater crashed north-west of Douai. No.48 Squadron had also seen action, claimed one destroyed and four out of control over Vimy, and had one gunner wounded by ground fire. Another victory was scored by the CO of 19 Squadron, Major H D Harvey-Kelly DSO. He had attacked a DIII between Graincourt and Cambrai at 1910, firing 60-80 rounds into it from 50 yards. It went down vertically and crashed about a mile outside of Cambrai. The German pilot had apparently tried to flatten out but then hit the ground.

German losses this day were Flieger Adam Föller and Unteroffizier Kaiser of Schusta 7 who had to make a crash landing but were otherwise unhurt. (Föller was to be killed over Gavrelle on 1 May.) Kampfgeschwader Nr.4 suffered several casualties: Leutnants Werner Steuber, Fritz von Massow, H Steibel, Eberhard Stettner and Oberleutnant Heinrich Möller.

Balloons were again attacked by the Jasta pilots, Vizefeldwebel Leopold von Raffay of Jasta 34 shooting at one near Belrupt. Others were also attacked but no claims made. Balloon Sections 5 and 16 both reported attacks, their balloons considerably hit but not destroyed. However, the balloon sections did sustain casualties: Lieutenant H E Goody of No. 16 Section and 2AM G W N Kidney of No. 3 were both wounded.

Left BE2f of 16 Squadron, shot down by Manfred von Richthofen on 23 April, its crew being killed. This picture was taken before this event and became the Baron's forty-seventh victory.

Right Otto Bernert, of Jasta Boelcke, scored heavily against the British during April 1917. In 1916 he had flown with Jasta 4 and achieved seven victories. He claimed no less than fifteen victories during April, including a record of five on 23 April; three BEs, one DH4 and a Strutter. His final claim, on 19 May, would have been his twenty-eighth had it been confirmed. He took command of the Jasta in June but did not add to his score. Wounded in August he did not see further action, and was destined to die in the influenza pandemic, in October 1918.

French Front

On the Nancy sector, a Nieuport two-seater crew of N.23, Maréchal-des-Logis Morizot and Lieutenant Gouin, brought down an Albatros Scout over the Bois de Avocourt, flown by Vizefeldwebel Arno Schramm of Jasta 7, who was reported killed over Montfaucon. Along the Châlons front Sous Lieutenant Juguin brought down a hostile aircraft north-west of Itancourt while the crew of a Farman of F.7 claimed another. A two-seater was also claimed by Capitaine Jean Derode, CO of N.102, over Prosnes, his 3rd of an eventual seven victories, although his machine was damaged in the action and he had to force-land. Leutnant Friedrich Feldmann of FA(A)252 was wounded over Prosnes, dying on the 26th, and it is likely he was hit during this fight.

On the debit side an observer in N.23 was wounded, and during Lieutenant Juguin's fight, his aircraft was set on fire but he got down without injury. A Caudron of C.8 was damaged and a gunner wounded, while a Morane Parasol of N.124 was shot down, claimed by Leutnant Willi Schunke of Jasta 20 for his first – and only – victory, south-west of St Quentin.

The Lafayette Escadrille, apart from having Nieuport Scouts, also had several other assorted aeroplanes, but not for general use over the lines. On this day, Sergeant Ron Hoskier, an American from New Jersey, son of a New York banker – and whose parents were now based in Paris – took the Morane up with Soldat Jean Dressy in the observer's cockpit. Dressy was the orderly to Lieutenant de Laage de Meux (having been with the family for years), who loved to fly but was not a regular aviator, although he hoped to become an air force gunner.

Having been told the Moranes would soon be taken away when Spads would totally equip N.124, Hoskier had decided to make one last flight in the old machine and Dressy asked to go too. They were attacked by three Albatros Scouts of Jasta 20, and after a struggle, in which Hoskier was wounded, the Morane fell into the French communication trenches, both occupants being killed instantly.

	A/C	KB		DES	OOC	KB
British losses	14	–	British claims	13	27	–
French losses	2	–	French claims	5		–
German claims	17	1	German losses	2		–†

† The Nachrichtenblatt records one large aircraft lost due to flak(!), one scout, and eight pilots wounded.

British Casualties

Aircraft type	No.	Squadron	Crew		
BE2e	7089	13 Sqdn	2/Lt H S Robertson	Safe	
			Lt G J Farmer	Safe	
BE2e	2840	15 Sqdn	Lt Vachell	Safe	*
			2AM F A Blunden	WIA	
FE2b	7681	22 Sqdn	2/Lt J A Rossi	WIA	
			2/Lt P H West	WIA	
BE2f	A3168	16 Sqdn	2/Lt E A Welch	KIA	
			Sgt A G Tollervey	KIA	
BE2f	A2876	16 Sqdn	2/Lt C M Crow	KIA	
			2/Lt E T Turner	WIA	

Aircraft type	No.	Squadron	Crew		
AWFK8	A2709	35 Sqdn	2/Lt F H Reynell	KIA	
			Capt S Barne MC	KIA	
AWFK8	A2694	35 Sqdn	2/Lt N C Yonge (O)	WIA	*
BE2e	7182	12 Sqdn	Lt A Ralphs	KIA	
			Lt L W Mott	KIA	
DH4	A7410	55 Sqdn	Lt T Webb	Safe	
			1AM W Bond	Safe	
DH4	A7408	55 Sqdn	Capt A T Greg	KIA	
			1AM R W Robson	WIA	
DH4	A2147	55 Sqdn	Lt I V Pyott DSO	Safe	*
			2/Lt A D Taylor	WIA	
Nieuport XVII	B1520	29 Sqdn	Lt W P T Watts	WIA	
Nieuport XVII	B1516	29 Sqdn	2/Lt J D Atkinson	Safe	
Nieuport XVII	A6752	29 Sqdn	Capt E F Elderton	WIA	*
Martinsyde G100	A7501	27 Sqdn	Lt M H Coote	WIA	*
RE8	A88	34 Sqdn	2/Lt H O W Hill	WIA	
			Lt H P Illsley	Safe	
FE2b	6929	22 Sqdn	Lt E A Barltrop	KIA	
			2/Lt F O'Sullivan	KIA	
DH2	7909	24 Sqdn	2/Lt M A White	KIA	
FE2b	A823	18 Sqdn	2/Lt E L Zink	WIA	*
			2/Lt G B Bate	Safe	
BF2a		48 Sqdn	Lt L E Porter (O)	WIA	*
		French Casualties			
Sopwith 2		N.23	Lt J Gouin (O)	DOW	*
Caudron R4		F.8	Sol Le Guino (G)	WIA	*
Morane Parasol	1112	N.124	Sgt R W Hoskier	KIA	
			Sol J Dressy	KIA	

24 APRIL 1917
M **T** W T F S S

British Front

A return to fine spring weather again brought forth increased activity with the resulting casualties, but they were not as heavy as the previous day. On the ground the intense fighting by the British extended their grip in the south, along the banks of the St Quentin canal near Vendhuile. In the north, though several counter-attacks were mounted by the Germans at Gavrelle, these had been broken up by well-directed and concentrated shellfire. Further gains to the north-east of Fampoux – at Greenland Hill – north of the Scarpe, and east of Monchy to the south of the Scarpe had also been achieved. Soon after first light, up to 3,000 German prisoners had been taken as the British blunted the attacks and counter-attacked themselves.

The first air loss of the day came at just after 0700(A), Oberleutnant Heinrich Lorenz, CO of Jasta 33, bringing down a Pup of 66 Squadron, part of an escort to a recce of Solesmes. The RFC pilot was last seen near Cambrai, Lorenz shooting him down near Bourlon, the first kill for the Jasta.

Six FE2s of 20 Squadron were across the lines by 0700 escorting a 45 Squadron Sopwith two-seater on a photo job, getting into a fight with an estimated 18 Albatros Scouts of Jastas 8 and 18 west of Ledeghem twenty minutes later. The crew of Lieutenant R E Johnson and Captain F R Cubbon claimed two of the V-Strutters shot down. In turn Jasta 8's Offizierstellvertreter Walter Göttsch and Leutnant Werner Junck claimed their 9th and 1st victories respectively by downing two of 20 Squadron's FEs, while Leutnant Walter von Bülow-Bothkamp of Jasta 18 claimed a third pusher over Ypres, on the British side. Göttsch's victim too came down on the British side, thus Junck must have brought down A6385, the only one of 20's machines that didn't recross the lines.

FE No.A5144 caught fire during the fight but Lieutenant Robertson, although wounded, got his burning aeroplane down. A6403 was in the running fight for the lines, the crew of Lieutenant E O Perry and 2AM E H Sayers claiming an Albatros down in flames, but they too had their machine set on fire but came down inside British lines. Jasta 18 had Leutnant Fritz Kleindienst killed. His Albatros caught fire north of Comines and he jumped to his death. The Staffelführer, Rittmeister Karl von Grieffenhagen, had his machine badly hit and he crash-landed, losing a leg and part of his lower jaw.

Confusing the issue somewhat is the fact that Marine Feld-Jagdstaffel I was also operating opposite Ypres this morning and they too claimed two FEs shot down, one near Ypres and another over Becelaere, the latter inside German lines. They also lost the pilot who was believed to have got these two pushers, Vizeflugmeister Josef Wirtz, who fell over Polygon Wood, possibly after colliding with the second FE. As Wirtz died in the crash, we have no way of confirming if he indeed caused the two FEs to go down, or even collided with one. Although MFJ claimed two victories, it is more probable that the 'live' pilots of Jasta 8 and 18 received official credit.

Later a letter was passed to the squadron from Major James Abbey, OC of the A/103 Battery, Royal Field Artillery, which read:

'I beg to report that an aeroplane, No.5144 [sic], belonging to your squadron, landed in flames on my battery position about 8 am this morning and was totally destroyed.

'The machine burst into flames at a great height and was landed safely in our lines owing to the gallant conduct and great presence of mind of the two occupants, the pilot Lt Robertson and observer Capt Knowles.

'Though both these officers were wounded, the pilot rather seriously in two places, and both were burnt slightly, they managed to keep the flames under control until within 200 feet of the ground, Knowles then jumped clear just before the machine turned over and pulled Robertson from under the burning wreckage.

'Captain Knowles was full of praise at the manner in which Lt Robertson piloted him safely to the ground.'

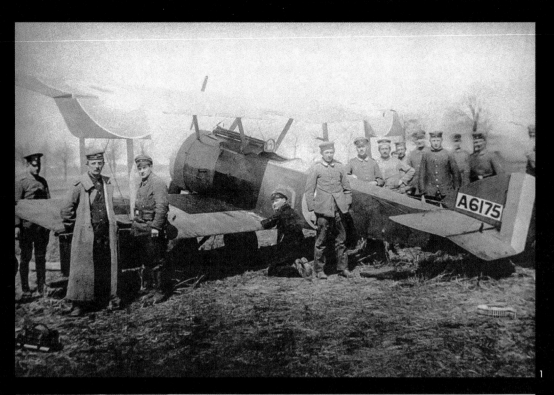

1

2

1 Sopwith Pup A6175 of 66 Squadron, downed by Oberleutnant Heinrich Lorenz, commander of Jasta 33 on 24 April. The pilot, 2/Lt R S Capon was wounded and taken prisoner. It was Lorenz's second victory, of his eventual five.

2 Tethered observation balloons were legitimate targets in WW1 and although dangerous to attack, a number of pilots on both sides became adept at bringing them down. One German pilot was Heinrich Gontermann of Jasta 5, who shot down two on the 16th and two more on the 22nd. Another on the 26th brought his score to seventeen, six being balloons. Killed in a crash in October 1917, his score stood at thirty-nine, seventeen of which were balloons.

3 Lt. G E Hicks of 9 Squadron became a prisoner on 24 April, following an encounter with Otto Bernert of Jasta 2, one of three 9 Squadron BE2s he shot down this day. In all Bernert shot down five RFC aircraft on the 24th. The arrows indicate the bombs that were still being carried when the BE crashed.

4 Francis Dominic Casey, from Clonmee, Ireland, served with 3 Naval Squadron in 1917, and his nine victories included seven achieved during April. One of these was a two-seater DFW, shared with J J Malone of the same unit, which they forced down inside British lines and captured. All his victories were whilst flying the Pup, but returning from leave in August he tested one of the new Sopwith Camels, got into a fatal spin and was killed.

Captain R M Knowles, an officer of the Norfolk Regiment attached to the RFC, had only recently received the Military Cross. By one of those strange quirks of fate, Knowles had shot down and wounded Göttsch on 3 February 1917; now Göttsch unknowingly had got his revenge.

The 1½ Strutters of 70 Squadron were up early, nine beginning a recce of Cambrai at 0535 hours, led by Captain Williams, escorted by some Pups. After some time they were engaged by six pilots of Jasta 2, and although the RFC men claimed two Halberstadt DIIs out of control the Jasta had no losses.

An Albatros attacked Sergeant Thomson's machine (A8213), his observer, 2AM Impey firing a drum at it. Hits were seen on the engine and it stalled and fell away. Impey changed the drum, then fired into its fuselage and saw it go down out of control. Lieutenant J H Gotch engaged another Albatros, his observer, Lieutenant L A Kiburz, scoring hits and it too went down, in a nose dive.

Otto Bernert, however, clawed one Strutter down, which fell in flames south of Vaucelles for his 20th victory. This was Lieutenant Halse and 2AM Bond. They were hit in the engine early in the fight and began to glide away, but they were then attacked again and shot down. Only the previous day had Bernert been notified of the award of the Pour le Mérite, and if this victory was in any way a celebration, then this day would see his celebrations extended.

Still with fuel and ammunition Bernert soon spotted other targets, three BE2e aircraft of 9 Squadron who had flown out on a bomb raid at 0540 without gunners so as to increase their bomb load. Bernert swooped down on them as they headed for home and between 0840 and 0845(G) shot down all three, one falling north of Joncourt, the second north of Levergies and the last south of Bellicourt, north of St Quentin. The mechanics at Morlancourt waited in vain for their three BEs to return. For some reason the squadron thought they had been brought down by AA fire, so the fact that the three aircraft had virtually no defence probably wasn't considered.

Within five minutes Bernert had spotted another victim, a DH4 bomber of 55 Squadron, also out early to bomb La Briquette. Bernert attacked it and it went down inside British lines where the pilot crash-landed west of Bony at 0850(G) with a dead gunner and a wounded pilot.

Five victories in one day would have been a record, but five victories in one sortie, all scored between 0830 and 0850, was outstanding. No other German pilot had achieved that sort of success, nor had any Allied pilot in France come to that. The fact that he wore spectacles didn't preclude success in air combat either, and he had now achieved 24 victories. He would add three more to his score before being wounded. He was destined to die of influenza a month before WWI ended.

Just on 0900(G), Heinrich Gontermann of Jasta 5 shot down a Triplane of 8 Naval Squadron near Bailleul, on the British side. One Naval pilot claimed an Albatros out of control.

During the morning, near Lens, German two-seater crews claimed two victories, a Sopwith to Unteroffizier Friedel Stegmann and Vizefeldwebel Merzel of Schusta 27 at 0750, and an unspecified type to Leutnant Reigel and Vizefeldwebel Tötsch of FA211 at 0930(A). There were no RFC losses at these times that match up in this area.

Naval 8's was the last loss until after lunch, although the RFC made claims for hostile aircraft brought down. 1 Naval Squadron claimed one destroyed and two

John Joseph Malone, born in the USA to Canadian parents, achieved ten victories in the early weeks of 1917, six of which were downed during April. He received the DSO but was killed in combat on 30 April, claimed by Paul Billik of Jasta 12, the first of this German's thirty-one victories.

out of control fighters in the Sailly-Noyelles area at 0815/40(A) while 18 Squadron's FEs claimed three destroyed – one in flames – over Barelle at the same time. One of these was probably Offizierstellvertreter Rudolf Weckbrodt of Jasta 26. He was wounded during a fight with some FEs, but he was back with the Jasta by the end of the month. At 1110(A) the SE5s of 56 Squadron attacked and claimed a two-seater destroyed over Bellone, credit going to Captain C M Crowe and Lieutenants L M Barlow and M A Kay.

Flight Lieutenant C D Booker of 8 Naval Squadron saw a two-seater being 'archied' (fired at by AA guns) near his aerodrome (Auchel, also known as Lozinghem), so gained height, following it towards Arras. He lost it momentarily then spotted it amongst some further AA bursts, chased after it and then attacked under its tail. The observer still managed to fire into the Triplane (N5482) and scored some hits, but Booker's fire also struck home and the observer disappeared into his cockpit, obviously hit. The German pilot then put his nose down and headed towards Douai, trailing a thin line of smoke but under control. Booker did not make a claim.

It is not certain who was in the two-seater, but Vizefeldwebel Richard Schleichardt of FA(A)224 made two flights over Allied lines this day, and on the second was forced down by a British fighter inside his own lines.

Two German two-seaters were brought down in the front lines around noon. The first, an Albatros C-type, came down at Grenier Wood, south-west of Armentières, after a combat with Second Lieutenant T F Hazell of 1 Squadron. Tom Hazell was on a Line Patrol at midday flying at 14,000 feet when he spotted two two-seaters 4,000 feet below. He dived on one, firing 30 rounds from 20 yards under its tail. Volumes of smoke came out of the bottom of the fuselage, and as it went down, it burst into flames, falling into the German front-line trenches. The crew of Unteroffizier Otto Haberland and Leutnant Heinrich Klofe of FA227 were both killed.

Another one of the great fighting pilots of WW1, Charles D Booker was with 8 Naval Squadron flying Sopwith Triplanes. He scored four victories in April 1917, and in 1918 would command 201 Squadron RAF, bringing his personal score to twenty-nine on 13 August, but was killed in action this date, shot down by Ulrich Neckel of Jasta 12, the German's twenty-second victory of a total of thirty.

Twenty-five kilometres to the south two Nieuport pilots of 40 Squadron, Lieutenants I P R Napier and J A G Brewis, engaged what they described as an Aviatik west of Lens. Flight Sub Lieutenant R A Little of 8 Naval then joined in flying a Triplane (N5469). The Australian Bob Little had been on his airfield at Auchel around noon, had received a message that a German aircraft was approaching, and was sent off to engage it. So for the second time this morning, 8 Naval had engaged enemy aircraft near their base. He spotted the two Nieuports and the two-seater right over Auchel as he gained height; the German turned north, Little following, firing whenever the opportunity arose. When he noticed the observer was not firing, he closed in, the two-seater starting to lose height; then it nose-dived and landed in a field inside British territory near Lens. It was a machine of FA 18 and the crew of Leutnants Hans Huppertz and Friedrich Neumüller were taken prisoner. Whether Little decided to capture his victims himself and attempted to land next to the downed machine, is uncertain. In his report he stated he could not get his engine going after the dive and had to land beside the two-seater. Whatever the reason, Little ran into a ditch and turned his Triplane over. Neumüller went to his aid and helped free him from the wreck! The German machine became G.24, recorded as a DFW CV.

At 1300 British time, Nieuports of 1 and 60 Squadrons went for a massed attack on the German balloon lines. Lieutenant A V Burbury of the former unit flamed one while Lieutenant W E Molesworth of 60 Squadron got another at Boiry Notre Dame.

Meanwhile, Second Lieutenant Reginald Burton Clark (Australian) of 60, while diving at a balloon, was attacked by four Albatros Scouts. He was hit in the upper part of his left leg and a subsequent shot hit him in the lower part of the same leg; his fuel tank was also holed. Despite his injuries, he tried to engage the enemy, firing off half a drum of Lewis at them but could not wait to see any effects. His Nieuport was hit again, his flying wires being cut and he quickly came down. The machine crunched into a shell hole and caught fire on landing but Clark was pulled clear by Corporal Summers of the 1st Canadian Pioneer Battalion. There were signs that he may have to lose the leg, but he gave his report of the fight before allowing his wounds and burns to be attended to, but he died of his injuries on 1 May. There is no German claim for his Nieuport.

Mid-afternoon saw patrols and fights by 56 Squadron, who claimed two EA out of control; then at 1650, Flight Lieutenant H T Travers of 3 Naval made it three two-seaters captured for the day, by bringing down another DFW CV, this time of FA26. Travers, with Flight Sub Lieutenants F D Casey and J J Malone engaged the German between Morchies and Louverval. It came down near to the front line at Doignies with its pilot, Unteroffizier Max Haase, and his observer Leutnant Karl Keim both wounded, the latter fatally. No sooner had the DFW landed than German artillery opened up and the two-seater was soon reduced to matchwood and scrap iron, the wreckage designated G.25 by the RFC. In the absence of tangible evidence, it was recorded as an Aviatik. However, the DFW's number was 5927/16. Malone's Pup developed engine trouble during the combat (although it is possible his motor was hit by Keim) and he had to make a forced landing, then had to take shelter in the same shell hole as his two victims until they could be rescued. Keim died ten minutes later, and Malone's Pup was also blown to pieces by shell fire.

The last RFC casualties of the day came in the late afternoon. A 10 Squadron BE2g on a special bombing mission was hit by ground fire but got back across the lines before being forced to crash-land. Then a 59 Squadron RE8, one of three flying a line patrol over Monchy-le-Preux, was hit by AA fire over Guémappe at 1845, wounding the observer, but the pilot brought him back safely. Flakbatterie 701 claimed a two-seater hit near Wancourt which was probably this machine.

Just on 1700, a six-man patrol of 60 Squadron – Fry, Horn, Young, Penny, Percival and Rutherford – were near Vis-en-Artois. They spotted four red-fuselaged Albatros Scouts, one with green wings, the others with red. One was going down on a BE at 1,500 feet. Three of the Nieuports dived to protect the two-seater, and joined by a Sopwith Triplane, they succeeded in driving off what was obviously Jasta 11. The Albatros pilots rapidly broke off and dived east.

At 1730, FE2s of 25 Squadron had a scrap with some Albatros Scouts over Billy Montigny, claiming one destroyed. Also during the day, 48 Squadron claimed three DIIIs destroyed around Arras, while Lieutenant R N Hall of 40 Squadron claimed a two-seater out of control east of Lens. This may have been a machine of FA(A)235 who lost Leutnants Richard Zeglin and Karl Timm who fell at Acheville, which is about three miles south-east of Lens.

French Front

French fighter pilots were busy this day, claiming at least five German two-seaters shot down – it was a bad day generally for German two-seaters – and two scouts, at least one being a DIII.

Adjutant Georges Madon of N.38 claimed an Albatros down at Cornilette which was not confirmed (of an eventual total of 65 such claims), and an Albatros C in flames for his 9th victory (of an eventual 41 confirmed). Capitaine Robert Massen-et-Royer de Marancour, commander of Groupe de Combat 14 (GC14) and Caporal Lejeune of N.83 crashed a two-seater also at Courson, near Courcy le Château at 1640 while Adjutant Baudoin of N.80 shot down a two-seater in flames at 1700 hours over l'Ange Gardien. Adjutant Raoul Lufbery, the American star of the Lafayette Escadrille, shot down an Aviatik two-seater east of Cerisy on the Somme – where N.124 were now operating – at 1725 for his 9th victory.

A fighter was claimed by Maréchal-des-Logis Marcel Henriot of N.65 at 1720 over the Forêt de Pinon, with Sergent Edmund Pillon of N.82 claiming a DIII down at Dannemarie for his 3rd victory (he was promoted to Adjutant the next day and ended the war with eight official victories). Pillon's victim was probably Vizefeldwebel Rudolf Rath of Bavarian Jasta 35 flying 2020/16, who came down at Hagenbach and was killed at 0722(G). The other known scout pilot brought down was Vizefeldwebel Max Wackwitz of Jasta 24, who was compelled to land at Bignicourt, near the Jasta's aerodrome after a combat with a French fighter, but was otherwise unharmed. This may well have been Madon's unconfirmed victory.

French losses were just two, both Nieuport XXIIIs, Sergent Boiteux-Levret of N.81 and Caporal Ménard of N.85. Two Nieuports were claimed, one by Vizefeldwebel Albert Haussmann of Jasta 23 over Beaurieux at 1605(G) for his 2nd victory, the other by Leutnant Ernst Udet of Jasta 15 for his 5th, shot down over Chavignon at 1930. A Spad was claimed by Offizierstellvertreter Felsman of Jasta 24, east of Prunay at 1012 in the morning but records do not identify the French unit. Similarly, a Caudron two-seater was claimed by Oberleutnant Eduard Dostler of Jasta 34 over Ablonville as his 6th victory.

German two-seaters lost over the French front were: Vizefeldwebel Otto Hartung and Leutnant Friedrich Krowolitski of FA252 killed at Nauroy by Madon; Leutnants Werner Hecht and Hugo Schneider of FA(A)222 killed over Courcy le Château by Baudoin of N.80; Leutnants Karl Jaeger and Walter Rudatis of FA253, killed in the Laon-Allemant area, by de Marancour and Lejeune of N.83. In addition Leutnant Karl Schmidt, observer in FA(A)251, was killed over Clermont, and Flieger Josef Reuber of FA250 was killed at Sissone, crashing on take-off, although his observer survived. AA fire wounded Leutnant Blum of FA46 south of St Mihiel.

A German pilot not claimed was Oberleutnant Rudolf Berthold, leader of Jasta 14, wounded during a combat with a Caudron, although not serious enough for him to leave his command.

	A/C	KB		DES	OOC	KB
British losses	12	–	British claims	16	10	3
French losses	2	–	French claims	7		–
German claims	22†	–	German losses	15‡		?

† Four by flak. ‡ The Nachrichtenblatt states 11 aircraft lost, including two behind enemy lines, three missing and one collided with enemy aircraft. In addition one officer was killed and three wounded.

Aircraft type	No.	Squadron	Crew		
Sopwith ½ Strutter	A1002	70 Sqdn	2/Lt C H Halse	KIA	
			2AM W Bond	KIA	
BE2e	7195	9 Sqdn	Lt G E Hicks	POW	
BE2e	A2937	9 Sqdn	2/Lt F A Matthews	KIA	
BE2e	A2941	9 Sqdn	Lt C L Graves	KIA	
DH4	A2149	55 Sqdn	Lt A M N de Lavison	WIA	
			2AM K Oliver	KIA	
FE2d	A5144	20 Sqdn	Lt N L Robertson	WIA	
			Capt R M Knowles MC	WIA	
FE2d	A6385	20 Sqdn	2/Lt A R Johnston	KIA	
			Lt H R Nicholson	KIA	
FE2d	A6403	20 Sqdn	Lt E O Perry	Safe	
			2AM E H Sayers	Safe	
Sopwith Pup	A6175	66 Sqdn	2/Lt R S Capon	POW/WIA	
Triplane	N5467	8N Sqdn	FSL E B J Walter	KIA	
Nieuport XXIII	A6777	60 Sqdn	2/Lt R B Clark	DOW	
BE2g	A2843	10 Sqdn	2/Lt A W Watson	Safe	
RE8	A3252	59 Sqdn	Capt W W Leete	Safe	*
			Lt R S Stone	WIA	
Pup	N6208	3N Sqdn	FSL J J Malone	Safe	

French Casualties

Nieuport XXIII	2937	N.81	Sgt Boiteux-Levret	MIA
Nieuport XXIII		N.85	Cpl R Ménard	WIA
Spad?				
Caudron?				

25 APRIL 1917
M T **W** T F S S

British Front

Low clouds again curtailed the intensity of air fighting, although the artillery flyers were able to operate often. This helped the movement of troops on the ground, the British line advancing slightly south of the Scarpe. It was announced that since the 23rd, over 3,000 German prisoners had been taken.

A successful zone call was made by a crew of 15 Squadron, Second Lieutenants W G Barker and C S Goodfellow, after spotting an estimated 1,000 enemy troops in trenches. They then directed the shellfire onto the trenches and followed this by directing gunfire on other troops and two gun batteries. Canadian Billy Barker later became one of the leading Allied air aces and won the Victoria Cross in October 1918.

Today was Jasta 11's day, but the first victim was a 59 Squadron RE8 that had taken off at 0515 to fly a recce-line patrol south-east of Arras. It failed to return, but as no German pilot made a claim for a British machine at this early hour, it must be assumed to have been brought down by AA fire. KFlak 63 claimed a BE on this date, brought down near Omissy which they may have mistaken for the RE. Both crewmen were captured, the pilot being the same Sergeant Smith who had brought back a wounded observer the previous evening.

The first air fight came at 1030(G) over Guémappe, Karl Allmenröder of Jasta 11 shooting down a BE right over the lines. A 12 Squadron BE2e is the only machine to fit the claim although the exact time it was lost has not been discovered, but the crew were both killed.

Jasta 11 also spotted six FE2bs shortly after this encounter, which were 25 Squadron aircraft escorting line-patrol aircraft between Lens and Arras, led by Captain A de Selincourt. Emil Schäfer went down behind A837 and shot it down between Willerval and Bailleul but inside British lines. A5505 was also hit by a Jasta pilot but it got back over the lines only to crash attempting a forced landing later, but the crew were unhurt.

By this time, however, Jasta 11 had become aware that one of its pilots was missing. Sebastian Festner had been part of the early patrol and near Oppy had spotted the 1½ Strutter of 43 Squadron. He attacked, but the rear gunner of A8232, crewed by Lieutenant C R O'Brien and Second Lieutenant J L Dickson, had hit the red Albatros (2251/16) at 0815(A) – 0915 German time – and Festner fell to his death. He had scored 12 victories, ten during Bloody April. He was also the only German aircraft claimed by the RFC on this morning, although British AA fire also claimed the Albatros over Gavrelle. The Albatros fell just inside British lines and was noted as G.26, but as it was under shell fire from the German artillery it was not salvaged. 43 Squadron had a gunner wounded in this fight but the pilot brought the Strutter home.

Not until the evening did further air action occur, Schäfer again being involved. 48 Squadron's Bristol Fighters were on a combined offensive patrol east of Arras, and AA observers reported seeing a machine go down during a combat with enemy fighters. Schäfer's claim for a Bristol down by the railway station at Roeux was confirmed. Lieutenant W T Price and his observer Lieutenant M A Benjamin claimed an Albatros destroyed at 1900 but Jasta 11 had no other losses.

Another BE was the last casualty, 10 Squadron having sent out a machine at 1725 for artillery observation work against the Cité St Pierre. At 1945(A) it was attacked by Albatros Scouts and shot up. The pilot, Lieutenant R V Kann, was flying fairly low to avoid the clouds when he and his observer, Second Lieutenant C Bousfield, saw five or six hostile aircraft approaching. The largest, painted red, opened fire and hit Kann in the back. Bousfield opened fire and his bullets seemed to enter the red machine's fuselage. Meantime, Kann had begun to spiral down, finally landing in a shell hole near to Cité St Pierre. So close was it to the line that it could not be salvaged. Nobody seems to have put in a claim for it.

French Front

Nothing of note to report.

	A/C	KB			DES	OOC	KB
British losses	6	–	British claims		2	–	–
French losses	–	–	French claims		–		–
German claims	4†	–	German losses		1		–

† One to flak.

British Casualties

Aircraft type	No.	Squadron	Crew	
RE8	A3213	59 Sqdn	Sgt F C Smith	POW
			Lt E J Dilnutt	POW
Sop 1½ Strutter	A7799	43 Sqdn	2/Lt C L Veitch	Safe
			2/Lt E S W Langton	WIA
BE2e	7191	12 Sqdn	Lt T Thomson	KIA
			Lt A M Turnbull	KIA
FE2b	A837	25 Sqdn	2/Lt C V Darnell	KIA
			2AM G Pawley	KIA
FE2b	A5505	25 Sqdn	2/Lt M A Hancock	Safe
			Lt V Smith	Safe
BF2a	A3352	48 Sqdn	2/Lt W J Clifford	KIA
			2/Lt H L Tomkies	KIA
BE2g	A2899	10 Sqdn	Lt R V Kann	WIA
			2/Lt C Bousfield	Safe
Nieuport XVII	A6790	1 Sqdn	2/Lt A V Collins	Injured†
Nieuport XVII	A6624	1 Sqdn	2/Lt L J Mars	Injured†

† Collision in bad weather on return from an OP; both men suffered severe concussion.

French Casualties

Nieuport		N.80	Adj G Langel	POW

26 APRIL 1917
M T W **T** F S S

British Front

The cloudy weather persisted until the evening, therefore most of the air action took place either after lunch or during the evening. On the ground the Germans made an attempt at retaking Gavrelle but they were heavily repulsed. An assault by British troops on some quarries on the eastern outskirts of Hargicourt was successful.

Ten FEs of 20 Squadron flew to Rumbeke aerodrome – home of Jasta 8 – each carrying two 112-pound bombs. Take-off was at 0600 and they were engaged by about eight Albatros Scouts, the gunners claiming two shot down out of control. One FE was hit, its observer being mortally wounded in the chest but the pilot regained the lines near Watou.

Ground fire hit a Nieuport XVII of 60 Squadron at 1010, while on an OP, compelling Second Lieutenant N P Henderson to make a forced landing in a lake, during

Top Julius Buckler was another balloon-buster, although he did not shoot down his first till 26 April, his sixth victory overall. By the end of the war, with a score standing at thirty-six, another six balloons had burned under his guns. **Bottom** This picture shows two French aces, Albert Deullin, of N.3, and Paul Tarascon of N.62. On 19 April Tarascon downed a German two-seater for his tenth victory, by which time his unit had become Spa.62 with the arrival of Spad fighters. Deullin, by April 1917 was flying with Spa.73, gaining his thirteenth victory on the 15th. The stork-marked Nieuport is that of N.3 of the Cigognes Group.

which he sustained a cut under one eye. The machine was unable to be salvaged and was therefore written off.

At midday, 1 Squadron mounted a balloon attack, Lieutenant Arthur V Burbury MC shooting down one in flames, and he was last seen heading his Nieuport down towards another but he failed to get back. He was hit by gunfire from KFlak 2 east of Wytschaete, coming down near Houthem to be taken prisoner.

Captain D C Rutter/Second Lieutenant B J Venn leading a squad of 43 Squadron was patrolling the line over Oppy at 1530, when he spotted four red Albatros Scouts coming from Douai – Jasta 11! They proceeded to attack a BE2c working over Oppy but Rutter led his patrol down and drove them off. The hostile scouts turned south and attacked another BE2c over the Scarpe River. Rutter followed as quickly as he could but they easily outpaced his Strutter. Seeing the danger, Rutter opened fire from 1,000 yards but he was too far away and before he could do anything further, the BE was going down in flames and the Albatri heading back towards Douai. That was Kurt Wolff at work.

Kurt Wolff brought his score to 21 with this kill at 1635(G), bringing down a BE of 5 Squadron working with the 57th Siege Battery near Gavrelle, despite the attempt by 43 to help. Thus Rutter and company had saved one Corps crew at the expense of a second. Such was fate – or luck.

Two hours later Karl Allmenröder and Lothar von Richthofen went down on two 16 Squadron BEs also engaged on artillery observation over Vimy. One fell in flames on the German side of the Ridge, the other crash-landing west of Vimy, its pilot wounded.

Jasta 30 claimed its first victory since 6 April: Leutnant Paul Erbguth, a former Schlasta pilot, shot down yet another BE, this one from 10 Squadron flying a photo sortie. It went down at 1725(A) between Hulloch and Wingles to crash at Haisnes right on the front line.

The FEs of 22 Squadron flew two sorties in the late afternoon, the first at 1615 being a photo op to Flesquières and the Bois de Vaucelles with six aircraft. They came under heavy AA fire, one FE being hit and wounding its pilot in the chin, but he got back. The second sortie, at 1735, went to bomb Bohain Station. One pusher

developed engine trouble and turned back, dumping its bombs into front-line trenches north-west of St Quentin.

The rest met Jasta 5 north of St Quentin and lost two of their number to Offizierstellvertreter Alfred Sturm for his first (and only) victory and Leutnant Rudolph Nebel for his first (of two) victory. Sturm got Hopkins and Stewart in A825, Nebel claiming Captain H R Hawkins, an Australian, and his gunner, Second Lieutenant G O McEntee. The Fees came down at Brancourt le Grand and Joncourt at 2000 and 2005(G) hours.

Jasta 5 claimed two balloons downed during the day, Gontermann one at Arras at 1150, Leutnant Kurt Schneider one at Seraucourt at 1600. In all there were three balloons claimed, the other by Vizefeldwebel Julius Buckler of Jasta 17 by Bois de Genicourt. Buckler's victim was French, 35 Cié. Gontermann's balloon was the 1st Brigade's 8th KB Section, which was destroyed after three determined attacks by the German, the last from below 500 feet.

There were numerous combats during the afternoon and evening, all except two against Albatros Scouts. The two were C-types engaged by FE8s of 41 Squadron near Hooge around midday, both being claimed as destroyed. Once more there were more claims for destroyed enemy aircraft than lost by the Germans, plus the usual crop of 'out of controls'.

The FEs of 25 Squadron were operating in the Lens-Arras area, claiming one of each category at 1720(A) near Drocourt, north-east of Arras. One FE had to make a forced landing near Lens after a fight with a German Scout but both crewmen were unhurt. In the same fight, Booker of 8 Naval Squadron claimed a DIII in flames, as did Flight Sub Lieutenant E D Crundall.

Naval Triplanes nearly added to the British losses during this late afternoon period by attacking Spads of 19 Squadron. No.19 had started an OP at 1740, saw the activity over Douai and went to investigate. Just north-east of Arras Lt J M Child (B1537) was attacked by five Triplanes which put shots through his tailplane, fuselage and both wings. Child put his Spad into a spin with engine full-on and managed to force-land at Bellevue at 1900. Lieutenant Holmes (B1588) also received the attention

Top Erich Hahn gained one victory with Jasta 1 in late 1916, before joining and commanding Jasta 19. During April 1917 he shot down three more French aircraft and two kite balloons. He was killed in action on 4 September. Hahn's fourth victory, on 26 April, had been a Spad VII, being flown by René Doumer of Spa.76, an ace with seven victories. **Bottom** William 'Bill' Thaw, was an American who flew with the Escadrille Lafayette in 1916-17. On 26 April he claimed his second victory, a German two-seater and by the end of the year had four victories in all. His fifth came in March 1918, by which time he was commanding the American 103rd Aero Squadron.

Lt A V Burbury of 1 Squadron was shot down in his Nieuport XVII, A6671, by ground fire during an attack on a German balloon on 26 April. He was lucky to survive the crash with only a wound, but ended up a prisoner.

of two Triplanes but managed to evade and get away. It is hoped that these were not the two Albatros Scouts 8 Naval claimed!

Further south another group of FEs were flying north of Cambrai shortly after 1900. Captain Albert Ball of 56 Squadron was operating in the same area, spotting the FEs approaching and also saw a number of Albatros Scouts climbing up from the direction of Cambrai itself. Biding his time until the Scouts came up to his height – 13,000 feet – he then attacked and claimed one went down and crashed.

He was then heavily engaged by five other Scouts and after a brief skirmish he headed away south-east but was chased by the Germans. One outpaced the others and when it was almost in range, Ball turned quickly and fired into it, the Albatros catching fire and falling in flames. Ball had then to fight his way back, which he managed successfully, finally landing at Vert Galant at 2030, with his SE5 badly shot about. It is believed that it was Jasta 3 that engaged Ball and they lost Vizefeldwebel Emil Eisenhuth in a DIII, 2207/16, who fell in flames near Hayencourt, north-west of Cambrai and was killed.

At 1920 hours, Lieutenant H E O Ellis of 40 Squadron, on an OP to Salome, made an attack on a balloon over the town but was attacked by four Albatros Scouts. Ellis manoeuvred into a favourable position and fired from 25 yards into one of them. This machine turned over on its starboard wing and crashed east of Salome, a second Albatros being seen to land close beside it.

Up over the coast, off Ostende, 7 Naval Squadron lost a Handley Page 0100, shot down by German seaplanes while four HPs were attempting to bomb a destroyer outside the port.

Credit went to Vizeflugmeister Müller of Seeflug 2, flying a Rumpler 6B1 (No.1037), the HP falling into the sea three miles north-west of Nieuport. The British pilot drowned but two others were rescued by the Germans. The fourth was rescued by a French FBA flying boat, one of two which attempted to get to the men, one being shot down by flak and then towed into Ostende by one of the German destroyers originally under attack. On board, so the Germans then discovered, were the other two Naval survivors. The HPs were from the Manston Squadron, but were operating from Coudekerque aerodrome under 5 Naval Wing.

French Front

There was more activity over the French sectors, with a total of at least seven German aircraft claimed as being shot down. N.48 brought down an Albatros C-type at La Ville-aux-Bois at 0615(A), credited to three of the Escadrille's pilots, Lieutenant Armand de Turenne, Caporal René Montrion and Caporal Conan. La Ville-aux-Bois is just to the east of Cerny where a machine of FA(A)255 had observer Leutnant Traugott Milbrandt killed.

Capitaine René Doumer of Spa.76, shot down by Erich Hahn, leader of Jasta 19, on 26 April 1917. Doumer had achieved his victories during 1916 and early 1917.

That evening N.48 made it two for the day as Sergent Bajac and Caporal Jacques Roques downed a hostile machine at Loivre at 1740. The Lafayette Escadrille claimed two. Sergeant Charles Johnson got another two-seater Albatros east of St Quentin at 1800, while Lieutenant William Thaw and Sergeant Willis Haviland sent a second down over Juvincourt, halfway between Laon and Reims, at 1830.

The other three victories were claimed by N.79 at Itancourt, and N.93 north of Res d'Ailette, while R.46 gunners shot down one over Fort Brimont. One German loss was the Staffelführer of Jasta 15 – Oberleutnant Max Reinhold – who went down near Lierval at 1930(G) after a fight with three Spads.

In addition to the German losses above, Observer Leutnant Sigismund Steinfeld of FA(A)271 died over Ripont and Leutnant Franz Blum of FA46 was killed at Chambley.

Three French losses are recorded. Capitaine Doumer of Spa.76 failed to return from a patrol having taken off at 1600 hours heading towards Fresnes, shot down by Oberleutnant Hahn of Jasta 19 north of Brimont; Caporal Egret of N.78 was downed by Leutnant Albert of Jasta 31 over Nauroy; and a Caudron G4 of C.56, was hit by ground fire south of Fort Brimont. The latter machine got back, but Lieutenant Burville, the pilot, had been wounded; it was claimed by Flakzug 87, 102 and 180 and KFlak 53.

	A/C	KB			DES	OOC	KB
British losses	10	3?		British claims	10	15	–
French losses	2	–		French claims	7		–
German claims	11†	3		German losses	2‡		1

† Two by flak. ‡ The Nachrichtenblatt states two scouts lost in combat, one balloon, two two-seaters FTL inside German lines and one officer killed by flak. This does not include the seaplane claimed at Zeebrugge.

British Casualties

Aircraft type	No.	Squadron	Crew		
FE2b	A6393	20 Sqdn	Lt F D Stevens	Safe	*
			Sgt A Clayton	KIA	
Nieuport XVII	B1549	60 Sqdn	2/Lt N P Henderson	WIA	
Nieuport Scout	A6671	1 Sqdn	Lt A V Burbury MC	POW	
BE2g	A2806	5 Sqdn	Lt H B T Hope	KIA	
			2/Lt L E Allan	KIA	
BE2g	A2859	16 Sqdn	Lt W K Mercer	WIA	
			Pvt Lea	Safe	
BE2e	A2826	16 Sqdn	2/Lt W S Spence	KIA	
			2/Lt W A Campbell	POW	

Aircraft type	No.	Squadron	Crew		
FE2b	A796	22 Sqdn	Lt L W Beal	WIA	*
			2/Lt G Bell	Safe	
BE2e	5870	10 Sqdn	Lt H F Roux	WIA/POW	
			2/Lt H J Price	WIA/POW	
FE2b	A825	22 Sqdn	2/Lt G M Hopkins	POW	
			Lt J D M Stewart	POW	
FE2b	4883	22 Sqdn	Capt H R Hawkins	POW	
			2/Lt G O McEntee	POW	
BE2	6266	9 Sqdn	Capt R J Lowcock (P)	WIA	*
			Lt E E Macartney	Safe	
BE2		2 Sqdn	2AM T Aspinall (O)	WIA	
Sopwith Baby	8171	SDF	F/Cdr W L Welch	Safe	
Handley Page 0/100	3115	7N Sqdn	FSL T S S Hood	Drowned	
			LM R H Watson	POW/Died	
			AM2 F C Kirby	WIA	
			ACM W C Danzey	POW/Died	

French Casualties

Aircraft type	No.	Squadron	Crew		
Spad VII	1447	N.76	Capt R Doumer	KIA	
Spad VII		N.78	Cpl Egret	MIA	
Caudron G4		C.56	Lt Burville (P)	WIA	*

27 APRIL 1917
M T W T **F** S S

British Front

There was no improvement in the weather, low clouds prevailing all day. With very little activity in the air, there were a number of 'shoots' – 59 targets being dealt with by artillery with aircraft observation, plus 26 by balloon observers. Crews of 8 and 13 Squadrons were particularly successful against German batteries.

A BE2c of 2 Squadron was brought down by AA fire while flying an artillery observation sortie for the 219th and 150th Siege Batteries at 1115 hours, following a successful shoot on German trenches. It was claimed by Flakzug 145, and as the machine fell one of the crew fell out near the Cité St Pierre. This must have been the pilot as the observer was later reported burnt to death. The whole episode was witnessed by another 2 Squadron crew, Captain W A Skeate and Second Lieutenant R V Waters, while working with the 224th Siege Battery.

The only other combat losses of the day came in the evening. FE2bs of 11 Squadron flew a line patrol, taking off at 1720, only to run into pilots of Jasta 11. Gunners claimed two Scouts destroyed south-west of Vitry, one in flames and another out of control. Lothar von Richthofen brought 4850 down at Fresnes where the crew were taken prisoner, while Kurt Wolff forced 7698 down to make a crash-landing south of Gavrelle, inside British lines. The victories were timed by the Germans at 2015 and 2020. Jasta 11 had no recorded losses.

Five minutes later Karl Allmenröder claimed a BE2f, in British lines, west of Fampoux. The only possible victim was a 12 Squadron BE, that reported a fight with a German scout who wounded the observer, but the two-seater was not a loss.

Two balloons were claimed by RFC pilots, Lieutenant Bishop of 60 Squadron attacking one at 0655 near Vitry-en-Artois, seen to go down smoking heavily, while Lieutenant H E O Ellis of 40 Squadron destroyed one at Salome at 1000 hours. 48 Squadron Bristols also claimed a two-seater destroyed, seeing it crash in the Scarpe River, near Vitry.

Two other losses of note were a 43 Squadron 1½ Strutter flown by Captain H H Balfour and Second Lieutenant E H Jones. Flying along the crest of Vimy Ridge they were hit in the engine by ground machine-gun fire, which promptly stopped. Balfour quickly turned for the lines, made it – just – then ploughed into the ground, catapulting him and his observer into the mud in front of the wreck. Despite a few moments of unconsciousness, both men were only slightly injured and rescued by Canadian troops. Balfour had been recently discussing whether a crew should strap themselves in firmly when about to crash-land, the majority of his squadron comrades thinking it was better not to do so. He disagreed, but in this final moment he changed his mind and undid his seat belt. When he scrambled back to his shattered Strutter, he saw that the engine had been smashed back into the cockpit where his legs would have been had he remained strapped in!

The other loss was a Nieuport XVII of 60 Squadron. Second Lieutenant F Stedman took off from No.2 ASD at Candas, to deliver a new machine to the squadron at Le Hameau. Instead of flying directly there, he obviously decided to take a look at the front (unless he became completely lost), for he ended up behind the German lines as a prisoner of war.

Another successful RNAS pilot was R A 'Bob' Little of 8 Naval Squadron. An Australian, he had flown Pups and now Sopwith Triplanes, and during April he brought down eight hostile aircraft with the new type. One of these, on the 24th, had been a two-seater, forced down on the Allied side of the lines. His score of twelve by the end of April was increased to forty-seven by May 1918, by which time he was with 203 Squadron RAF. He was mortally wounded on the 27th of that month.

French Front

The French claimed just three German aircraft during the day. One was a two-seater of FA14 crewed by Leutnants Herbert Zimmermann and Ernst Naumann. They were brought down at Gerardner and were either killed or died of wounds in a French hospital. A scout was claimed by the crew of a Farman of F.71, which was probably Leutnant Friedrich Vonschott of Jasta 14 who came down near Montchâlons with wounds so severe he died on 14 May. Two other fighter pilots were casualties, Leutnant Eissfeldt of Jasta 10, severely wounded in combat and Leutnant Rudolf Hepp of Jasta 24. Hepp's machine, Albatros DIII 1731/16, was badly damaged and he crashed at Leflincourt, but without injury. It is possible he was shot up by Alfred Auger of N.3 who forced a hostile machine to land north of Bétheniville.

A Farman 42 of Escadrille F.19 was attacked by an Albatros and forced to land inside French lines with 49 bullet holes in it, the observer having been wounded. There is no German claim for this action, although KFlak 93 did claim a Caudron shot down over Essigny-le-Grand.

Jasta 36 pilots made attacks on the French balloon lines, claiming three destroyed, Leutnant Albert Dossenbach claiming one – which was not confirmed – Leutnant Heinrich Bongartz two, one at Berry-au-Bac the other south-east of Thillois.

	A/C	KB			DES	OOC	KB
British losses	4	–	British claims		3	2	2
French losses	–	?	French claims		4		–
German claims	6†	2	German losses		1‡		–

† Three by flak. ‡ The Nachrichtenblatt records one aircraft missing, one officer and one NCO killed with four officers.

British Casualties

Aircraft type	No.	Squadron	Crew		
BE2c	2713	2 Sqdn	2/Lt W J Stonier	KIA	
			2/Lt F R Croker	KIA	
Nieuport XVII	B1570	60 Sqdn	2/Lt F Stedman	POW	
Sop 1½ Strutter		43 Sqdn	Capt H H Balfour	Injured	
			2/Lt E H Jones	Injured	
FE2b	4850	11 Sqdn	2/Lt J A Cairnes	POW	
			1AM E G Perry	POW	
FE2b	7698	11 Sqdn	2/Lt P R Robinson	WIA	*
		12 Sqdn	2AM H Tilley	WIA	
BE2			2AM T C Coe (O)	WIA	*

French Casualties

Farman 42		F.19	Sgt Bouchon	Unhurt	*
			Lt Fabre	WIA	

28 APRIL 1917
M T W T F **S** S

British Front

Low cloud once more prevailed over the shattered Western Front. On the ground the British attacked along a front of several miles to the north of the Scarpe; fighting became severe. Canadian troops captured Arleux-en-Gohelle, three miles east of Vimy Ridge, and progress was made north-east of Gavrelle as well as the western slopes of Greenland Hill. South of the Scarpe ground was gained north of Monchy-le-Preux.

In the air it was to be the Germans' day with virtually no losses despite a few claims by RFC. It began soon after dawn with a 13 Squadron BE2e on a contact patrol over 17 Corps' area being brought down by ground fire from the trenches, so they knew they had made 'contact'! The machine was later salvaged.

A second 13 Squadron BE took on the job of artillery spotting an hour later, but this time it was a red Albatros Scout that ended the squadron's task. Manfred von Richthofen shot down the BE into the south-east corner of the wood east of Pelves at 0930(G). The BEs were persistent, and at 1120, Kurt Wolff sent a machine of 16 Squadron down south of Oppy for his 23rd victory.

It wasn't going to be a good day for 16 Squadron either. Another dawn patrol machine had already been brought down by ground fire at 0600, being forced down with its fuel tank shot through, only to crash into a front-line shell hole with a wounded observer. At 1005 two Canadians, Major E O McMurty and Lieutenant H D Mason, had taken off to patrol over Thelus. They were nearing the end of a long sortie when ground observers saw their BE come down – the apparent victim of Allied shellfire. McMurty, from Montreal, having served in France with the Canadian Infantry since 1915, had only joined the RFC in January, became a pilot and had returned to duty in France on 18 April – ten days earlier.

Sopwith 1½ Strutters of 43 Squadron had left their base at 1050 to fly a line patrol between Lens and Neuvireuil and one failed to get home. The only Sopwith claimed this day was by Offizierstellvertreter Edmund Nathanael of Jasta 5. The Sopwith two-seater went down at La Vacquerie at 1315(G) for his 12th victory. Flak did claim one Sopwith on the British front, south of Tournai, but it is doubtful that a 43 Squadron machine from this sortie would have been so far over, so what it was is a mystery; but then again, Nathanael's victim was some distance from the patrol line but had obviously seen the Jasta 5 machines and the Strutters had had a go.

Not long after Major McMurty was killed by 'friendly fire', a BE2c of 2 Squadron was also hit by Allied shells while working with the 219th and 150th Siege Batteries, but this time the crew managed to get their damaged machine home. 5 Squadron's BEs also suffered. Second Lieutenant A E Clark was attacked by a German fighter soon after lunch and he was wounded in the leg but got back. At 1745(G) another 5 Squadron BE received the attention of Kurt Wolff, while on a photo op to Gavrelle.

Second Lieutenants Buckton and O'Sullivan had been trying for some time to get across to take photos that were of some importance but had been thwarted three times. Determined to carry out his assignment, Buckton made a fourth attempt. Seeing two Nieuport Scouts nearby, Buckton fired off two red lights and the two British fighters took up an escort position, but as they headed for the line again, six Halberstadt Scouts appeared, so Buckton circled, hoping they would fly off. This seemed to let the Nieuports off the hook as they flew away, leaving the BE unprotected once more.

Buckton saw the Halberstadts head away and quickly crossed the trenches to complete his task. They had exposed just one plate when the Jasta 11 pilots came

Sopwith 1½ Strutter (A993) of 43 Squadron, shot down by Edmund Nathanael of Jasta 5, on 28 April, his twelfth victory. Nathanael shot down seven British aircraft and two balloons during April, and on 6 May scored his fifteenth victory. He was killed in action on 11 May.

back, Wolff swooping down from the low cloud. O'Sullivan began firing in defence but the BE was driven down, riddled with bullets from the German's fire. At least twenty holes were punched in the petrol tank, Buckton quickly switching off the engine to prevent fire.

O'Sullivan's fire kept at least two of the Halberstadts at bay, but Wolff's fire had taken effect, Buckton being forced to crash-land into the British lines west of Gavrelle. The BE broke in two, Buckton and O'Sullivan being obliged to get beneath the wreckage as one of the Halberstadts – perhaps Wolff himself – came down to strafe them, the German trenches being just 140 yards away. British soldiers began firing white lights at the German who then broke away and headed east.

Another BE brought down was a 52 Squadron machine at 1410(A). Second Lieutenants W D Thom and B H Armstrong were patrolling near the front, 2,000 yards north-east of Villers Plouich. Attacked by a German fighter, Thom began to spiral down, his observer's gun then jamming. The fighter followed them down, Thom force-landing south of Villers Plouich just inside British lines, the German being driven off by ground fire.

Flakbatterie 709 claimed an FE2b shot down over Villers Plouich, south-west of Cambrai but for once there were no pusher casualties on the 28th. Leutnant Julius Schmidt of Jasta 3 claimed a balloon south of Marœuil, behind Arras at 1815 hours, presumably the one lost by the 6th KBS.

What claiming the RFC did was limited to a two-seater shot down over Salome at 1000 by Lieutenant Ellis of 40 Squadron, another over Oppy at 1225 by Flight Sub Lieutenant Bob Little of 8 Naval Squadron. Later, Captain Albert Ball crashed an Albatros two-seater over Fontaine, west of Cambrai, at around 1630 while Flight Commander Ray Collishaw of 10 Naval claimed an Albatros Scout destroyed over Ostende at 2000. However, there are no German losses recorded despite all three claimants being very experienced air fighters. Collishaw, of course, may have claimed a Marine Albatros, but loss records are not available.

The Ball fight was witnessed by others of 56 Squadron, for the Flight had attacked three of the C-type machines and seen one go down and land, then saw another fall to pieces and crash. After chasing another two-seater, Ball's SE5 (A4850) was hit by AA fire which left his port elevator controls connected by a single thread and the fuselage badly damaged, but he brought it home to a safe landing.

The main feature of the fighter aircraft this day was in ground strafing, notably by aircraft of 56, 32 and 23 Squadrons, while three 56 Squadron SE5s led by Captain C M Crowe patrolled defiantly over one of the German airfields at Douai at 3,500 feet but were not challenged.

French Front

There are no records of any losses or claims on the 28th, despite the fact that Jasta 26 engaged French Sopwith two-seaters, claiming two and receiving credit for one destroyed. Vizefeldwebel Langer claimed an 'enemy aircraft' south of St Quentin at 1830(G), thinking this might have been a 1½ Strutter. He didn't receive confirmation of his claim as it went down on the Allied side.

Leutnant Hermann Göring also claimed a French Sopwith two-seater at approximately the same time, noted as being from Escadrille Sop.27, this and Langer's unconfirmed claim both being from this unit.

Leutnant Jakob Wolff of Jasta 17 also received confirmation of a claim over a Caudron at Brimont and KFlak 41 also reported shooting down a French Sopwith two-seater near Reims.

	A/C	KB		DES	OOC	KB
British losses	6	1	British claims	4	–	–
French losses	–	–	French claims	–	–	–
German claims	9†	1	German losses	–	–	–

† Three by flak.

British Casualties

Aircraft type	No.	Squadron	Crew		
BE2e	A1843	13 Sqdn	2/Lt J H Jones	Safe	
			2/Lt G Hall	Safe	
BE2e	A2896	16 Sqdn	Capt Bird	Safe	*
			2/Lt A G Perryman	WIA	
BE2e	7221	13 Sqdn	Lt R W Follit	DOW	
			Lt F J Kirkham	WIA/POW	
BE2e	A2745	16 Sqdn	2/Lt J V Wischer	WIA/POW	
			2/Lt A A Baerlein	POW	
BE2e	A2944	16 Sqdn	Maj E O McMurtry	KIA	
			Lt H D Mason	KIA	
Sopwith 1½ Strutter	A993	43 Sqdn	2/Lt C M Reece	POW	
			2A M A Moult	WIA/POW	
BE2e	7165	52 Sqdn	2/Lt W D Thorn	Safe	*
			2/Lt B H Armstrong	Safe	
BE2f	2551	5 Sqdn	2/Lt A E Clark	WIA	*
			AM A Morley	Safe	
BE2c	2543	2 Sqdn	2/Lt F W Crawford	Safe	*
			Lt F B Scullard	Safe	
BE2g	2557	5 Sqdn	2/Lt N C Buckton	Safe	
			2/Lt G R O'Sullivan	Safe	

French Casualties

None recorded

29 APRIL 1917
M T W T F S **S**

British Front

Fine weather at last, but with it came the blood-letting of the final two days of April. Ground fighting continued on a large scale with British troops capturing trench systems to the south of Oppy along a mile-long front. First figures of captured German soldiers came to 976 over the two days 28/29th.

Contact patrols were again flown, trying to locate front-line troops and positions so that the generals could plan. Among the first of these was a 12 Squadron BE2e

Top On 29 April 1917, three pilots of 19 Squadron ran into aircraft of Jasta 11. The patrol was led by the squadron commander, Major H D Harvey-Kelly DSO, famous for being noted as the first RFC officer to land in France after war had been declared. All three Spads were shot down, Harvey-Kelly by Kurt Wolff ....

Above ...Richard Applin was shot down by Manfred von Richthofen, the Rittmeister's 49th victory, and killed ...

Right ... W N Hamilton went down following the attentions of Lothar von Richthofen, his thirteenth victory, and taken prisoner.

brought down by machine-gun fire soon after its 0610 take-off time. The crew were both wounded, the machine wrecked.

Nieuports of 40 Squadron patrolled from 0645; Lieutenant J A G Brewis and Second Lieutenant W A Bond came under intense ground fire which hit Brewis' machine which crashed, killing its pilot. Flak 61 and 68 claimed him, north of Hendécourt.

Two hours later – 1015 – 57 Squadron's FEs were flying a line patrol between Lieven and Noreuil. They saw two SE5s fighting five or six enemy fighters over Dury and joined in. Captain N G McNaughton and Second Lieutenant H G Downing (A6365) attacked an Albatros; the German pilot, as he dived, was seen to fall from it before the machine hit the ground. The FEs were engaged in turn by the Albatros Scouts from Jasta 12. Unteroffizier Friedrich Gille came down on A6355 and as the rest of the FEs fought their way west – claiming one Albatros destroyed and two out of control – they saw their companions turning on to the tail of one Albatros near Noyelles, but that was the last they saw of them. The dog-fight drifted south, but finally Gille got the upper hand and sent the FE down north of Barelle at 1055(G) where the crew got down but were taken prisoner. Gille had his first victory of an eventual six. Jasta 12 itself did not record any losses in personnel.

It was a good day for German flak gunners too, with so many low flying RFC machines over the front, either on contact work or low strafing sorties. 29 Squadron's Nieuports came in for some rough handling during a late morning OP where they obviously dropped down to try some strafing mayhem on the ground but came under fire from MFlak 63 south of Dury. Two of the nimble Nieuports were hit and brought down, putting two more young pilots in a prison camp.

The Naval boys were much in evidence in the last hour before noon, 1 and 3 Naval claiming three hostile aircraft destroyed, one in flames, plus six out of control, including a C-type. Shortly before midday, Lieutenant Bishop of 60 Squadron claimed a Halberstadt DII in flames east of Épinoy. Once again there is a lack of recorded losses by the Germans. However, the two-seater, although only claimed as 'out of control', may well have been the FA2 machine that came down near Barelle,

north-west of Cambrai, in which Leutnants Bruno Kittel and Hermann Waldschmidt died. Flight Sub Lieutenants C B Ridley and H V Rowley claimed the two-seater near Villers-les-Cagnicourt, which is just to the west of Barelle.

The 3 Naval's Pups had been escorting FEs, led by Flight Lieutenant H G Travers with five machines, and Flight Lieutenant Lloyd Breadner with another five. They had picked up the pushers south of Cambrai and saw them safely back from their recce job, keeping position between the sun and the FEs at 14,000 feet. They attacked three enemy machines over Villers Outreaux but they quickly dived away east. It was in the subsequent fight with eight scouts that Flight Sub Lieutenant S L Bennett was lost while Breadner's men fought them. Travers then returned having seen the FEs safely across the lines.

Obviously Jasta 5 was one of the units involved in the fighting, for Leutnant Kurt Schneider claimed a Pup over Elincourt, inside German lines, Bennett going down near this location. 3 Naval claimed three scouts out of control, but needless to say the Germans were again spinning down out of trouble.

The most serious loss to the Royal Flying Corps this day was the CO of 19 Squadron, Major H D Harvey-Kelly DSO. As is well known, Harvey-Kelly was the first RFC pilot to land in France after war had been declared, as a pilot with 2 Squadron on 13 August 1914. He had been commissioned into the Royal Irish Rifles in 1900 and had transferred to the RFC in 1913. He had received the DSO in February 1915 and took command of 19 Squadron in January 1916.

In the late morning of this day, Harvey-Kelly led a three-man patrol between Lens, Fontaine and Noreuil in their Spad VIIs – Jasta 11 country. Shortly after they took off, General Hugh Trenchard and his right-hand man, Major Maurice Baring, arrived at Vert Galant where 19 (66 and 56 Squadrons too) were based. They had come to see Harvey-Kelly and have lunch, only to learn that he had just flown off

Left Manfred von Richthofen (left), Constantin Krefft, Kurt Wolff and Otto Brauneck of Jasta 11 in April 1917, outside the château at Roucourt.
Right Observation kite balloon were legitimate targets on the Western Front and were fiercely defended by air cover and ground gunners. Usually, at the first hint of danger the observer in the basket went over the side, having a parachute pack fixed to the side of the basket.

but would be back in an hour or so. They had lunch but were destined never to see Harvey-Kelly again.

The three Spads were spotted by von Richthofen, flying with several of his Jasta, and attacked them near Lecluse, south of Douai just after midday German time. Von Richthofen shot his man down into the swamps – Second Lieutenant Richard Applin's Spad falling in pieces – while brother Lothar brought down Lieutenant W N Hamilton near Izel after a chase north-west. It fell to Wolff to bring down Harvey-Kelly, shot down over Sailly-en-Ostrevent. This brought the Baron's score to 49. Would he reach 50 before the end of April?

Back at Vert Galant, with lunch over and no sign of the three pilots, Trenchard took his leave saying, 'Tell Harvey-Kelly I was very sorry to miss him.' Baring was to record that the tone of Trenchard's voice made it clear that he never expected the message to be delivered and neither did Baring.

FE2bs of 18 Squadron took off at 1420 to escort a photo machine to the 5th Army area and clashed with Jasta 11 over the front lines. They just had time to refuel, rearm and have some quick refreshment before they were off once more. Manfred von Richthofen and Kurt Wolff each despatched one FE, the Baron's falling inside German lines, south-west of Inchy, Wolff's in British front-line trenches with a dead gunner. Another 18 Squadron pilot was wounded in the fight but he brought his machine back to base. It also brought von Richthofen's score of kills to 50 and Wolff's to 26 – and the day was far from over.

The FE crews later reported being attacked by three Albatros Scouts (in fact there were five), the gunners claiming one Scout shot down in flames and another out of control. The 'surviving' Albatros shot up Second Lieutenants G H Dinsmore and Bate's FE, but Dinsmore succeeded in recrossing the lines, followed closely by Wolff, who watched it force-land south of Pronville. As Wolff headed back, troops from the Border Regiment helped Dinsmore get the wounded Bate from the machine but he died soon afterwards.

The British troops confirmed the action and saw one of the enemy machines wrecked on the ground and the other falling. As Jasta 11 had no casualties in this action, one wonders what they saw. Probably they were seeing the other FE go down – it fell in flames and the crew fell or jumped out – and von Richthofen reducing height as he followed it down.

One of the FEs to escape the main fight was that flown by Second Lieutenant G A Critchley (A851) whose observer, Lieutenant Oliver Partington, noted in his logbook:

> 'Duty: Photography. Ht. 10,000 ft. Five photos taken, large camera. Six HA attacked the formation E of Cagnicourt, no combat owing to pilot diving and losing touch with the rest of formation. AA normal, visibility fair.'

Partington sounded a bit miffed, but if he had known it was von Richthofen and his pilots, he may have thought Critchley's move a good one.

More FEs, this time 20 Squadron's, headed for the northern part of the front, taking off between 1545 and 1600 hours, carrying bombs to raid Bisseghem Dump, just outside Courtrai. Jasta 18 rose from Halluin and met the pushers west of Courtrai, Leutnants Paul Strähle and Ernst Wiessner each bringing down one. 20 Squadron reported being attacked by 20 Albatros Scouts, and in the fight that ensued claimed two shot down in flames, a third crashed and another out of control, while losing two FEs. Another FE, its fuel tank holed, force-landed at 42 Squadron's base, but was otherwise unharmed.

A third FE was crewed by the veterans Second Lieutenant E O Perry and 2AM T E Allum, both wounded north-west of Sanctury Wood – by AA fire, so they said – although Leutnant Gustav Nolte also claimed an FE shot down into British lines at Hooge. Perry got A29 down safely but the machine was burnt out. Jasta 18 suffered no losses.

Meantime, Jasta 11 had again landed and refuelled. No sooner had they done so than reports of more aircraft over the front sent the Richthofen brothers to their machines. Two 12 Squadron BE2s were working with artillery over the front, having taken off at 1645 and 1648 respectively. The brothers attacked them at 1925(G) – 1825 British time – Manfred's victim falling without its wings near Roeux on the Scarpe, near the front-line trenches, Lothar's crashing north-east of Monchy-le-Preux, again right by the front lines.

Lieutenants J H Westlake and C J Pile, in the BE attacked by Lothar von Richthofen, also had wing problems. The lower wing was shot away and the upper was damaged. Westlake got it down under some sort of control but it collapsed as soon as he touched down. Cyril Pile suffered injuries including a broken thigh, but died while being carried to the aid station of the 9th Battalion of the Essex Regiment.

There were several other skirmishes throughout the day, mainly against the artillery observation squadrons, several machines returning with wounded pilots or observers, as well as one wounded 55 Squadron bomber pilot. The final flurry of aerial activity embraced a large dog-fight between Spads, Nieuports and Triplanes near Hénin-Liétard and which netted for Manfred von Richthofen his 52nd victory, and his fourth for the day.

For many years the results of this battle have been wrongly assessed merely because von Richthofen did not mention the actual type of aircraft that he shot down. In his combat report he certainly notes all three of the above types and early historians looked for an obvious victim and came up with Captain F L Barwell of 40 Squadron (Nieuports) who was lost during this evening. However, Barwell took off at 1820 and Richthofen's timing of his combat at 1940 German time seemed to fit, although it would have been 1840 British time; i.e. 20 minutes after Barwell left Lozinghem.

Richthofen had only just shot down his 12 Squadron BE a short time before when he became embroiled in this final action of the day. If the earlier historians were to be believed, Barwell, in his final 20 minutes, had to fly the 25 km to the lines while gaining height, then have a 'long' air fight. An infantry report of the fight between the red Albatros and the British machine said that it lasted almost half an hour! So much for the 20 minutes Barwell had from take-off to falling. In any event, Richthofen stated his victim fell after 'a short time' so we can discount the half an hour fight as being with Richthofen.

Richthofen's 52nd victim was Canadian Flight Sub Lieutenant A E Cuzner of 8 Naval in a Triplane – the same type as recorded in the Nachrichtenblatt as Richthofen's victim. Richthofen and Jasta 11 were in action mainly with the Triplanes of 1 and 8 Naval, one ace (Little) and two future aces being in evidence: R P Minifie and Victor Rowley of 1 Naval, Bob Little of 8 Naval. So it was these men who were in action with Richthofen and Jasta 11. In fact it was Little who saw a red Albatros bring down a BE over Monchy (Lothar von Richthofen) and dived on it. Only

Top Flight Sub Lieutenant A H V Fletcher of 6 Naval Squadron, brought down on 29 April by Hermann Göring, for his sixth victory.
Bottom Captain F L Barwell of 40 Squadron, believed shot down by Nathanael of Jasta 5 on 29 April in Nieuport XVII A6745. Earlier, historians thought Barwell had been shot down by von Richthofen.

heavy AA fire deflected Little from closing in, which allowed the younger Richthofen to escape. Little and Minifie then got into a fight with an Albatros which ended with a German fighter crashing on Douai aerodrome. Minifie was then worked over by several enemy fighters, which put several holes through his Triplane and one through the left longeron. On his way back, Richard Minifie shot up some troops on a road for good measure. His shared victory was his second of the day and his second of an eventual 21 victories.

But what of Barwell? Who shot him down at the end of the half-hour combat? There were two claims for aircraft at around this time: Edmund Nathanael of Jasta 5 and Hermann Göring of Jasta 26. However, Jasta 26 was operating too far to the south-east of St Quentin, so that discounts Barwell. 6 Naval did have a scrap at 1855(A) over Guise, near St Quentin, claiming one EA in flames and two out of control, Göring shooting down Flight Sub Lieutenant A H V Fletcher north-east of St Quentin at 1945(G). Flight Sub Lieutenant R R Winter in a Nieuport XVIIbis (N3199) was badly shot up but got back. Perhaps the late confirmation of Ober-leutnant Bruno Loerzer, Jasta 26's commander, at 1930 near Bellenglise which was eventually credited as his 5th victory.

According to Jasta 5 records, Nathanael shot down a Triplane at 2100(G) over Beaumont, inside German lines. In the Nachrichtenblatt Nathanael's victory is recorded as a Rumpf Eins – single-seat with fuselage! (As opposed to a pusher type without the usual fuselage body, i.e: gitter-rumpf.) Nathanael's claim is timed at 2100 (ie: 2000 British time) which is a better fit for Barwell, who would have been in the air for an hour and 40 minutes by then.

1 Naval Squadron had put up three Triplanes at 1700(A) and 45 minutes later, over Beaumont, they had an indecisive fight with two hostile scouts. Soon afterwards, when east of Lens, Flight Sub Lieutenant A P Heyward engaged another enemy machine which dived vertically, but then Heyward was attacked by three more scouts and was wounded in the arm but got back and landed south of Béthune.

Another 1 Naval Squadron patrol set out at 1805 with five Triplanes. Near Gavrelle, Flight Sub Lieutenant H V Rowley attacked a red 'Nieuport' and fired 50 rounds at 50 yards, the hostile scout going down out of control for his first victory of an eventual nine, but he was then engaged by three more scouts. His engine was hit so he made straight for the lines and made an emergency landing in a field south of Béthune, but his machine turned over when landing on soft ground. As far as time is concerned, Nathanael's 'Triplane' claim seems to fit Rowley better than Heyward, despite the German saying his victim came down inside German lines, which Rowley did not – nor did Heyward. To add to all this confusion, another 1 Naval Triplane came down in the area south of Béthune. Flight Sub Lieutenant H D M Wallace developed engine trouble and was forced to land, but thinking he was in enemy territory, set fire to his machine which burnt out before he knew he was on the right side of the lines. So, if Nathanael's Rumpf Eins was not a Triplane, but a Nieuport, then Barwell had to have been brought down by him.

The crew of a BE2g, flying a recce sortie between Bailleul-Sir-Berthoult and Gavrelle, just north-east of Arras, had a lucky escape. Lieutenant A E Illingworth and Second Lieutenant F Tymms (6277) were at 5,000 feet when they spotted six German fighters almost directly overhead; two were coloured red, so one can assume they were Jasta 11 aircraft. It was 1815 as Arthur Illingworth saw the leader commence

a dive. Illingworth side-slipped and endeavoured to manoeuvre his BE out of the attacker's line of fire. The other fighters came down too and each made at least two attacks on the two-seater as it headed west, twisting and turning as it went. As they reached Mont St Eloi (which is within sight of Vimy Ridge) the fighters gave up the chase, but none had come too close for fear of the observer's rear gun, although Tymms had had no opportunity to fire, hoping in vain that one of the hostile machines would come in close.

An Albatros two-seater was claimed out of control near Pont Rouge on the River Lys just north of Armentières, by Captain E D Atkinson of 1 Squadron, at 1740. Atkinson (A6678) saw the two-seater approaching the lines opposite Ploegsteert Wood at 16,000 feet. The British pilot climbed between Ploegsteert and Armentières, then attacked as the two-seater turned and headed for Lille, its observer firing back at the Nieuport. Over Pont Rouge he got in 25 rounds from 30 yards which caused smoke to stream from the engine. The observer appeared to have been hit but then the machine went down in a vertical dive, in fact going over beyond the vertical. Atkinson then saw three Albatros Scouts below in his line of dive, so he pulled out and headed back. Apart from the two-seater 1 Naval claimed, this is the only other C-type accounted for this day. The Germans did incur some two-seater casualties but it is difficult to tie up victories with victims.

Oberleutnant Georg Kraft, observer with FA4 was killed over Arras; Vizefeldwebel Rener of FA(A)48 was wounded over Carvin, north-east of Lens; his observer, Leutnant Alois Stegmann, was killed.

French Front

Four hostile aircraft were claimed by French fighter pilots, one two-seater Albatros being claimed at 1343(A) at Fleuricourt by Sous Lieutenant 'Père' Dorme of N.3. It was Dorme's 21st victory. A scout fell north-east of Nauroy at 1500, shot down by Lieutenant Beraud-Villars of N.102. This was probably flown by the Staffelführer of Jasta 29, Leutnant Ludwig Dornheim, who was killed over Biene-Nauroy.

Sous Lieutenant Baudoin of N.80 shot down a two-seater at Moulins, the crew being captured, while Sous Lieutenant Lebeau of N.12 claimed his fourth victory by downing a machine over Orainville at 1745 hours.

FE2d A6355 of 57 Squadron, brought down by Friedrich Gille of Jasta 12 on 29 April. It was his first confirmed victory, having had a BE2 unconfirmed on the 22nd, and he would have another unconfirmed on the 30th. However, by September his score stood at six. The crew of this FE were both taken prisoner after being forced down near Barelle.

Losses for the Germans on this front were Leutnant Peckmann of Jasta 15, wounded; observer Leutnant Erich Bamm of FA(A)201, killed over Marchais, near Liesse; Flieger Ernst Deutchmann of Schutzstaffel 22, killed over Bray-en-Laonnois.

On the debit side a Caudron G4 of C.9 was attacked by two enemy machines on the Nancy front, wounding the pilot, Caporal Luizet. On the Soissons sector, Maréchal-des-Logis Ravet, piloting a Morane Parasol of C.122, was also wounded along with his gunner, Soldat Cassonnet, Ravet being forced to make an emergency landing near Ferme d'Alger.

Sergent Henri Leroy of N.12 was wounded and his Spad VII damaged, while a Letord of C.46 failed to return from a mission. This was probably the 'Caudron' claimed by Leutnant Walter Böning of Jasta 19 for his 3rd victory which fell at Brimont. Two other Caudrons were claimed during the day, one by Gefreiter Reichardt and Leutnant Zupan of FA7 near Marcoing at 1150, while Leutnant Heinrich Geigl of Jasta 34 claimed one south of Pont-à-Mousson at 1415(G), which was inside French lines. This may have been the Caudron of C.222 that returned with a wounded observer.

A Voisin of VB.114 also failed to get home. This machine suffered from engine trouble which forced the pilot to put down north of Pouvres where he and his observer were taken into captivity.

Leutnant Richard Ernert of Jasta 34 claimed a balloon at Fort Genicourt which was that of 87 Cié.

	A/C	KB		DES	OOC	KB
British losses	20	–	British claims	11	21	–
French losses	2	–	French claims	4		?
German claims	23†	1	German losses	4‡		1

† Four to flak. ‡ The Nachrichtenblatt records two aircraft in German lines, two missing, one balloon lost; three airmen killed in action plus three wounded.

British Casualties

Aircraft type	No.	Squadron	Crew	
BE2e	6768	12 Sqdn	Lt N H Mackrow	WIA
			Lt J M Musson	WIA
Nieuport XVII	A6739	40 Sqdn	Lt J A G Brewis	KIA
FE2d	A6355	57 Sqdn	2/Lt F A W Handley	POW
			2/Lt E W Percival	POW
Nieuport XXIII	B1579	29 Sqdn	Lt H B M Milling	POW
Nieuport XXIII	A6684	29 Sqdn	Sgt G Humble	POW
Sopwith Pup	A6160	3N Sqdn	FSL S L Bennett	KIA
Spad VII	A6681	19 Sqdn	Maj H D Harvey-Kelly	KIA
Spad VII	A6753	19 Sqdn	Lt W N Hamilton	POW
Spad VII	B1573	19 Sqdn	2/Lt R Applin	KIA
Nieuport XVII	N3192	6N Sqdn	FSL A H V Fletcher	POW/WIA
FE2b	4898	18 Sqdn	Sgt G Stead	KIA
			Cpl A Beebee	KIA

Aircraft type	No.	Squadron	Crew		
FE2b	A5483	18 Sqdn	2/Lt G H Dinsmore	Safe	
			2/Lt G B Bate	KIA	
FE2b	A5466	18 Sqdn	2/Lt R C Doughty (P)	WIA	*
			2/Lt R W Reid	Safe	
FE2d	A29	20 Sqdn	2/Lt E O Perry	WIA	
			2AM T E Allum	WIA	
FE2b	A19	20 Sqdn	Sgt S Attwater	POW	
			2/Lt J E Davies	POW	
FE2b	A6391	20 Sqdn	2/Lt V L A Burns	POW	
			2/Lt D L Houghton	POW	
BE2e	7092	12 Sqdn	Lt J H Westlake	WIA	
			Lt C J Pile	DOW	
BE2e	A2738	12 Sqdn	Lt D E Davies	KIA	
			Lt G H Rathbone	KIA	
Sop Triplane	N5484	1N Sqdn	FSL A P Heyward	WIA	*
Sop Triplane	N5441	1N Sqdn	FSL H M D Wallace	Safe	
Sop Triplane	N5463	8N Sqdn	FSL A E Cuzner	KIA	
Nieuport XVII	A6745	40 Sqdn	Capt F L Barwell	KIA	
BE2c	6266	9 Sqdn	2/Lt H J Grogarty (P)	WIA	
BE2c		7 Sqdn	2/Lt J H Haywood (P)	WIA	
DH4		55 Sqdn	Lt C G Sturt (P)	WIA	

French Casualties					
Caudron G4		C.9	Cpl Luizet (P)	WIA	*
Morane Parasol		C.122	MdL G Ravet	WIA	*
			Sol M Cassonnet	WIA	
Spad VII		N.12	Sgt H Leroy	WIA	*
Letord	90	C.46	Lt J Campion	KIA	
			MdL M Lamy	KIA	
			Cpl Bousque	KIA	
Voisin	1746	VB.114	Adj Durand	POW	
			Lt Lalaune	POW	
Caudron G4		C.222	S/Lt de Bussy (O)	WIA	*

30 APRIL 1917
M T W T F S S

British Front

Weather-wise it was another fine day for this last day of April. While British troops continued to fight along their front, the French made an attack in the Champagne region, taking several German trenches at Mont Carnillet to the south of Beine. Also significant was the announcement that General Henri Philippe Pétain had been appointed as Chief of the French General Staff, replacing General Nivelle, thus becoming the new commander-in-chief.

Captain R Oxspring MC and Bar, 66 Squadron. Badly injured on 30 April in a collision with a Bristol Fighter. In WW2 his son also became a fighter ace, DFC and Bar, AFC.

For the RFC this last day of April was to be another period of losses to the German Jasta pilots and ground gunners. This day also heralded a new phase in German air policy. For the first time four German Jastas were grouped together into one fighting formation. The four units were Jastas 3, 4, 11 and 33, all based in the Douai area.

While it would be difficult for the four units actually to fly together in formation, simply because up to 20-25 aircraft in one group was almost unheard of, it was almost impossible for a single man even to attempt to control such numbers in the air. In reality, however, the units continued to fight individually, but sometimes in two Jasta strength. The main reason for the grouping was so that a large body of fighting aeroplanes could be moved as a mass unit to various parts of the battle front, wherever they were needed most. This grouping became more official in June 1917 upon the formation of Jagdesgeschwader Nr.1 (Jastas 4, 6, 10 and 11) under the leadership of Manfred von Richthofen.

Due to the constant moving of the group from sector to sector, plus the highly imaginative colouring schemes being painted on their scouts by individual German fighter pilots, it was little wonder that the group soon became known as the Circus. Late on 30 April, however, von Richthofen left the front for some well-earned leave, his brother Lothar taking temporary command of the Jasta.

Dawn on this Monday saw the BEs rising from their aerodromes to start the day's work of contact patrols and artillery registration sorties. Always ready for the rich pickings, just like anglers on a river bank at first light, the German fighter pilots too headed for the front lines, their keen eyes ready to pick out the early 'fish'.

Sopwith 1½ Strutters of 45 Squadron provided escort for a photo sortie first thing, on the northern part of the front. Vizefeldwebel Max Müller saw the British machines flying near Armentières and attacked one of the escorts. The one he singled out, flown by Second Lieutenant W A Wright with his gunner 2AM B G Perrott, put up a good fight, but Perrott was hit and dropped out of sight into his cockpit. Bill Wright, a future ace on both Strutters and later Camels, got his machine back across the lines and put down at Lillers, where the machine was written-off, only to find his rear man dead.

Second Lieutenants N A Lawrence and G R Y Stout of 16 Squadron (Stout was about to receive the MC) took off from Bruay at 0540 to fly a contact patrol 3,000 yards east of Vimy Ridge. They were almost at the end of their patrol time when the sharp stutter of machine guns heralded a diving Albatros. Lothar von Richthofen watched as his victim nosed over and went down in flames to crash; victory number 15.

Meantime, 57 Squadron flew a line patrol between Lieven and Noreuil, led by Captain Harker, and ran into a grinder in the shape of Jastas 11,12 and 33 (not the new group formation!) near Douai.

Lothar von Richthofen was still in the air following his downing of the 16 Squadron BE forty minutes earlier. Seeing the FEs he attacked and brought down one at Izel. Adolf von Tutschek, leader of Jasta 12, clawed down a second FE at the same location and time – 0755(G). The fight must have broken up for these two FEs were the only ones lost, but some of the surviving FEs obviously continued with their mission, for more than half an hour later, Leutnant Geiseler from Jasta 33 attacked an FE and chased it over the lines near Oppy, but he did not have his victory confirmed. The FE finally made a forced landing near Roclincourt and although the machine was wrecked, the crew were unhurt. They were Lieutenants C S Morice and F Leathley, who had claimed one Albatros out of control. They then flew west, followed by four or five fighters, having their radiator hit. They continued to evade the worst of the enemy's fire as they also lost height, then had to run the gauntlet of ground fire as they flashed over the trenches at 500 feet. Finally the FE's engine seized and they force-landed at Roclincourt, 3,000 yards inside British territory.

Amidst all this, the squadron CO, Major L A Pattinson, with Lieutenant Angus Mearns, had taken off to do an engine test. They saw the fight going on over the lines and despite the engine overheating flew to help out, claiming one Albatros down out of control and another driven down with a dead engine, but by this time the main casualties had occurred.

This wasn't the end of 57 Squadron's misery, for another patrol took off at 0900 and also ran into hostile aircraft, Lieutenant J H Ryan being mortally wounded and his gunner, Second Lieutenant B Soutten, also hit. Ryan got his machine down inside British lines at Miraumont at 1020 but died soon afterwards.

Near Armentières at 0855(A), Captain C J Quintin Brand of 1 Squadron closed in on two two-seaters he'd seen going west over Wytschaete five minutes earlier. He finally engaged one south of Neuve Eglise, firing from 100 yards. He hit the observer, who was seen to drop down into his cockpit. Now free to close right in, he did so, shooting the two-seater down into Allied lines at Houplines. This was an Albatros C of FA204 flown by Vizefeldwebel Max Baatz and Leutnant Alexander Schleiper. Both men were killed and the machine was numbered G.27 by the British.

Later this morning, 16 Squadron had sent out another BE to photograph sections east of Vimy but this had the bad luck to run into a machine of FA(A)233 crewed by Vizefeldwebel Brokmann and Leutnant Pedell who shot the British machine down over Fresnoy at 1010(G). This was just inside British lines; the BE was wrecked but both men scrambled clear relatively unharmed.

More FEs ran into trouble on this sunny morning, 18 Squadron flying escort to their own photo machines. They were attacked by fighters and fought a defensive battle back to the lines, one with a dead gunner and a wounded pilot, while a second had to make a crash landing but the crew were unhurt. There were no German claims as they had no firm idea how much damage had been inflicted. Once again

Line-up of Sopwith Pups of 66 Squadron at Vert Galand. Nearest the camera is A6152 '3' which was shot up in combat on 24 April, 2/Lt C C Morley unhurt; A7323 '6' was being flown on the 30th by Captain R Oxspring MC when it collided with a BF2a, resulting in Oxspring being badly injured.

Oliver Partington was observer to G A Critchley and noted in his logbook:

'Photography: FE A851. 0810-1030. Ht. 11,000 ft – two photos taken, large camera. AA normal, visibility fair. Formation attacked by about 20 HA Scouts over Baralle. One HA came direct for our tail, fired half drum from back gun into him; he swerved past on left and I fired another half drum from front gun. HA then dived with engine trailing cloud of smoke. Fired three-quarters of a drum from front gun at another HA flying E about 1,500 ft below; he nose-dived, apparently out of control.'

The new SE5s of 56 Squadron flew an OP between Vitry and Villiers on this morning, taking off at 0805. They were engaged by some Albatros Scouts of Jasta 5 and Lieutenant M A Kay was shot down east of Fresnoy by Edmund Nathanael. Lieutenant J O Leach was then reported to have attacked the victorious German pilot having seen him shoot down Maurice Kay. The Albatros caught fire and crashed, but as far as is known, Nathanael was not shot down nor did Jasta 5 lose any pilots in this action. In fact Nathanael would claim one more victory (his 15th) before being killed in May 1917.

There were more combats taking place along the front during mid-morning operations. An OP by 1 Naval, led by Dallas, provided escort for 48 Squadron's Bristols. An estimated 20 enemy fighters tried persistently to engage the two-seaters south of Douai for more than 20 minutes but only succeeded in wounding one observer. Dallas claimed a two-seater Rumpler crashed near Hayencourt (see later). As the two-seaters headed home, the Triplanes went to help some FEs and managed to drive the Albatros pilots away, Dallas sending one down out of control.

Another 9 Squadron BE was in the air at 1000, flying a photo op east of Vimy – the generals were determined to get their pictures – but the German fighter pilots were equally determined to stop it. Hans Klein of Jasta 4 went down on this BE at noon German time, sending it crashing at Ribécourt, the first kill by Jasta 4 since the 14th.

The Spads of 19 Squadron took off at 1130 to fly an OP between Lens, Le Forêt, Fontaine and Noreuil, led by Captain D A L Davidson MC. This was the squadron's third OP of the day. On the second Davidson and Lieutenant J M Child had a fight with three EA near Vitry but had to return with gun jams. Taking off again they found a two-seater of Schutzstaffel 19 over the front, but in the attack, Davidson's Spad was hit badly and disintegrated – blown to pieces was one description – and fell to earth. The German crewmen were Vizefeldwebels Karl Voigt and Woldt, their victim falling over Sallaumines on the outskirts of Lens at 1320(G).

Further north, Nieuports of 1 Squadron escorted FE2s on a bomb raid late morning, and as the formation turned west after dropping their bombs, a number of German fighters engaged them between Gulleghem and Ypres. The Nieuports were led by Captain C J Quintin Brand, who had brought down a two-seater a couple of hours earlier, and in the fight, a couple of Germans were sent down out of control, while the FEs drove down another.

After lunch it was the turn of 15 Squadron to have problems during an artillery shoot in their Corps area. A crew took off at 1330 and did some good work for two hours, almost at the end of their duty, but the BE was a tempting target and finally it was hit by fire from KFlak 61 and Flakzug 28. Lieutenant Paris couldn't make the trenches and he and his observer were taken prisoner after a forced landing east of Chérisy.

Yet another BE was brought down in mid-afternoon, 13 Squadron having put up a machine to take photos over the 17th Corps front at 1508. Kurt Wolff of Jasta 11 was watching and waiting west of Vitry, swooping down with Spandaus blazing at 1735(G). His fire knocked out the observer and wounded the pilot, but he got his machine over the lines and force-landed west of Fresnes. 13 Squadron had another observer wounded during the day and so too did 12 Squadron; in fact it had two observers wounded in air fights.

Nieuports of 29 Squadron were on escort duty over the front at this time and were engaged by Jasta 3. Second Lieutenant R H Upson was in a brand-new machine when fire from Karl Menckhoff smashed his engine and forced him to put down at Cantin at 1850(G) after one hour's flying time. As the Nieuport only had a total of one hour 45 minutes recorded, it must have just run up about 45 minutes of flight testing and delivery time prior to this sortie, and its career was now at an end. Menckhoff had his 3rd victory of an eventual 39.

One other Nieuport, but one which was not confirmed, had been attacked by Leutnant Karl Deilmann of Jasta 6 near Roupy. It came down near Monchy-le -Preux, after a fight with Albatros Scouts. This had been flown by Major A J L 'Jack' Scott, CO of 60 Squadron, but he was safe and unharmed.

The final loss of April was a Pup of 3 Naval Squadron. The Naval boys were providing escort to FEs of 18 Squadron west of Cambrai, the Pups having taken off at 1615. Flight Sub Lieutenant J J Malone was on his second sortie of the day, having flown escort to 4 Squadron BEs bombing railway yards at Cambrai that morning. The Pups got tangled up with Albatros Scouts from Jasta 12, and despite his experience – John Malone had achieved ten victories in air combat since the beginning of March and won the DSO – he was bested in this action by the embryo pilot Leutnant Paul Billik, who shot him down over Remaucourt at 1810(G). It was Billik's first confirmed victory – the first of an eventual 31. He had been with Jasta 12 just over a month.

On the RFC side, once again a number of German aircraft had been claimed shot down; in fact seven destroyed and 23 out of control. Among the destroyed had been a Rumpler two-seater by Roderic Dallas of 1 Naval Squadron over Haynecourt at 0835 and another C-type by Captain J O Andrews of 66 Squadron between Brebières and Vitry at 0845. Of two machines that came down inside British lines this Monday, one became G.28 in the RFC numbering system, noted as a DFW CV, brought down by ground fire, its crew taken prisoner, the other recorded as an Albatros C, and numbered G.27, which was Quintin Brand's victim.

Another German artillery unit – FA(A)233 – recorded the loss of observer Leutnant August Rodenbeck on the 30th, killed near Oppy, which was right on the British front line. Yet another – FA(A)238 – recorded the death of Oberleutnant Hermann Benckiser at Roucourt. A third two-seater crew from the 2 Armee area, FA(A)259, Vizefeldwebel Max Reichle and Leutnant Erich Hampe were reported missing. These two men force-landed at Hendicourt with a damaged machine and are obviously the crew of G.28 reported captured.

Another crew who came off second best were Leutnants Tüxen and Wissemann of FA250, who were both slightly wounded. Kurt Wissemann would later become a fighter pilot and fly with Jasta 3 the following month and be credited with bringing down the French ace Georges Guynemer in September.

It is also noted that Lieutenant W A Bishop of 60 Squadron claimed a two-seater crashed south-east of Lens at 1115 and another forced to land south of Lens shortly afterwards, both inside German lines.

The only recorded casualty of a German fighter pilot was Leutnant Friedrich Mallinckrodt of Jasta 20, a six-victory ace, severely wounded while operating over the southern sectors of the British front, possibly the victim of Captain W J C K Cochran-Patrick of 23 Squadron, who claimed an Albatros in flames at 1640, west of Cambrai.

The Belgian pilot, Andre de Meulemeester of 1ere Escadrille, claimed a C-type this day, over Lecke – just inside German lines – flying a Nieuport. It was his first victory of an eventual 11.

Two interesting events occurred on this day. The first concerns the crew of a BE2e of No. 9 Squadron who were attacked by a formation of enemy scouts near Havrincourt Wood. The pilot, Second Lieutenant D McTavish, was wounded in the foot and thigh and had his engine set on fire. They crashed inside German lines, the BE erupting in flames. McTavish managed to scramble clear of the wreckage but his observer, Captain A S Allen MC (Canadian) was trapped in the fire. Unable to effect a rescue a German soldier shot him to end his suffering. They had been downed by Leutnant Friedrich Kempft of Jasta 2, his first victory.

Later a 16 Squadron crew, Second Lieutenants E L Bishop and P A B Lytton, were out taking important photographs near Fresnes when they too were attacked. An accompanying BE2 was driven off while Bishop levelled out at low level, but seeing the enemy machines head away, Bishop regained height, returned to the area of importance and he and his observer took 36 photographs before heading for home. Edwin Bishop received the Military Cross for his actions this day.

French Front

A claim was made by a French fighter pilot, Lieutenant Bailly of N.81 when he shot down a two-seater in flames at Moronvilliers, for his first victory. This is believed to have been a machine from KG2 that fell over Reims, Leutnants Karl Beckmann and Ernst Poetsch being killed. Adjutant Lucien Jailler of N.15 gained his 8th victory near Laon at 0940, type not recorded.

One of the iron men of French fighter aviation, Lieutenant Jacques Leps of Spa.81, took on two Albatros Scouts – and lost. Shot up, he crashed his Spad VII on Mont Cornillet, after just making it back across the lines. Leps would score 12 victories by the end of the war.

Two more fighters were brought down. A Nieuport Scout of N.38, flown by Caporal Leroy, failed to return, being forced down in a combat with Leutnant Otto von Breiten-Landenberg of Jasta 9 at 1100 hours, near St Hilaire le Petit. Sergent H Baudson of N.15 was wounded flying a Spad VII in the Soissons sector. Jasta 9 claimed three Spads: Leutnant Friedrich von Hartmann south-west of Nauroy at 0925(G) and Leutnant Hermann Pfeiffer at 1030 at Moronvilliers, and finally Leutnant Adolf Frey at 1115, again over Moronvilliers. One of them was probably Leps.

Frey, however, was then shot down in flames near Nauroy while attacking a Caudron R4, and Leutnant Werner Marwitz was also killed over Nauroy, although there are no records to indicate how Marwitz met his end.

Jasta 19 attacked the French balloon lines in force, claiming three destroyed at Guyencourt and two near Reims. Oberleutnant Erich Hahn claimed two, Vizefeldwebel Arthur Rahn two and Leutnant Walter Böning one. Leutnant Matthaei of Jasta 21 claimed a sixth balloon at 1440, over Montbré. The French lost balloons Cié 19, 59, 62 and 91.

	A/C	KB		DES	OOC	KB
British losses	15	–	British claims	8‡	23	–
French losses	2	?	French claims	1		–
German claims	19†	6	German losses	8*		–

† Three by flak. ‡ Plus one more if indeed ground fire brought down G.28. * The Nachrichtenblatt records six aircraft lost in combat plus two more missing, with two officers killed and four wounded.

British Casualties

Aircraft type	No.	Squadron	Crew		
BE2g	A2942	16 Sqdn	2/Lt N A Lawrence	KIA	
			2/Lt G R Y Stout	KIA	
BE2g	A2949	9 Sqdn	2/Lt D McTavish	POW	
			Capt A S Allen MC	KIA	
Sop 1½ Strutter	A1080	45 Sqdn	2/Lt W A Wright	Safe	
			2AM B G Perrott	KIA	
FE2d	A6402	57 Sqdn	Lt P T Bowers	POW	
			2/Lt S T Wills	POW	
FE2d	A6352	57 Sqdn	2/Lt E D Jennings	POW	
			2/Lt J R Lingard	POW	
FE2d	A1966	57 Sqdn	Lt C S Morice	Safe	
			Lt F Leathley	Safe	
FE2d	A6380	57 Sqdn	Lt J H Ryan	DOW	*
			2/Lt B Soutten	WIA	
FE2b	A5143	20 Sqdn	Lt D Y Hoy	Safe	
			Sgt E H Sayers	Safe	
BE2g	A2851	16 Sqdn	2/Lt V F Stewart	Safe	
			2/Lt A Boyle	Safe	
SE5	A4866	56 Sqdn	Lt M A Kay	KIA	
FE2b	6998	18 Sqdn	Sgt T Whiteman	WIA	*
			2AM J H Wynn	DOW	
BE2e	A2916	9 Sqdn	2/Lt R P C Freemantle	KIA	
			2/Lt P Sherman	KIA	
Spad VII	B1562	19 Sqdn	Capt D A L Davidson	KIA	
BE2e	7060	15 Sqdn	Lt D K Paris MC	POW	
			2/Lt A E Fereman	POW	
BE2e	A2910	13 Sqdn	2/Lt W K Trollope	WIA	
			2/Lt A Bonner	KIA	
Nieuport XVII	B1601	29 Sqdn	2/Lt R H Upson	POW	
Sopwith Pup	N6175	3N Sqdn	FSL J J Malone DSO	KIA	

Aircraft type	No.	Squadron	Crew		
BE2c		12 Sqdn	2AM J J Cameron (O)	WIA	*
BE2c		12 Sqdn	2AM D W Imber (O)	WIA	*
BE2c		13 Sqdn	1AM L Baines (O)	WIA	*
BF2a		48 Sqdn	Cpl R Edwards (O)	KIA	*
FE2b	A5481	18 Sqdn	2/Lt S H Bell	Safe	
			Lt D W Macleod	Safe	

French Casualties

Aircraft type	No.	Squadron	Crew		
Nieuport XVII		N.38	Cpl Leroy	MIA	
Spad VII		N.15	Sgt H Baudson	WIA	*
Spad VII		Spa.81	Lt A L J Leps	Safe	

Appendix 1

RFC Victory Claims

Time	Pilot/Crew	Sqdn	Vic No	E/A	Location	How
			1 April 1917			
1050	2/Lt D Gordon &	12	1	Albatros DIII	Arras	DF
	2/Lt H E Baker	12	1			
			2 April 1917			
0745	2/Lt C S Hall	60	1	Albatros DIII	Fontaine Notre Dame	OOC
0800	Lt O M Sutton	54	1	2-seater	Péronne	OOC
0850	Lt S Cockerall	24	5	Albatros DII	Gouzeaucourt	D
0855	Lt K Crawford	24	4	Albatros DII	Gouzeaucourt	DF
	Capt C R Cox &	24	2			
	Lt L C Welsford	24	1			
0945	2/Lt E E Pope &	57	1	Albatros DIII	SE Arras	DF
	Lt A W Naismith	57	1			
0945	2/Lt E E Pope &	57	2	Albatros DIII	SE Arras	DF
	Lt A W Naismith	57	2			
1105	2/Lt C de Berigny	43	1	Albatros DIII	E Vimy	DF
	2AM E Bowen	43	1			
	1st Army AA			Albatros DII	Lens	POW
	2nd Army AA			2-seater	Pilkem	DF
	5th Army AA			2-seater		POW
			3 April 1917			
1435	Lt H H Balfour &	43	2	Albatros DIII	Izel	DF
	2/Lt A Roberts	43	2			
			5 April 1917			
1000	Lt P Pike &	48	1	Albatros DII	Douai	OOC
	2/Lt H B Griffith	48	1			
1015	Capt W Leefe Robinson &	48	2	Albatros DII	Douai	OOC
	2/Lt E D Warburton	48	2			
1100	Lt H W Woollett	24	1	2-seater	E Honnecourt	D
1135	Capt G J Mahony-Jones &	20	1	Albatros DII	Courtrai	OOC
	Capt R M Knowles	20	2			
1140	Capt G J Mahony-Jones &	20	2	Albatros DII	Courtrai	OOC
	Capt R M Knowles	20	3			
1145	2/Lt H G White &	20	1	Albatros DIII	Neuve Eglise	POW
	Pvt T Allum	20	1			
1145	Lt C R O'Brien &	43	2	Albatros DII	E La Bassée	OOC
	Lt J L Dickson	43	1			
1200	Sgt J Dempsey &	25	1	Albatros DII	Vimy Ridge	OOC
	Sgt C H Nunn	25	1			
1200	F/C R S Dallas	1N	8	Albatros DIII	E St Quentin	OOC
1200	2/Lt V H Huston &	18	2	Albatros DII	Inchy	OOC
	Lt G N Blennerhasset	18	2			
1200	2/Lt V H Huston &	18	3	Albatros DII	Inchy	OOC
	Lt G N Blennerhasset	18	3			
1200	Capt R H Hood &	18	1	Albatros DII	Inchy	OOC
	2/Lt J R Smith	18	4			

Time	Pilot/Crew	Sqdn	Vic No	E/A	Location	How
1200	Capt A M Wilkinson &	48	11	Albatros DII	Douai	OOC
	Lt L G Allen	48	11			
1245	FSL R J O Compston	8N	2	Halberstadt DII	SE La Bassée	OOC
1345	2/Lt F H Kolligs &	22	1	Albatros DII	Honnecourt	OOC
	2/Lt J O Stewart	22	1			
	2/Lt G M Hopkins &	22	1			
	2/Lt G O McEntee	22	1			
1645	Lt G A H Pidcock &	60	1	Albatros DIII	Reincourt	D
	Lt T Langwill	60	1			
1645	2/Lt C S Hall	60	2	Albatros DIII	Reincourt	OOC
1645	Lt J M Elliott	60	1	Albatros DIII	Reincourt	OOC
1700	F/C E W Norton	6N	4	Albatros DIII	W Douai	D
1700	F/C E W Norton	6N	5	Albatros DIII	W Douai	OOC
1700	FSL A L Thorne	6N	1	Albatros DIII	Douai	OOC
1700	FSL R R Thornely	6N	1	Albatros DIII	W Douai	OOC
1835	2/Lt E J Pascoe	29	1	Albatros DIII	Vitry-en-Artois	OOC
1835	Lt C V Rogers	29	1	Albatros DIII	Vitry-en-Artois	OOC
1900	2/Lt B Scott-Foxwell	29	1	Albatros DIII	Douai	OOC
	Capt R G H Pixley,	54	2	Balloon	Gouy	DF
	Lt M D G Scott,	54	2			
	Capt F N Hudson &	54	3			
	2/Lt R M Charley	54	1			
	2/Lt H S Pell	40	1	Albatros DII	S Bailleul	D
	Lt Lavarack &	12	1	Albatros DII		D
	Lt Baker-Jones	12	1			
	Patrol	48	–	Albatros DIII	Douai	D

6 April 1917

Time	Pilot/Crew	Sqdn	Vic No	E/A	Location	How
0730	Capt F N Hudson	54	4	2-seater	Le Catelet	OOC
0730	Capt K C McCallum	23	1	2-seater		D
0800	Lt D Stewart	54	1	Albatros DIII	St Quentin	D
0800	Capt C M Clement &	22	3	Albatros DIII	St Quentin	D
	2/Lt L G Davies	22	1			
	Lt Gladstone &	22	1			
	1AM H Friend	22	1			
	Lt J V Aspinall &	22	3			
	Lt M K Parlee	22	2			
	Lt J F A Day &	22	3			
	2/Lt J K Campbell	22	2			
0855	2/Lt D P Walter &	25	1	Albatros DIII	SW Arras	OOC
	2/Lt C Brown	25	1			
1000	2/Lt H C Todd	40	2	Balloon	Neuvireuil	DF
1000	2/Lt Parkinson	18	2	Albatros DII	Beaumetz-Beugny	D
	2/Lt Power	18	1			
	2/Lt R W Reid &	18	1			
	Lt G N Blennerhasset	18	1			
1000	Capt R H Hood	18	2	Albatros DII	Écoust St Main	POW
	2/Lt J R Smith	18	5			
1010	2/Lt F D Ferry &	20	1	Albatros DIII	Ledeghem	D
	Pvt T Allum	20	2			
1015	2/Lt E J Smart &	20	1	Albatros DIII	Roulers	D
	2/Lt H N Hampson	20	1			
1020	2/Lt E J Smart &	20	2	Albatros DIII	S Roulers	OOC
	2/Lt H N Hampson	20	2			
1020	2/Lt E J Smart &	20	3	Albatros DIII	S Roulers	OOC
	2/Lt H N Hampson	20	3			
1020	F/Lt L S Breadner	3N	1	Halberstadt DII	Bourlon Woods	D

Time	Pilot/Crew	Sqdn	Vic No	E/A	Location	How
1020	FSL J S T Fall	3N	1	Halberstadt DII	Bourlon Woods	D
1020	FSL A W Carter	3N	1	Halberstadt DII	Bourlon Woods	OOC
1020	FSL F C Armstrong	3N	1	Halberstadt DII	Bourlon Woods	OOC
1030	2/Lt G H Cock &	45	1	Albatros DII	Lille	D
	2/Lt Murison	45	1			
1030	2/Lt P T Newling &	45	1	Albatros DII	Templeuve	OOC
	2AM B G Perrot	45	1			
1030	2/Lt A Roulstone &	25	1	Albatros DIII	E Givenchy	DF
	2/Lt E G Green	25	2			
1045	2/Lt B King &	25	1	Halberstadt DII	E Vimy	D
	Cpl L Emsden	25	4			
1135	Lt C R Kerry &	24	1	2-seater	Havrincourt Wood	OOC
	2/Lt T C Arnot	24	1			
1145	F/C B C Clayton	1N	1	Albatros DIII	NE St Quentin	OOC
1150	FSL T G Culling	1N	1	2-seater	SE St Quentin	OOC
	Lt G O Smart	60	1	Albatros DIII	Arras	OOC
	Lt F P Holliday &	48	1	Albatros DII	NE Arras	OOC
	Capt A H W Wall	48	1			
	2/Lt W T Price &	48	1	Albatros DII	NE Arras	OOC
	2/Lt M A Benjamin	48	1			
	Capt A J M Clarke	27	1	Halberstadt DII		OOC
	2/Lt E W Kirby &	27	1			
	Lt W H S Wedderspoon	27	1			
	Capt A J M Clarke	27	2	Halberstadt DII		OOC
	2/Lt EW Kirby &	27	2			
	Lt W H S Wedderspoon	27	2			

7 April 1917

Time	Pilot/Crew	Sqdn	Vic No	E/A	Location	How
1700	Lt W A Bishop	60	3	Albatros DIII	Arras	OOC
1710	Lt W A Bishop	60	4	Balloon	Vis-en-Artois	DF
1745	2/Lt C S Hall &	60	3	Albatros DIII	Mercatel	D
	2/Lt G O Smart	60	2			
1748	Lt H C Todd	40	3	Balloon	Sallaumines	DF
1830	Lt N L Robertson &	20	1	Albatros DIII	Tourcoing	D
	2/Lt L G Fauvel	20	1			
1830	2/Lt S N Pike &	20	1	Albatros DIII	Tourcoing	OOC
	2AM E H Sayers	20	1			
1930	FSL R A Little	8N	7	Albatros DIII	SE Lens	D
	F/L C D Booker	8N	1	Albatros DIII	Lens	OOC

8 April 1917

Time	Pilot/Crew	Sqdn	Vic No	E/A	Location	How
0820	2/Lt E S T Cole	1	2	Balloon	Quesnoy	DF
0930	Lt W A Bishop	60	5	Albatros DIII	NE Arras	OOC
0930	Maj A J L Scott &	60	2	2-seater	Fouquières	D
	Lt W A Bishop	60	6			
1010	Lt W A Bishop	60	7	Albatros DIII	Vitry-en-Artois	OOC
1130	2/Lt F M Kitto &	43	3	Albatros DIII	NE Vimy	OOC
	2AM A W Cant	43	1			
1130	Capt C J Q Brand	1	5	Balloon	Moorslede	DF
1400	2/Lt G N Brockhurst &	48	1	Albatros DIII	Rémy-Éterpigny	OOC
	2/Lt C B Boughton	48	1			
	2/Lt R E Adeney &	48	1			
	2/Lt L G Lovell	48	1			
	2/Lt A G Riley &	48	1			
	2/Lt L G Hall	48	1			
1400	Capt D M Tidmarsh &	48	4	Albatros DIII	Rémy-Éterpigny	OOC
	2/Lt C B Holland	48	1			

Time	Pilot/Crew	Sqdn	Vic No	E/A	Location	How
1445	F/C R S Dallas	1N	9	2-seater	E Cambrai	OOC
1500	FSL F D Casey	3N	2	Albatros DIII	NE Pronville	OOC
1500 to	Capt G W Roberts	66	1	Halberstadt DII		OOC
1735	Lt C C Montgomery	66	1	Halberstadt DII		OOC
	2/Lt A J Lucas	66	1	Halberstadt DII		OOC
1510	F/Lt H G Travers	3N	3	Albatros DIII	NE Pronville	OOC
1700	Lt C M Clement &	22	4	Albatros DIII	Beugny	D
	2/Lt L G Davies	22	2			
	Lt L W Beale &	22	1			
	Lt G G Bell	22	1			
	Lt J F A Day &	22	3			
	2/Lt Taylor	22	1			
	Lt J V Aspinall &	22	4			
	Lt M K Parlee	22	3			
	Lt C M Furlonger &	22	1			
	Lt C W Lane	22	1			
	2/Lt J Campbell &	22	3			
	2/Lt H Spearpoint	22	1			
1910	2/Lt A Sutherland	29	2	Albatros DIII	SE Arras	D
	Capt R W Oxspring	54	1	2-seater		D

9 April 1917

Time	Pilot/Crew	Sqdn	Vic No	E/A	Location	How
1145	FSL R A Little	8N	8	Halberstadt DII	Noyelles-Lens	OOC
1145	FSL F C Norton &	6N	6	Albatros DIII	Cambrai	OOC
	FSL A L Thorne	6N	1			
1200	F/C E W Norton	6N	7	Albatros DIII	Cambrai	OOC
am	Capt A M Wilkinson &	48	12	2-seater	Lens	D
	2/Lt H B Griffith	48	3			
am	Capt A M Wilkinson &	48	13	2-seater	Lens	OOC
	2/Lt H B Griffith	48	4			
am	2/Lt W T Price &	48	2	2-seater	E Arras	D
	2/Lt M A Benjamin	48	2			
1800	Capt A M Wilkinson &	48	14	Albatros DIII	E Arras	D
	Lt L G Allen	48	1			
	Lt J H T Letts &	48	1			
	Lt H G Collins	48	1			
1800	Capt A M Wilkinson &	48	15	Albatros DIII	E Arras	OOC
	Lt L G Allen	48	2			
	Lt J H T Letts &	48	2			
	Lt H G Collins	48	2			
1905	Lt T H Southon &	25	1	Albatros DIII	Lievin	OOC
	2/Lt H Freeman-Smith	25	1			

10 April 1917

Time	Pilot/Crew	Sqdn	Vic No	E/A	Location	How
1900	Capt D M Tidmarsh &	48	5	Albatros DIII	Rémy	OOC
	2/Lt C B Holland	48	2			
	2/Lt G N Brockhurst &	48	2			
	2/Lt C B Boughton	48	2			

11 April 1917

Time	Pilot/Crew	Sqdn	Vic No	E/A	Location	How
0800	Capt D M Tidmarsh &	48	6	Albatros DIII	Fampoux	D
	2/Lt C B Holland	48	3			
	2/Lt R E Adeney &	48	2			
	2/Lt L G Lovell	48	2			
	2/Lt G N Brockhurst &	48	3			
	2/Lt C B Boughton	48	3			
	2/Lt A G Riley &	48	2			
	2/Lt L G Hall	48	2			

Time	Pilot/Crew	Sqdn	Vic No	E/A	Location	How
0800	Capt D M Tidmarsh &	48	7	Albatros DIII	Fampoux	OOC
	2/Lt C B Holland	48	4			
	2/Lt R E Adeney &	48	3			
	2/Lt L G Lovell	48	3			
	2/Lt G N Brockhurst &	48	4			
	2/Lt C B Boughton	48	4			
	2/Lt A G Riley &	48	3			
	2/Lt L G Hall	48	3			
0820	2/Lt A G Riley &	48	4	Albatros DIII	Fampoux	OOC
	2/Lt L G Hall	48	4			
0845	F/C L Breadner	3N	3	Albatros C	Cambrai	DF
0855	F/C L Breadner	3N	4	Albatros DII	Cambrai	D
0900	FSL J S T Fall	3N	2	Albatros DII	Cambrai	OOC
0900	FSL P G McNeil	3N	1	Albatros DII	Cambrai	OOC
0905	FSL J S T Fall	3N	3	Albatros DII	Cambrai	OOC
0905	FSL J S T Fall	3N	4	Albatros DII	Cambrai	OOC

12 April 1917

Time	Pilot/Crew	Sqdn	Vic No	E/A	Location	How
1030	F/C R G Mack	3N	2	Albatros DII	Pronville	D
1030	FSL A T Whealy	3N	1	Albatros DII	Pronville	OOC
1030	FSL E Pierce &	3N	1	Albatros DII	Pronville	OOC
	FSL F C Armstrong	3N	2			
1030	FSL E Pierce	3N	2	Albatros DII	Pronville	OOC
1040	2/Lt E L Zink &	18	3	Albatros DII	Cagnicourt	OOC
	Pte N G Jones	18	1			
1040	2/Lt E W A Hunt &	18	1	Albatros DII	Cagnicourt	OOC
	2/Lt K Fearnside-Speed	18	1			
1040	Capt A M Wilkinson &	48	16	Albatros DIII		OOC
	Lt L G Allen	48	4			
	2/Lt W O B Winkler &	48	1			
	2/Lt E S Moore	48	1			

13 April 1917

Time	Pilot/Crew	Sqdn	Vic No	E/A	Location	How
0840	Lt G S Buck	19	1	Albatros DIII	Brebières	OOC
1130	Lt H E O Ellis	40	1	Albatros C	Courrières	D
am	Capt R Oxspring	66	–	Albatros C	Douai	DD
am	Lt J T Collier	66	–	Albatros DIII	Douai	DD
1620	2/Lt B Scott-Foxwell	29	2	Albatros DII	Monchy-le-Preux	OOC
1830	Lt J V Aspinall &	22	5	Albatros DIII	Itancourt	D
	Lt M K Parlee	22	4			
1930	Capt J L Leith &	25	2	Albatros DIII	Sallaumines	D
	Lt G M A Hobart-Hampden	25	2			
1930	2/Lt R G Malcolm &	25	3	Albatros DIII	Hénin-Liétard	D
	Cpl L Emsden	25	5			
pm	Capt A M Wilkinson &	48	17	Albatros DIII	Vitry-en-Artois	D
	Lt L G Allen	48	5			
	Lt J W Warren &	48	1			
	2/Lt H B Griffith	48	4			
pm	Capt A M Wilkinson &	48	18	Albatros DIII	Vitry-en-Artois	OOC
	Lt L G Allen	48	6			
	Lt J W Warren &	48	2			
	2/Lt H B Griffith	48	5			

14 April 1917

Time	Pilot/Crew	Sqdn	Vic No	E/A	Location	How
0810	2/Lt M B Cole	54	1	2-seater	Gonnelieu	OOC
0815	Capt W V Strugnell	54	4	2-seater	Buissy-Inchy	OOC
0820	F/C T F N Gerrard	1N	1	Albatros DII	Épinoy	OOC
0905	FSL E D Crundall	8N	1	2-seater	Hénin-Liétard	OOC

Time	Pilot/Crew	Sqdn	Vic No	E/A	Location	How
0910	FSL E D Crundall	8N	2	2-seater	E Douai	D
0910	F/L C D Booker	8N	2	2-seater	Hénin-Liétard	OOC
0950	2/Lt A G Jones-Williams	29	1	Albatros DII	Neuvireuil-Vitry	OOC
1200	Lt W E Reed	19	1	2-seater	Douai	OOC
1720	Lt D de Burgh &	40	1	Albatros DII	Méricourt	D
	Lt I P R Napier	40	1			
1930	Sgt W Burkenshaw &	25	1	Albatros DIII	Lens	OOC
	Capt A Binnie MC	60	3			
	Sgt J H Brown	25	3	Albatros DII	Hénin-Liétard	D
	2/Lt R G Malcolm &	25	4			
	2/Lt J B Weir	25	2			
	2/Lt R C Savery &	11	2	Albatros DIII		OOC
	2AM Tollerfield	11	2			
	2/Lt W R Exley &	11	1	Albatros DII		OOC
	Capt J A Le Royert	11	1			
	Capt L C Coates &	5	1	Albatros DIII	Willerval	D
	2/Lt J C Cotton	5	1			
			16 April 1917			
0830	2/Lt S J Young &	18	1	Albatros DIII	Cagnicourt	OOC
	2/Lt G N Blennerhasset	18	5			
0830	2/Lt E W A Hunt &	18	2	Albatros DIII	Cagnicourt	OOC
	2/Lt O J Partington	18	2			
			21 April 1917			
1730	FSL F D Casey &	3N	2	Albatros DIII	Heudécourt	D
	FSL H S Broad	3N	1			
1730	F/Lt H G Travers	3N	4	Albatros DII	Cagnicourt	OOC
1740	FSL J J Malone	3N	3	Albatros C	N Quéant	OOC
1810	Lt R H Stocken	23	1	2-seater	Sauchy-Lestrées	OOC
1840	2/Lt R L Keller	23	1	Albatros DIII	Cagnicourt	OOC
1840	FSL F D Casey	3N	3	Albatros DIII	Cagnicourt	OOC
1850	F/C A R Arnold &	8N	2	Albatros DIII	Thelus	POW
	Lt R G Malcolm	25	5			
	2/Lt J B Weir	25	3			
1855	FSL R A Little	8N	9	Albatros DIII	NE Oppy	D
1855	Capt J L Leith &	25	8	Albatros DIII	Oppy-Rouvroy	OOC
	Lt G M A Hobart-Hampden	25	3			
			22 April 1917			
0705	2/Lt H G Ross	60	1	Balloon	N Dury	DF
0705	2/Lt G L Lloyd	60	1	Balloon	NE Boiry	DF
0705	2/Lt E M Wright	1	1	Albatros DIII	Flers	OOC
0705	Capt E D Atkinson	1	2	Albatros DIII	Lille	OOC
0710	Capt E D Atkinson	1	3	Albatros DIII	Lille	OOC
0715	Lt W E Reed	19	2	Albatros C	S Quiery	DF
0720	2/Lt E S T Cole	1	5	Balloon	Wervicq	DF
0730	2/Lt A R Penny	60	1	Balloon	Vis-en-Artois	DF
0730	FSL A R Knight	8N	1	Albatros DIII	E Oppy	OOC
0745	2/Lt J T Collier	66	2	Albatros DIII	Vitry	OOC
1120	Lt W A Bishop	60	8	Albatros DIII	E Vimy	OOC
1121	Lt W A Bishop	60	9	Albatros DIII	E Vimy	OOC
1350	2/Lt W T Walter	40	1	2-seater	Hénin-Liétard	D
1720	Lt W E Molesworth	60	1	Albatros DIII	Vitry	OOC
1720	FSL T G Culling	1N	2	Albatros DIII	Arleux	OOC
1722	F/C R S Dallas	1N	10	DFW C	Arleux	D
1725	F/C R S Dallas	1N	11	DFW C	Arleux	DF

Time	Pilot/Crew	Sqdn	Vic No	E/A	Location	How
1820	2/Lt R L Keller	23	2	Albatros DIII	E Cambrai	OOC
1830	Capt C K C Patrick	23	4	Albatros DIII	Fontaine Notre Dame	OOC
1900	Capt C K C Patrick	23	5	Albatros DIII	Flesquières	OOC
1910	FSL H S Kirby	3N	1	Albatros C	Cambrai	OOC
1915	FSL E Pierce	3N	3	Albatros DIII	Cambrai	OOC
	Capt A M Wilkinson &	48	19	Albatros DIII	Vitry-en-Artois	OOC
	Lt L G Allen	48	7			
	Capt E F Elderton	29	1	Balloon		DF
	2/Lt J S Leslie &	16	1	EA		OOC
	Lt A R Sortwell	16	1			
				Anti-Aircraft	Albatros DIII	D

23 April 1917

Time	Pilot/Crew	Sqdn	Vic No	E/A	Location	How
0630	FSL H F Beamish	3N	1	Albatros DIII	Croiselles	OOC
0630	FSL G B Anderson	3N	1	Albatros DIII	Croiselles	OOC
0630	FSL E Pierce	3N	3	Albatros DIII	Croiselles	OOC
0630	FSL J J Malone	3N	4	Albatros DIII	Croiselles	OOC
0645	Capt A Ball	56	32	2-seater	Abancourt	D
0710	Lt R H Upson	29	1	Albatros DIII	Biache-Sailly	D
0715	FSL J J Malone	3N	5	Albatros DIII	Croiselles	OOC
0745	FSL J J Malone	3N	6	Albatros DIII	Havrincourt	OOC
0800	F/C R S Dallas	1N	12	DFW C	W Douai	OOC
0800	FSL T G Culling	1N	3	DFW C	W Douai	OOC
1020	F/Lt L Breadner	3N	4	Gotha G	Vron	POW
1105	2/Lt N H England &	43	1	Albatros DIII	SE Méricourt	D
	Lt L F Bettinson	43	1			
	1AM E Bowen &	43	2			
	2/Lt C de Berigny	43	2			
1140	Lt K MacKenzie &	40	1	2-seater	Lens	OOC
	Lt H E O Ellis	40	2			
1145	Capt A Ball	56	33	Albatros DIII	Selvigny	DF
1520	Lt J M Child	19	1	2-seater	NW Douai	OOC
1530	Lt W A Bishop	60	10	2-seater	Vitry-en-Tardenois	D
1559	Lt W A Bishop	60	11	Albatros DIII	E Vitry	D
1630	2/Lt A Sutherland	29	3	Albatros DIII	Vitry	OOC
1630	2/Lt A G Jones-Williams	29	3	Albatros DIII	Vitry	OOC
1630	2/Lt A G Jones-Williams	29	4	Albatros DIII	Vitry	OOC
1630	2/Lt J D Atkinson	29	1	Albatros DIII	Vitry	OOC
1640	2/Lt F A Handley &	57	1	Albatros DIII	SE Arras	OOC
	2/Lt E Percival	57	1			
1730	2/Lt H A Trayles &	18	1	Albatros DIII	Baralle	OOC
	Cpl A Beebee	18	1			
1730	2/Lt E L Zink &	18	4	Albatros DIII	Baralle	OOC
	2/Lt G B Bate	18	1			
1730	2/Lt R W Reid &	18	2	Albatros DIII	Baralle	OOC
	2/Lt Fearnside-Speed	18	2			
1730	Capt C E Bryant &	18	1	Albatros DIII	Baralle	OOC
	2/Lt N Couve	18	1			
1730	FSL A W Carter	3N	2	Albatros DIII	Épinoy	D
1730	FSL H S Kerby	3N	2	Albatros DIII	Le Pave	D
1730	FSL H S Kerby	3N	3	Albatros DIII	Le Pave	D
1730	F/Lt L Breadner	3N	5	Albatros DIII	Bourlon Wood	OOC
1730	FSL J S T Fall	3N	5	Albatros DIII	Bourlon Wood	OOC
1800	FSL F D Casey	3N	4	Albatros DIII	Saudemont	OOC
1800	FSL A W Carter	3N	3	Albatros DIII	Épinoy	OOC

Time	Pilot/Crew	Sqdn	Vic No	E/A	Location	How
1810	FSL A T Whealy	3N	2	Albatros DIII	N Cambrai-Arras Road	OOC
1910	2/Lt F Williams	66	1	Albatros DIII	Lecluse	OOC
1932	Maj H D Harvey-Kelly	19	3	Albatros DIII	Cambrai	D
	Lt F P Holliday &	48	2	Albatros DIII	Vimy	D
	Capt A H W Wall	48	2			
	Lt F P Holliday &	48	3	Albatros DIII	Vimy	D
	Capt A H W Wall	48	3			
	Lt W O B Winkler &	48	2			
	2/Lt E S Moore	48	2			
	Lt R B Hay &	48	1			
	?????	48	–			
	Lt W T Price &	48	3			
	Lt M A Benjamin	48	3			
	Capt E R Manning &	11	1	Albatros DIII		OOC
	Lt H D Duncan	11	1			
	2/Lt I V Pyott &	55	2	Albatros DIII	Bove	OOC
	2AM W Bond	55	1			
			24 April 1917			
0640	Lt J H Gotch &	70	1	Halberstadt DII	SE Cambrai	OOC
	2/Lt L A Kiburz	70	1			
0640	Sgt Thomson &	70	1	Halberstadt DII	SE Cambrai	OOC
	2AM Impey	70	1			
0720	Lt R E Johnson &	20	1	Albatros DIII	W Ledeghem	D
	Capt F R Cubbon	20	1			
0720	Lt R E Johnson &	20	2	Albatros DIII	W Ledeghem	D
	Capt F R Cubbon	20	2			
0725	2/Lt R H Stocken	23	2	Albatros DIII	NW Cambrai	OOC
0755	Lt E O Perry &	20	2	Albatros DIII	Becelaere	DF
	2AM E H Sayers	20	2			
0815	F/C R S Dallas	1N	13	Albatros DIII	SE Lens	OOC
0815	F/C T F N Gerrard	1N	2	Albatros DIII	Noyelles	D
0815	Sgt J Whiteman &	18	1	Albatros DIII	Baralle	DF
	Lt Fearnside-Speed	18	4			
0815	Collided	18		Albatros DIII	Baralle	D
0815	Collided	18		Albatros DIII	Baralle	D
0830	F/C T F N Gerrard	1N	3	Albatros DIII	Noyelles	OOC
0840	FSL G G Simpson	8N	2	Albatros DIII	Sailly	OOC
1010	F/Lt A M Shook	4N	1	Fokker D	Ghistelles	OOC
1110	Capt C M Crowe	56	1	2-seater	Bellone	D
	Lt L M Barlow &	56	1			
	Lt M A Kay	56	1			
1200	2/Lt T F Hazell	1	2	Albatros C	Bois Grenier	POW
1200	Lt I P R Napier	40	2	Aviatik C	Lens	POW
	Lt J A G Brewis &	40	1			
	FSL R A Little	8N	10			
1300	Lt A V Burbury	1	1	Balloon		DF
1300	Lt R B Clark	60	1	Albatros DIII	S Tilloy	D
1305	Lt W E Molesworth	60	2	Balloon	Boiry-Notre Dame	DF
1515	Lt G C Maxwell &	56	1	Albatros DIII	NE Cambrai	OOC
	2/Lt C R W Knight	56	1			
1645	2/Lt K J Knaggs	56	1	Albatros DIII	Fresnoy	OOC
1650	F/Lt H G Travers	3N	5	DFW C	Morchies	POW
	FSL F D Casey &	3N	5			
	FSL J J Malone	3N	7			
1730	Lt A Roulstone &	25	2	Albatros DIII	Billy-Montigny	D
	2/Lt E G Green	25	2			

Time	Pilot/Crew	Sqdn	Vic No	E/A	Location	How
1900	Lt W T Price &	48	4	Albatros DIII	E Arras	D
	Lt M A Benjamin	48	4			
	Lt L M S Essell	29	1	Balloon		DF?
	Lt Le Gallais	29	1	Balloon		DF?
	Lt F P Holliday &	48	4	2-seater	SE Arras	D
	Capt A H W Wall	48	4			
	Lt F P Holliday &	48	5	Albatros DIII	Cagnicourt	D
	Capt A H W Wall	48	5			
	2/Lt W O B Winkler &	48	3			
	2/Lt E S Moore	48	3			
	Lt R B Hay &	48	2			
	????	48	–			
	Lt R N Hall	40	1	2-seater	E Lens	OOC

25 April 1917

Time	Pilot/Crew	Sqdn	Vic No	E/A	Location	How
0815	Lt C R O'Brien &	43	3	Albatros DIII	Oppy	D
	2/Lt J L Dickson	43	2			

26 April 1917

Time	Pilot/Crew	Sqdn	Vic No	E/A	Location	How
1155	2/Lt E Bartlett	41	2	2-seater	Hooge	D
1200	Patrol	41		2-seater		D
1530	FSL A J Chadwick	4N	1	Albatros DIII	S Bruge	OOC
1615	FSL Collins	SDF	1	Seaplane	Zeebrugge	D
1720	Sgt J H R Green &	25	4	Albatros DIII	Drocourt	OOC
	Lt H Freeman-Smith	25	2			
1720	Lt C Dunlop &	2	3	Albatros DIII	Izel-lès-Équerchin	D
	Lt J L B Weir	25	4			
1720	F/C C D Booker	8N	3	Albatros DIII	Drocourt	DF
1720	FSL E D Crundall	8N	3	Albatros DIII	Drocourt	D
1830	Capt K C McCallum	23	2	Albatros DIII	Cambrai	OOC
1830	Capt K C McCallum	23	3	Albatros DIII	Cambrai	OOC
1840	2/Lt R L Keller	23	3	Albatros DIII	Fontaine-Notre Dame	OOC
1840	2/Lt G C Stead	23	1	Albatros DIII	Fontaine-Notre Dame	OOC
1900	Lt D Y Hay &	20	1	Albatros DIII	Moorslede	OOC
	2AM T E Allum	20	3			
1910	Capt F N Hudson	54	5	Albatros DIII	Prémont	OOC
1910	2/Lt R M Charley	54	1	Albatros DIII	Prémont	OOC
1910	Lt S G Rome	54	1	Albatros DIII	Prémont	OOC
1915	Lt H L Stachell &	20	1	Albatros DIII	SW Roulers	D
	2AM M Todd	20	1			
1915	FSL C J Moir	4N	1	Albatros DIII	Dixmuide	OOC
1915	FSL F D Casey	3N	6	Albatros DIII	Cambrai	OOC
1915	FSL J J Malone	3N	7	Albatros DIII	Cambrai	OOC
1920	Lt H E O Ellis	40	3	Albatros DIII	E Salome	D
	FSL R R Thornely	6N	1	Albatros DIII		OOC
	FSL G G Simpson	8N	3	Albatros DIII		OOC
1930	Capt A Ball	56	34	Albatros DIII	Hayencourt	D
1930	Capt A Ball	56	35	Albatros DIII	E Cambrai	DF

27 April 1917

Time	Pilot/Crew	Sqdn	Vic No	E/A	Location	How
0655	Lt W A Bishop	60	12	Balloon	Vitry-en-Artois	DF
1000	Lt H E O Ellis	40	4	Balloon	Salome	D
2000	2/Lt D S Kennedy &	11	1	Albatros DIII	SW Vitry	DF
	Capt J A Le Royer	11	2			

Time	Pilot/Crew	Sqdn	Vic No	E/A	Location	How
2000	2/Lt D S Kennedy &	11	2	Albatros DIII	SW Vitry	D
	Capt J A Le Royer	11	3			
	Lt W T Price &	48	5	2-seater	Vitry	D
	Lt M A Benjamin	48	5			
	Lt R B Hay &	48	3			
	?????	48	–			
	Patrol	6		Albatros DIII		OOC

28 April 1917

Time	Pilot/Crew	Sqdn	Vic No	E/A	Location	How
1225	Lt R A Little	8N	11	2-seater	Oppy	D
1630	Capt A Ball	56	34	Albatros C	Fontaine	D
2000	FSL R Collishaw	10N	5	Albatros DII	Ostende	D

29 April 1917

Time	Pilot/Crew	Sqdn	Vic No	E/A	Location	How
1000	Capt H Meintjes	56	5	Albatros DIII	Hamel-Récourt	OOC
1020	2/Lt A Erlebach &	57	1	Albatros DIII	Noyelles	OOC
	2/Lt C H Trott	57	1			
1030	Capt N G McNaughton &	57	1	Albatros DIII	Noyelles	OOC
	2/Lt H G Downing	57	1			
1030	Lt J H Ryan &	57	1	Albatros DIII	Noyelles	OOC
	2/Lt B Soutten	57	1			
1100	FSL F D Casey	3N	7	Albatros DIII	Bantouzelle	DF
1100	FSL J S T Fall	3N	6	Albatros DIII	Bois de Gard	D
1110	F/C T F N Gerrard	1N	4	Albatros DIII	Épinoy	OOC
1110	FSL R P Minifie	1N	1	Albatros DIII	Épinoy	D
1115	F/Lt L Breadner	3N	6	Albatros DIII	SE Cambrai	OOC
1115	FSL A W Carter	3N	4	Albatros DIII	SE Cambrai	OOC
1115	FSL H S Broad	3N	2	Albatros DIII	SE Cambrai	OOC
1150	FSL C B Ridley &	1N	1	2-seater	Cagnicourt	OOC
	FSL H V Rowley	1N	1			
1155	Lt W A Bishop	60	13	Halberstadt DII	E Épinoy	DF
1315	F/C E W Norton &	6N	7	Albatros DIII	E Honnecourt	OOC
	FSL A H V Fletcher	6N	1			
1400	FSL E D Crundall	8N	4	Albatros DIII	Hénin-Liétard	DF
1500	Capt C M Crowe	56	2	Albatros DII	Waziers	OOC
1500	Lt J O Leach	56	1	Albatros DII	Bugnicourt	OOC
1550	2/Lt G Dinsmore &	18	1	Albatros DIII	Inchy-Proville	DF
	2/Lt G B Bate	18	3			
1700	2/Lt F E Conder &	20	1	Albatros DIII	Courtrai	OOC
	2/Lt H G Neville	20	1			
1705	Capt F H Thayre &	20	2	Albatros DIII	E Menin	DF
	Capt F R Cubbon	20	3			
1710	Capt F H Thayre &	20	3	Albatros DIII	E Zillebeke	DF
	Capt F R Cubbon	20	4			
1725	2/Lt E J Smart &	20	4	Albatros DIII	Courtrai-Ypres	D
	2/Lt T A M S Lewis	20	1			
1740	Capt E D Atkinson	1	4	Albatros C	Pont Rogue	OOC
1800	FSL A P Heywood	1N	1	Albatros DII	E Lens	OOC
1830	2/Lt E S T Cole	1	5	Albatros DII	Ypres-Menin Road	OOC
1850	FSL R R Winter	6N	1	Albatros DIII	Guise	OOC
1855	F/C E W Norton	6N	8	Albatros DIII	Guise	DF
1855	F/C E W Norton	6N	9	Albatros DIII	Guise	OOC
1900	FSL F H M Maynard	1N	1	Albatros DIII	Fresnoy	OOC
1915	FSL R P Minifie &	1N	2	Albatros DIII	Douai	D
	FSL R A Little	8N	12			

Time	Pilot/Crew	Sqdn	Vic No	E/A	Location	How
1930	FSL H V Rowley	1N	2	Albatros DIII	Gavrelle	OOC
	Lt Knight &	6	1	Albatros DIII		OOC
	F/Sgt Cardno	6	1			

30 April 1917

Time	Pilot/Crew	Sqdn	Vic No	E/A	Location	How
0630	Lt G A Hyde	54	2	Albatros DIII	Walincourt	OOC
0645	FSL R J O Compston	8N	2	Albatros C	E Douai	OOC
0700	FSL R J O Compston	8N	3	Albatros C	W Douai	OOC
0700	FSL C D Booker	8N	4	Albatros DIII	W Douai	OOC
0710	FSL R A Little	8N	13	Albatros DIII	E Arras	OOC
0725	FSL R A Little	8N	14	Albatros DIII	E Arras	OOC
0835	F/C R S Dallas	1N	13	Rumpler C	Hayencourt	D
0845	Capt C M Crowe	56	3	Albatros DIII	E Douai	D
0845	Lt M A Kay &	56	1	Albatros DIII	E Douai	OOC
	Lt J O Leach	56	2			
0845	Capt J O Andrews	66	8	2-seater	Brebières-Vitry	D
0855	Capt C J Q Brand	1	6	Albatros C	Houplines	POW
0920	F/C R S Dallas	1N	14	Albatros DIII	Hayencourt	OOC
0930	2/Lt M M Kaizer &	18	1	Albatros DIII	Baralle-Bourlon	D
	Sgt F Russell	18	2			
0930	2/Lt S H Bell &	18	1	Albatros DIII	Marquion	OOC
	Lt D W MacLeod	18	1			
0930	2/Lt I C Barkley &	18	1	Albatros DIII	Baralle	OOC
	2AM L B Adcock	18	1			
0930	2/Lt M M Kaizer &	18	2	Albatros DIII	Baralle-Bourlon	OOC
	Sgt F Russell	18	3			
0930	2/Lt S H Bell &	18	2	Albatros DIII	Marquion-Bourlon	OOC
	Lt D W MacLeod	18	2			
0930	2/Lt G Critchley &	18	1	Albatros DIII	Baralle	OOC
	2/Lt O Partington	18	1			
0945	2/Lt D Marshall &	57	1	Albatros DIII	Buissy	OOC
	Lt J T Anglin	57	1			
0945	Lt C S Morice &	57	1	Albatros DIII	Buissy	OOC
	Lt F Leathley	57	1			
1115	Capt W A Bishop	60	14	Albatros C	E Lens	D
1145	Lt E S T Cole	1	6	Albatros DIII	N Ypres	OOC
1150	FSL A R Knight	8N	1	Albatros DIII	E Lens	OOC
1245	FSL L F W Smith	4N	1	Albatros DIII	E Nieuport	OOC
1640	Capt W J C K Cochran-Patrick	23	7	Albatros DIII	Inchy-en-Artois	DF
1640	2/Lt S C O'Grady	23	1	Albatros DIII	Inchy-en-Artois	OOC
1730	FSL R Collishaw	10N	6	Albatros DIII	E Cortemarck	D
1900	FSL C J Moir	4N	2	Albatros DIII	S Nieuport	OOC
	2/Lt T Middleton &	48	1	Albatros DIII		OOC
	Lt C G Claye	48	1			
	Lt H Game &	48	1			
	2/Lt C Malcomson	48	1	Albatros DIII		OOC

D = Destroyed DF = Destroyed in flames OOC = Out of Control P= Probable Victory POW = Captured

Appendix 2

French Victory Claims

Time	Pilot/Crew	Sqdn	Vic No	E/A	Location	How
			1 April 1917			
	Sgt L Goux	N.67	1	2-seater		D
			5 April 1917			
	S/Lt J Chaput	N.57	9	EA		D
	S/Lt J Chaput	N.57	10	EA		D
			6 April 1917			
1805	Adj C Jeronnez	N.26	2	Balloon	Montchâlons	DF
	S/Lt V Régnier	N.112	5	Balloon	Époye	DF
	Adj G Douchy	N.38	6	Balloon	Hauvine	DF
	Brig P Leroy	N.78	1	Balloon	Ardeuil	DF
	S/Lt P Tarascon	N.62	9	Albatros	Marechalpot	DF
	Lt J Mistarlet	N.31	1	Balloon	Lavannes	D
	Cpl Montagne	N.112	1	EA		
			7 April 1917			
	S/Lt L Bucquet	N.3	1	EA	Forges	DF
	Lt A Lorillard	N.48	–	Balloon		P
			8 April 1917			
1330	Lt A de Laage de Meux	N.124	–	EA	N St Quentin	FTL
1350	Lt A de Laage de Meux	N.124	3	2-seater	N Moy	FTL
1530	Cpl Damanez (P)	R.46	–	EA	Orgeval	P
	Cpl Rivière (G) &	R.46	–			
	MdL C Théron (G)	C.46	–			
1615	Lt Bloch,	R.46	1	EA	Aguilcourt	D
	Sgt L Joussen (G) &	C.46	2			
	Sgt Roye (G)	R.46	1			
	Brig Brunet (P)	R.214	1	EA	N Berry-au-Bac	D
	Sgt R Levy (G) &	R.214	1			
	Sgt Gerard (G)		1			
			9 April 1917			
	S/Lt P Tarascon	N.62	10	LVG C	Pinon	D
			11 April 1917			
	Adj C Jeronnez	N.26	3	EA	Cerny-le-Laonnois	D
	Lt A Pinsard	N.78	6	Albatros D	SE St Souplet	D
			12 April 1917			
	Lt A Pinsard	N.78	7	Albatros D	S Époye	D
	MdL M J M Nogues	N.12	2	EA	Boise de Cheval	D
	Adj L Jailler	N.15	7	Scout	Rethel	FTL

Time	Pilot/Crew	Sqdn	Vic No	E/A	Location	How
13 April 1917						
1730	Adj R Lufbery	N.124	8	EA	NW St Quentin	D
	MdL L Gros (P) &	F.41	1	EA	Mont Sapigneul	D
	S/Lt de Dreux (O)	N.57	1			
	Adj A Bertrand	F.2	2	EA	Guignicourt	D
	Adj N Paulli-Krause (P) &	F.2	1	EA		WIA
	S/Lt H Clave (O)		1			WIA
14 April 1917						
0600	S/Lt H Languedoc	N.12	5	EA	Bois de Noyelle	D
1030	Cpl Benedictus (P)	R.214	1	EA	Mont Sapigneul	D
	Soldat Bassière (G) &		1			
	S/Lt Lullert (O)		1			
1030	Capt G Guynemer	N.3	36	Albatros	Neuville	DF
1100	MdL de Belleville	N.49	1	EA	Elbach	D
1215	Capt D Lecour Grandmaison	C.46	5	EA	S Craonne	D
	Adj M Vitalis (G) &	C.46	7			
	MdL A Rousseau (G)	C.46	5			
1315	S/Lt Mauduit (P)	F.41	1	EA	SW Condé	D
	Lt Tartet (O) &	F.41	1			
	Brig Kissel (G)	F.41	1			
	Adj G Daladier	N.516	1	2-seater	Ste Marie-aux-Mines	D
	MdL P Vieljeux	N.93	1	2-seater	Bonhomme	D
	Adj J Hamel	N.93	1	Balloon	Saulxures	DF
	Adj Grelat (P) &	GB4	3	EA	Brisach	D
	Lt Cavinet (O)	GB4	3			
	Lt A Pinsard	N.78	8	EA	N Somme-Py	D
	Lt E Thiriez	N.15	1	EA	Corbeny	DF
	71st Balloon Co		–	EA		DF
	Capt G Matton	N.48		2-seater		P
15 April 1917						
	Lt A Deullin	N.73	13	EA	Festieux	DF
	S/Lt P de Larminat	N.48	–	EA		P
	Lt A Deullin	N.73	–	EA	Festieux	P
16 April 1917						
0600	S/Lt H Languedoc	N.12	6	EA	E Cauroy	D
1025	Brig R Rigault	N.73	2	EA	Cormicy	DF
1030	Lt Balme (P) &	C.222	1	EA	Hermonville	D
	Lt Liort (O)	F.72	1			
1510	Brig R Rigault	N.73	2	Balloon	Bruxières	DF
1520	Cpl A Cordonnier	N.57	1	Balloon	S Bois de Grands Usages	DF
	Brig E Thomassin	N.26	1	EA	Juvincourt	D
	Sgt G Triboulet	N.57	–	EA		P
19 April 1917						
1451	S/Lt R Dorme	N.3	19	EA	W Orainville	D
	S/Lt Tarascon	N.62	10	LVG C	E Trucy	D
	????			EA	W Moronvilliers	D
	????			EA	SE Fresnes	D

Time	Pilot/Crew	Sqdn	Vic No	E/A	Location	How
	21 April 1917					
	Lt A Pinsard	N.78	9	EA	Nauroy	D
	Lt A Pinsard	N.78	10	EA	Nauroy-Moronvilliers	D
	S/Lt H Languedoc	N.12	7	EA	Somme-Suippes	POW
	Adj de Fourneaux	N.78	1	EA	Somme-Suippes	D
	22 April 1917					
1710	Adj F Bergot	N.73	–	EA	Aumenaucourt	P
1750	Lt A Deullin	N.73	14	EA	W Craonne	D
1835	S/Lt R Dorme	N.3	20	EA	Beaurieux	D
1910	Capt A Auger	N.3	4	EA	Lierval	D
	Sgt P Pendaires	N.69	–	EA		P
	23 April 1917					
1815	S/Lt Juguin	N.84	1	Rumpler C	NW Itancourt	D
	MdL L Morizot (P) &	N.23	1	EA	Bois de Avocourt	D
	Lt J Gouin (O)	N.23	2			
	Sgt Reyzal (P)	F.7	1	EA		D
	Lt Climens (O) &	F.7	1			
	Brig Leclair (G)	F.7	1			
	Adj E Pillon	N.82	3	LVG CV		D
	Capt J Derode	N.102	3	2-seater	Prosnes	D
	????			EA	Épine de Chevigny	D
	24 April 1917					
1640	Cpl R Lejeune &	N.83	1	2-seater	Courson	D
	Capt R de Marancour	GC14	3			
1700	Adj R Baudoin	N.80	2	2-seater	L'Ange Gardien	DF
1720	MdL M Henriot	N.65	1	Scout	Forêt de Pinon	D
1725	Adj R Lufbery	N.124	9	2-seater	E Cérisy	D
1800	S/Lt F Battesti	N.73	2	EA	Ste Croix	D
	Adj G Madon	N.38	8	2-seater	Courson	D
	Adj G Madon	N.38	9	Albatros	Cornilette	D
	Adj E Pillon	N.82	4	Albatros D	Dannemarie	D
	????	M26	–	EA	W Bois de l'Enclume	D
	MdL C Soulier	N.57	–	EA		P
	Sgt G Triboulet			EA		P
	26 April 1917					
0615	Lt A de Turenne,	N.48	2	Albatros C	Ville-aux-Bois	D
	Cpl R Montrion &	N.48	1			
	Cpl J Conan	N.48	1			
1000	S/Lt R Baudoin	N.80	–	Scout	Reservoir-Trucy	P
1740	Sgt R Bajac &	N.48	1	EA	Loivre	D
	Cpl J Roques	N.48	1			
1800	Sgt C Johnson	N.124	1	Albatros C	E St Quentin	D
1830	Lt W Thaw &	N.124	2	Albatros C	Juvincourt	D
	Sgt W Haviland	N.124	1			
	Lt G Luc Pupat	N.79	1	EA	Itancourt-St Quentin	D
	Sgt Gendronneau	R46	2	EA	N Ft Brimont	D
	Asp Breuil &	R46	1			
	Cpl Cadot	R46	1			
	????			EA	Gratreuil	D

Time	Pilot/Crew	Sqdn	Vic No	E/A	Location	How
	27 April 1917					
	Sgt E Breton &	N.501	1	2-seater	N Reservoir d'Ailette	D
	Sgt P Barthes	N.501	1			
	Cpl Sigaud (P)	F71	1			
	S/Lt Guye (O) &	F71	1	EA		D
	Sol Lehemade (G)	F71	1			
	????			EA	Gerardmer	D
	????			EA	S Beine	D
	Sgt J Naegely	N.15	–	Albatros	Coucy-lès-Eppes	FTL
	29 April 1917					
0545	S/Lt R Baudoin	N.80	3	2-seater	Moulins	POW
1343	S/Lt R Dorme	N.3	21	Albatros C	Fleuricourt	D
1745	S/Lt G Lebeau	N.12	4	EA	Orainville	D
	Lt J Beraud-Villars	N.102	2	EA	NE Nauroy	D
	????			EA	Aguilcourt	D
	30 April 1917					
0940	Lt L Jailler	N.15	8	EA	Laon	D
	Lt R Bailly	N.81	1	EA	N Moronvilliers	DF
	Adj H Peronneau	N.81	–	EA		P
	MdL Diesbach	N.15	–	EA	Berry-au-Bac	P

D = Destroyed DF = Destroyed in flames POW = Prisoner of War FTL = Forced to Land

P = Probably destroyed (P) = Pilot (O) = Observer (G) = Gunner (B) = Bombardier

Appendix 3

German Victory Claims

Time	Pilot/Crew	Sqdn	Vic No	E/A	Location
			1 April 1917		
1045	Ltn O Bernert	B	10	Balloon	Villers-au-Flos
1145	Ltn W Voss	B	23	BE2c	E St Leger
	Flakzug 145 & MFlak 14			FE	Pont de Courriers
			2 April 1917		
0830	Ltn O Bernert	B	11	Nieuport	Quéant
0835	Oblt M v Richthofen	11	32	BE2d	Farbus
0930	Ltn K Allmenröder	11	5	BE	Angres
1000	Vfw S Festner	11	3	FE2d	SE Auby
1000	Ltn C Krefft	11	1	FE2d	Oignies
1120	Oblt M v Richthofen	11	33	Sop 1½	Givenchy
	OfStv E Nathanael	5	6	FE2b	NE Gouzeaucourt
		FTL		Nieuport	Poix Terron
			3 April 1917		
1440	Ltn G Nernst	30	2	Nieuport	Ésquerchin
1450	Uffz L Weber	3	1	BE2e	NE Brebières
1615	Oblt M v Richthofen	11	34	FE2d	Cité St Pierre
1620	Ltn K Schäfer	11	9	FE2d	La Coulotte
1635	OfStv E Nathanael	5	7	DH2	N Bourssies
1655	Vfw E Eisenhuth	3	2	FE2b	Hendécourt
1717	Vfw S Festner	11	6	FE	Lens
1719	Ltn A Schulte	12	6	FE	NE St Leger
1720	Vfw S Festner	11	7	FE	Hendécourt
1720	Hptm P v Osterroht	12	2	FE	N Bullecourt
1910	Ltn O Bernert	B	12	Balloon	Ervillers
1922	Ltn O Bernert	B	13	Balloon	N Bapaume
1955	????			Balloon	Athies-Thelus
	Ltn Schumacher &	FA40	1	Nieuport	S St Quentin
	Uffz Scheinig	FA40	1		
	Flakzug 28,47 & 185			FE	S Feuchy
	Lt A Schulte	12	–	DH2	
			4 April 1917		
0840	Ltn H Klein	4	1	BE2e	SE Arras
0905	Ltn H Malchow	4	1	FE	SW Arras

Time	Pilot/Crew	Sqdn	Vic No	E/A	Location

5 April 1917

Time	Pilot/Crew	Sqdn	Vic No	E/A	Location
1100	Vfw S Festner	11	4	BF2a	Meincourt
1105	Ltn F Röth	12	2	FE2b	Gouzeaucourt
1105	Ltn A Schulte	12	–	FE2b	Lepave
1108	Oblt M v Richthofen	11	35	BF2a	Lewarde
1110	Ltn O Splitgerber	12	2	FE2b	Honnecourt
1120	Ltn G Simon	11	1	BF2a	N Monchecourt
1128	Oblt M v Richthofen	11	36	BF2a	Quincy
1200	Ltn G Schlenker	3	6	FE2b	SW Moeuvres
1205	Ltn G Nernst	30	3	Sopwith 2	W Rouvroy
1300	Vfw S Festner	11	5	Nieuport	SW Bailleul
1806	Ltn H Auer	26	1	Nieuport/Spad	Sennheim
2230	Ground fire			FE	Bailleul
	Vfw K Menckhoff	3	2	Nieuport	W Athies
	Ltn E Wiessner	18	1	FE2d	S Ypern
	Ltn E Voss	20	1	Nieuport	Omissy
	Ltn A Dossenbach	36	10	Caudron	Sillery
	Ltn Wolluhn &	FAA210	1	EA	Ribécourt
	Uffz Mackeprang	FAA210	1		
	Flakzug 407 &				
	Beh Flakbatt 4.64			Sopwith	Origny
	Forced to land			Martinsyde	La Bouteille

6 April 1917

Time	Pilot/Crew	Sqdn	Vic No	E/A	Location
0815	Ltn J v Bertrab	30	1	Martinsyde	Ath
0815	Ltn H Gontermann	5	6	FE2d	Neuville
0820	OfStv E Nathanael	5	8	FE2d	Douchy
0825	Ltn O Splitgerber	12	3	FE2d	Thiaut
0830	Hptm P v Osterroht	12	5	FE2d	Lagnicourt
0830	Oblt A v Tutschek	B	9	FE2d	Anneux
0830	Ltn J v Bertrab	30	2	Martinsyde	SE Leuze
0830	Ltn A Schulte	12	–	FE2b	Anneux
0850	Ltn W Frankl	4	16	FE2b	Fauchy
0850	Ltn W Frankl	4	17	FE2b	Arras
0945	Ltn W Voss	B	24	BE2e	S Lagnicourt
1000	Ltn W Frankl	4	18	BE2e	NE Boiry
1010	MFlak 60			Nieuport	Neuvireuil
1015	Ltn O Bernert	B	17	RE8	Roeux
1015	Vfw K Menckhoff	3	1	RE8	Fampoux
1015	Ltn K Wolff	11	6	RE8	Bois Bernard
1018	?????			EA	Loosbogen
1020	Ltn K Schäfer	11	10	BE2d	Givenchy
1037	Ltn K Schäfer	11	11	BE2c	SW Vimy

Time	Pilot/Crew	Sqdn	Vic No	E/A	Location
1048	Ltn J v Bertrab	30	3	Sopwith 2	N Becq
1048	Oblt H Bethge	30	5	Sopwith 2	NE Templeuve
1050	Ltn J v Bertrab	30	4	Sopwith 2	NE Pecq
1215	Hptm P v Osterroht	12	3	Triplane N	Hénin-Liétard
1810	Ltn H Baldamus	9	16	Spad	NW Fresnes
1930	Ltn J Jacobs	22	2	Balloon	Blanzy-Vailly
	Ltn W Frankl	4	19	FE2b	Quiery-la-Motte
	OfStv W Göttsch	8	7	FE2d	NE Polygonwald
	Ltn Kreuzner	13	1	Caudron	S Vailly
	Oblt R Berthold	14	10	Caudron	Malval-Ferme
	Vfw G Strasser	17	1	Caudron	N Pontavert
	Ltn W Böning	19	1	Caudron	S Berry-au-Bac
	Ltn D Collin	22	–	Farman	Terny-Sorny
	Ltn E Kreuzer	36	2	Caudron	Berry-au-Bac
	Ltn H Bongartz	36	1	Spad	Vitry-les-Reims
	Ltn Zywitz &	FA228	1	Nieuport	Berry-au-Bac
	Ltn Lexow	FA228	1		
	Ltn Hansen &	FA212	1	Caudron	Berneuil
	Vfw Gonella	FA212	1		
	KFlak 35			EA	Fayet-Gricourt
	KFlak 82			FE	Richtung-Holnon
	Flakbatt 505			FE	Lagnicourt
	Flak 709, Flak 507 or a				
	pilot			FE	Anneux
	Forced to land			Triplane	Mons
	Forced to land			Sopwith 2	N Laon
	MG fire from ground			FE	Quiery-le-Motte
	????			Caudron	Souain

7 April 1917

Time	Pilot/Crew	Sqdn	Vic No	E/A	Location
1645	Ltn H Klein	4	2	Balloon	W Arras
1710	Vfw L Patermann	4	1	Nieuport	NW Biache
1710	Ltn O Bernert	B	14	Nieuport	S Roeux
1745	Oblt M v Richthofen	11	37	Nieuport	NE Mercatel
1745	Ltn K Wolff	11	7	Nieuport	NE Mercatel
1745	Ltn K Schäfer	11	12	Nieuport	NE Mercatel
1750	Vfw S Festner	11	6	Nieuport	Mont St Eloi
1815	Ltn W v Bülow-Bothkamp	18	10	FE2d	S Ploegsteertwald
1815	OfStv M Müller	28	6	FE2d	Ploegsteertwald
1910	Ltn W Frankl	4	18	Nieuport	SE Fampoux
	Hptm H v Hünerbein	8	1	Nieuport	Becelaere
	MFlak 60			Nieuport	Fresnes

8 April 1917

Time	Pilot/Crew	Sqdn	Vic No	E/A	Location
0440	Ltn H Klein	4	3	FE2b	SE Douai
0930	Vfw S Festner	11	7	Nieuport 23	E Vimy
1140	Rittm M v Richthofen	11	38	Sopwith 2	Farbus
1330	Ltn W Frankl	4	20	EA	Arras
1430	Ltn K Wolff	11	8	DH4	NE Blécourt

Time	Pilot/Crew	Sqdn	Vic No	E/A	Location
1440	Ltn K Schäfer	11		DH4	Épinoy
1510	Ltn O Bernert	B	18	BF2a	SE Éterpigny
1510	Ltn O Bernert	B	l9	RE8	N Bailleul
1640	Rittm M v Richthofen	11	39	BE2g	W Vimy
1900	KFlak 12, Flakzug 38, Flakzug 46, Flakzug 72, & MFlak 70			FE2b	N La Bassée
1910	Ltn G Schlenker	3	7	Nieuport 23	NE Croiselles
	Ltn H Gontermann	5	8	Balloon	W St Quentin
	OfStv W Göttsch	8	8	BE2d	E Dixmuide
	Ltn W v Bülow-Bothkamp	18	11	Nieuport	E Ypres
	Oblt E Hahn	19	2	Caudron	N Loivre
	Ltn Weinschenk &	FA23	1	Caudron	Effigny
	Ltn Camphausen	FA225	1		
	Vfw Finkendel &	FA225	n	Nieuport	SW St Quentin
	Ltn Weber				
	Flakzug 17			Grosskampf	Amigny
	KFlak 43			Nieuport	E Arras

9 April 1917

Time	Pilot/Crew	Sqdn	Vic No	E/A	Location
1900	Ltn K Schäfer	11	14	BE2d	Aix Noulette

10 April 1917

Time	Pilot/Crew	Sqdn	Vic No	E/A	Location
	Forced to land			Nieuport	Aleucourt

11 April 1917

Time	Pilot/Crew	Sqdn	Vic No	E/A	Location
0845	Ltn G Röth	12	1	BE2c	NE Abancourt
0855	Ltn A Schulte	12	7	BE2d	Tilloy
0900	Ltn H Frommherz	B	1	Spad	Cuvillers
0900	Vfw S Festner	11	8	BE	N Monchy
0905	Ltn A Schulte	12	8	Pup	W Neuvireuil
0910	Ltn K Schäfer	11	15	BF2a	SW Fresnes
0910	Ltn K Wolff	11	9	BF2a	N Fresnes
0915	Ltn L v Richthofen	11	2	BF2a	N Fresnes
0925	Rittm M v Richthofen	11	40	BE2d	Willerval
1020	Ltn H Klein	4	4	BE	Biache
1100	Ltn H Klein	4	5	BE	Feuchy
1145	Oblt R Berthold	14	11	Spad	S Corbeny
1145	OfStv Hüttner	14	2	Spad	Berry-au-Bac
1230	Ltn O Bernert	B	15	Spad	Arras
1235	Ltn L v Richthofen	11	3	BE2e	NE Fampoux
1240	Ltn O Bernert	B	16	Morane	NW Lagnicourt
1250	Ltn K Schäfer	11	16	BE2c	E Arras
	Ltn G Salzwedel	24	1	Nieuport	Xures
	Ltn A Dossenbach	36	"	Farman	Berry-au-Bac

Time	Pilot/Crew	Sqdn	Vic No	E/A	Location

12 April 1917

Time	Pilot/Crew	Sqdn	Vic No	E/A	Location
1035	Hptm P v Osterroht	12	4	Pup	NW Bourlon
1035	Vfw A Schorisch	12	2	FE2b	SE Éterpigny
1040	Ltn A Schulte	12	9	FE2b	N Baralle
1100	Uffz E Horn	21		Sopwith 2	S Nauroy
1900	Ltn H Baldamus	9	17	Spad	N Pont Faverger
	Ltn K Schneider	5	2	BE2c	Herbécourt
	Oblt E Hahn	I9	3	Caudron	Orainville
	Flakzug 54			Caudron R4	Le Beau Château
	Forced to land			Spad	Attigny
	Forced to land			Nieuport	Leffincourt

13 April 1917

Time	Pilot/Crew	Sqdn	Vic No	E/A	Location
0854	Vfw S Festner	11	9	RE8	N Dury
0855	Ltn L v Richthofen	11	4	RE8	NE Biache
0856	Ltn H Klein	4	6	RE8	SW Biache
0856	Ltn K Wolff	11	10	RE8	N Vitry
0856	Rittm M v Richthofen	11	41	RE8	E Vitry
0900	Ltn K Schneider	5	3	FE2d	S Gavrelle
0905	Ltn H Gontermann	5	3	FE2d	S Gavrelle
1235	Ltn K Wolff	11	11	FE2b	S Bailleul
1245	Rittm M v Richthofen	11	42	FE2b	W Monchy
1400	Ltn A Dossenbach	36	12	Spad	Sapigneul
1520	Flak			EA	Quiery-la-Motte
1630	Ltn K Wolff	11	12	Nieuport	S Monchy
1700	Ltn H Bongartz	36	2	Caudron	Cormicy
1830	Ltn K Schäfer	11	17	FE2b	SW Monchy
1830	Ltn E Dostler	34	–	Balloon	Gernicourt
1852	Ltn K Wolff	11	13	Martinsyde	Rouvroy
1910	Ltn H Klein	4	7	FE2d	Vimy
1915	Ltn E Bauer	3	1	FE2b	La Bassée
1930	Vfw S Festner	11	10	FE2b	E Harnes
1935	Rittm M v Richthofen	11	43	FE2b	Noyelle-Godault
1935	Ltn J Jacobs	22	4	Farman	Barisis
1935	OfStv E Nathanael	5	9	Balloon	W St Quentin
1940	Ltn H Gontermann	5	9	Balloon	S St Quentin
	Ltn L v Richthofen	11	5	RE8	Pelves
	Uffz S Ruckser	37	1	Balloon	SW Oppy
	Ltn Stobe	3	1	BE2g	Gavrelle
	Ltn K Schneider	5	4	FE2d	W St Quentin
	Ltn G Bassenge	5	–	Gitterrumpf	Willerval
	KFlak 12			BE	Brebières
	Flakzug 155			FE	
	KFlakbatt: 101, KFlak 12,			Bristol	Courcelles
	Flakzug 31, Flakzug 75,				
	Flakzug 145 & Flakzug 188				

Time	Pilot/Crew	Sqdn	Vic No	E/A	Location

14 April 1917

Time	Pilot/Crew	Sqdn	Vic No	E/A	Location
0500	MG Ground fire			BE2f	Salome
0810	Ltn H v Schöll	30	1	Sopwith 2	Douai
0915	Rittm M v Richthofen	11	44	Nieuport	S Bois Bernard
0920	Ltn K Wolff	11	14	Nieuport	SE Drocourt
0920	Ltn L v Richthofen	11	6	Nieuport	W Fouquières
0923	Vfw S Festner	11	11	Nieuport	Gavrelle
0930	Ltn H Frommherz	B	2	BE2f	Ribécourt
0934	Vfw K Menckhoff	3	–	EA	Écoust St Mein
0934	Oblt K v Döring	4	1	Nieuport	SE Fresnoy
1140	Ltn F Pütter	9	1	Balloon	E Suippes
1140	Ltn H Baldamus	9	18	Nieuport	St Marie-à-Py
1200	Uffz H Kramer	14	1	Caudron	Juvigny
1200	Oblt R Berthold	14	12	Spad	Bois de Marais
1200	Ltn J Veltjens	14	1	Spad	Craonne
1705	Ltn K Schäfer	11	18	FE2b	SW Lievin
1720	Ltn K Schäfer	11	19	BE	La Coulotte
1823	Ltn L v Richthofen	11	7	Spad	SE Vimy
1829	Ltn K Wolff	11	15	Spad	Bailleul
	Ltn H Adam	24	2	Balloon	W St Mihiel
	Ltn H Gontermann	5	11	BE2e	Metz-en-Couture
	Vfw O Gerbig	14	2	Caudron	Craonelle
	Oblt E Dostler	34	5	Nieuport	SW St Mihiel
	Vfw G Schindler	35	1	Sopwith 2	Schlettstadt
	Vfw R Rath	35	1	Sopwith 2	Scherweiler
	Flakbatt 511			Nieuport	Crenay-les-Reims
	Flakzug 79			Nieuport	Rotbach-Rainhof
	Flakzug 21			Spad	Lauchensee
	Flakzug 50			EA	Monchy
	Flakbatt 507, 509 &				
	Flakzug 30			EA	Sains-les-Marquion
	Flakzug 79, 171 & 413			Spad	SE Moyenmoutier

15 April 1917

Time	Pilot/Crew	Sqdn	Vic No	E/A	Location
1030	Uffz M Zachmann	21	1	Spad	Sery
	Vfw J Buckler	17	4	Spad	Prouvais
	Ltn Dotzel	19	1	Nieuport	La Neuvillette
	Ltn W Albert	31	3	Spad	Nauroy
	Ltn A Dossenbach	36	13	Nieuport	Bétheny
	Ltn A Dossenbach	36	14	Spad	St Ferguex
	Vfw H Mitkeit	36	2	Spad	Thugny
	Uffz Rath	SchSt10	1	Farman	Oulcher Wald
	Gefr Musch		1		
	Forced to land			Nieuport	Barricourt
	Cause unknown			Nieuport	Prosnes
	Cause unknown			Spad	Nauroy
	Ltn R Matthaei	21	–	Spad	Nauroy-Moronvilliers

Time	Pilot/Crew	Sqdn	Vic No	E/A	Location
			16 April 1917		
1030	Ltn L v Richthofen	11	8	Nieuport	E Roeux
1030	Ltn K Wolff	11	16	Nieuport	NE Roeux
1030	Vfw S Festner	11	12	Nieuport	NE Biache
1030	Ltn R Oertelt	19	FTL	Caudron	Laneuville
1040	Ltn Glinkermann	15	FTL	Farman	Juvincourt
1130	Vfw G Strasser	17	3	Caudron	S Cormicy
1505	Ltn E Thuy	21	2	Caudron	N Berry-au-Bac
1650	Ltn H Gontermann	5	10	Balloon	Manancourt
1700	Ltn H Gontermann	5	11	Balloon	Manancourt
1730	Rittm M v Richthofen	11	45	BE2e	NW Gavrelle
	Ltn H Wendel	15	1	Nieuport	Prouvais
	Vfw J Buckler	17	5	Nieuport	Berry-au-Bac
	Ltn J Jacobs	22	5	Balloon	Laffaux
	Gefr May &	SchSt 3	1	Spad	Corbeny
	Uffz Wiehle	SchSt 3	1		
	Vfw Jehle &	FA295	FTL		
	Ltn Calliebe	FA295	FTL	Farman	Juvincourt
	Uffz Janning &	SchSt 5	FTL		
	Gefr Reimers	5		Nieuport	NW Reims
	Ltn Rose &	FA22	1		
	Ltn Parlow	FA22	1	Caudron	E Cernay
	Ltn Figulla &	SchSt 4	1		
	Uffz Steudel	SchSt 4	1	Sopwith	Douai
	KFlak 63			BE	NW St Quentin
	KFlak 93			BE	SW St Quentin
	KFlak 47			Nieuport	Craonne
			18 April 1917		
0800	Ltn H Joens	31	1	Voisin	Auberive
	MFlak 54			Spad VII	Donnrein
			19 April 1917		
1000	Ltn W Marwitz	9	1	Spad	SW Auberive
1145	Ltn A Frey	9	2	Farman	S Moronvilliers
	Ltn R Wenzl	31	1	Spad	S Moronvilliers
	Ltn W Daugs	36	1	Morane	Prosnes
			20 April 1917		
0745	Ltn Peters &	FA235	1	Vickers	Vimy
	Vfw Schopf	FA235	1		
0940	Vfw A Schorisch	12	3	BE2e	Écoust St Mein
	Ltn Schurz	13	1	Farman	Landricourt
	Flakzug 31, 188,			BE2f	Fresnes-Oppy
	KFlak 105 & Flakbatt 503				
	Flakzug 46			Sopwith	NE Beaucamp
	KFlak 1,8,96 & 112			Bristol	E Urvillers
			21 April 1917		
1728	Ltn L v Richthofen	11	9	BE2g	SE Vimy

Time	Pilot/Crew	Sqdn	Vic No	E/A	Location
1730	Ltn K Wolff	11	17	BE2g	N Willerval
1745	Ltn K Wolff	11	18	Nieuport	E Fresnes
1745	Ltn K Schäfer	11	20	Nieuport	Fresnes
	KFlak 105			BE2g	N Vimy
	Flakzug 103			BE	E Ypern

22 April 1917

Time	Pilot/Crew	Sqdn	Vic No	E/A	Location
0630	Uffz F Gille	12	–	BE	Croiselles
0810	Ltn A Hanko	28	1	Nieuport	Wavrin
0935	Ltn H Gontermann	5	23	Balloon	Arras
1130	Ltn K Schneider	5	6	Balloon	Épehy
1145	Ltn K Schneider	5	7	Balloon	Essigny-le-Grand
1430	OfStv E Nathanael	5	10	Balloon	Bus
1710	Ltn K Wolff	11	19	FE2b	Hendécourt
1710	Rittm M v Richthofen	11	46	FE2b	Lagnicourt
2005	OfStv E Nathanael	5	11	Spad	Ribécourt
2005	Ltn K Wolff		20	Morane	Havrincourt
2005	Hptm P v Osterroht	12	6	Spad	S Marcoing
2005	Ltn F Röth	12	2	EA	Marcoing
2010	Vfw R Jörke	12	2	Spad	W Havrincourt
2020	Ltn K Schäfer	11	21	BE2e	W Monchy
	Ltn Gerlt	19	1	Caudron	St Etienne

23 April 1917

Time	Pilot/Crew	Sqdn	Vic No	E/A	Location
0815	Ltn K Schneider	5	8	FE2b	Bellenglise
0830	Uffz F Gille	12	–	Sopwith	Javrincourt
0920	Ltn Pedell &	FA 233	1	EA	Gavrelle
	Vfw Brockmann	FA 233	1		
1200	Vfw A Schorisch	12	4	Sopwith	Wancourt
1200	Hptm P v Osterroht	12	7	Sopwith	Fontaine
1205	Rittm M v Richthofen	11	47	BE2f	Méricourt
1205	Ltn K Schock	12	1	Sopwith	Dainville
1205	Vfw Grigo	12	2	Sopwith	Neuville
1210	Ltn L v Richthofen	11	10	BE2g	N Vimy
1400	Ltn W Schunke	20	1	Morane	SW St Quentin
1700	Vfw Frantz	33	1	Sopwith 2	Boisleux
1715	Vfw L v Raffay	34	1	Balloon	Belrupt
1720	Ltn H Göring	26	4	FE2b	NE Arras
1800	OfStv R Weckbrodt	26	2	DH4	SW Itancourt
1925	Ltn H Gontermann	5	13	RE8	SE Arras
2000	Vfw Grigo	12	4	DH4	St Martin
	Ltn K Schneider	5	9	FE2b	Bellenglise
	Ltn K Schneider	5	10	DH2	Bellenglise
	Ltn Rohr	22	2	Farman	Leuilly

Time	Pilot/Crew	Sqdn	Vic No	E/A	Location
			24 April 1917		
0805	Oblt H Lorenz	33	2	Pup	Bourlon
0830	Ltn O Bernert	B	20	Sopwith 2	S Vaucelles
0840	Ltn O Bernert	B	21	BE2e	N Joncourt
0842	Ltn O Bernert	B	22	BE2e	N Levergies
0845	Ltn O Bernert	B	23	BE2e	S Bellicourt
0850	Ltn O Bernert	B	24	DH4	W Bony
0850	Ltn C Krefft	11	–	EA	Arras
0850	Uffz Stegmann &	SchSt 27	1	Sopwith	Lens
	Vfw Menzel	SchSt 27	1		
0900	Ltn H Gontermann	5	14	Triplane	Bailleul
1012	OfStv P Felsmann	FA 24	2	Spad	E Prunay
1030	Ltn Reigel &	FAA 211	1	Sopwith	Lens
	Vfw Tötsch	FAA 211	1		
1605	Vfw A Haussmann	23	2	Nieuport	Beaurieux
1930	Ltn E Udet	15	5	Nieuport	Chavignon
	OfStv W Göttsch	8	9	FE2d	E Ypern
	Ltn W Junck	8	1	FE2d	Ypern
	Ltn W Kypke	14	–	Spad	Berry-au-Bac
	Ltn W v Bülow-Bothkamp	18	11	FE2d	Ypern
	Oblt E Dostler	34	6	Caudron	Ablonville
	Vflgmt Wirtz	MFJI	2	FE2d	Polygon Wald
	KFlak 94 or pilot			BE	S Krylon Ferme
	Flakbatt 701			BE	Wancourt
	Flakbatt 512			FE	E Ypern
	Flakzug 120			BE	Seidelli
	Cause unknown			FE	NW Menin
			25 April 1917		
1030	Ltn K Allmenröder	11	7	BE2e	Guémappe
1040	Ltn K Schäfer	11	22	FE2b	N Bailleul
2030	Ltn K Schäfer	11	23	BF2a	Roeux Station
	KFlak 63			BE	Richtung-Omissy
	Forced to land			BE	S Valenciennes
			26 April 1917		
0920	Vfw J Buckler	17	7	Balloon	Bois de Genicourt
1150	Ltn H Gontermann	5	15	Balloon	Arras
1600	Ltn Schneider	5	15	Balloon	Seraucourt
1635	Ltn K Wolff	11	21	BE2g	E Gavrelle
1818	Ltn P Erbguth	30	1	BE2e	SE Haisnes
1840	Ltn L v Richthofen	11	11	BE2g	SE Vimy Ridge
1845	Ltn K Allmenröder	11	8	BE2g	Vimy Ridge
2000	OfStv A Sturm	5	1	FE2b	Brandcourt
2005	Ltn R Nebel	5	1	FE2b	Joncourt
	Oblt E Hahn	19	4	Spad	N Brimont
	Ltn W Albert	31	4	Spad	Nauroy
	KFlak 2			Nieuport	Houthem
	Flakzug 87, 102, 180 &			Caudron G4	S Ft Brimont
	KFlak 53				
	Cause unknown			EA	Cambrai

Time	Pilot/Crew	Sqdn	Vic No	E/A	Location
27 April 1917					
0900	KFlak 93			Caudron	Essigny-le-Grand
2015	Ltn L v Richthofen	11	12	FE2b	Fresnes
2020	Ltn K Wolff	11	22	FE2b	S Gavrell
2025	Ltn K Allmenröder	11	9	BE2	W Fampoux
	Ltn A Dossenbach	36	–	Balloon	
	Ltn H Bongartz	36	3	Balloon	Berry-au-Bac
	Ltn H Bongartz	36	4	Balloon	SE Thillois
	KFlak 12			BE	S Bois Bernard
	Flakzug 145			BE	E Loos
28 April 1917					
0830	Ltn J Wolff	17	2	Caudron	Brimont
0930	Rittm M v Richthofen	11	48	BE2e	SE Pelves
1120	Ltn K Wolff	11	23	BE2g	Oppy
1315	OfStv E Nathanael	5	12	Pup	La Vacquerie
1710	Flakbatt 709			FE2b	Villers Plouich
1745	Ltn K Wolff	11	24	BE2f	W Gavrelle
1815	Ltn J Schmidt	3	2	Balloon	S Marœuil
1830	Ltn H Göring	26	5	Sopwith two-seater	St Quentin
1830	Vfw Langer	26	–	EA	S St Quentin
	KFlak 41			Sopwith	Reims
	Beh Flakzug der Etlnsp	6		Sopwith	S Tournai
29 April 1917					
1055	Uffz F Gille	12	1	FE2d	Baralle
1130	Ltn K Schneider	5	11	Pup	Elincourt
1150	Gefr Reichardt &	FA 7	1	Caudron	Marcoing
	Ltn Zupan	FA 7	1		
1205	Rittm M v Richthofen	11	49	Spad	E Lecluse
1210	Ltn K Wolff	11	25	Spad	Sailly
1215	Ltn L v Richthofen	11	13	Spad	Izel
1415	Ltn H Geigl	34		Caudron	S Pont-à-Mousson
1655	Rittm M v Richthofen	11	50	FE2b	SW Inchy
1700	Ltn K Wolff	11	26	FE2b	S Pronville
1900	Ltn G Nolte	18	1	FE2d	Hooge
1925	Rittm M v Richthofen	11	51	BE2e	S Roeux
1925	Ltn L v Richthofen	11	14	BE2e	NE Monchy
1930	Oblt B Loerzer	26	–	EA	Bellenglise
1940	Rittm v Richthofen	11	52	Triplane	N Hénin-Liétard
1945	Ltn Kempf	B	1	BE2c	SW La Pave
1945	Ltn H Göring	26	6	Nieuport 17	Rémicourt
2045	Ltn H Stutz	20	–	FE2b	Douai

Time	Pilot/Crew	Sqdn	Vic No	E/A	Location
2100	OfStv E Nathanael	5	13	Pup	Beaumont
	Ltn P Strahle	18	4	FE2d	N Courtrai
	Ltn E Wiessner	18		FE2d	Courtrai
	Ltn W Böning	19	3	Caudron R11	Brimont
	Ltn R Ernert	34	1	Balloon	Génicourt
	Vfw T Himmer	34	1	Farman	Génicourt
	Flakzug 28,40 &			Nieuport	N Hendécourt
	KFlak 61 and 68				
	MFlak 63			Nieuport	S Dury
	MFlak 63			Nieuport	S Dury
	Flakbatt 530			Nieuport	E Lunéville
	Forced to land			Vickers	N Courtrai
	Forced to land			Voisin	N Pauvres

30 April 1917

Time	Pilot/Crew	Sqdn	Vic No	E/A	Location
0700	OfStv M Müller	28	7	Sopwith 2	E Armentières
0715	Ltn L v Richthofen	11	15	BE2g	SE Vimy
0755	Ltn L v Richthofen	11	16	FE2d	Izel
0755	Oblt A v Tutschek	12	4	FE2d	Izel
0820	Uffz F Gille	12		EA	Récourt
0845	Ltn H Geiseler	33	–	FE2d	Oppy
0925	Ltn v Hartmann	9	1	Spad	SW Nauroy
1005	OfStv E Nathanael	5	14	SE5	E Fresnoy
1010	Vfw Brokmann &	FAA223	2	BE	Fresnoy
	Ltn Pedell	FAA233	2		
1030	Ltn H Pfeiffer	9	10	Spad	Moronvilliers
1100	Ltn v Breiten-Landenberg	9	I	Nieuport	St Hilaire-le-Petit
1115	Ltn A Frey	9	3	Spad	Moronvilliers
1200	Ltn H Klein	4	8	BE2e	Ribécourt
1200	Vfw W Wagener	21	4	Sopwith 2	Prosnes
1320	Vfw A Franz	33	–	EA	Monchy
1320	Vfw Voigt &	SchSt 19	1	Spad	Sallaumines
	Vfw Woldt	SchSt 19	1		
1440	Ltn R Matthaei	21	3	Balloon	Montbré
1735	Ltn K Wolff	11	29	BE2e	W Fresnes
1810	Ltn P Billik	12		Pup	Romaucourt
1850	Vfw K Menckhoff	3	3	Nieuport	Cantin
	Ltn W Böning	19	2	Balloon	Guyencourt
	Oblt E Hahn	19	5	Balloon	Guyencourt
	Oblt E Hahn	19	6	Balloon	Guyencourt
	Vfw A Rahn	19	1	Balloon	Reims
	Vfw A Rahn	19	2	Balloon	Reims
	Ltn K Deilmann	6	–	Sopwith	Roupy
	Ltz S T Osterkamp	MFJI	FTL	Nieuport	Oostkerke
	KFlak 93			BE	N Fayette
	KFlak 61 & Flakzug 28			BE	E Chérisy
	Flakzug 165			Farman	Rapes

Appendix 4

Known German Casualties

NB. Although compiled from official sources this list of casualties cannot be taken as complete, but is given as an aid to the overall picture. Although we have tried to list the known operational casualties, there may well be a few non-operational losses included.

1 April 1917

Ltn Alfred Mohr	J3	Alb DIII 2012/16, KIA 1150 nr Arras, 6 Armee
Ltn Werner (O)	FAA288b	Severely WIA, 6 Armee

2 April 1917

Ltn Erich König	J2	KIA over Wancourt
Ltn Hans Wortmann	J2	KIA over Vitry-en-Artois
Vfw Rudolf Nebel	J35	Alb DIII 2107/16 – POW, (Escaped 5 May)
Ltn Karl Haan	FA19	KIA over Langmarck, 4 Armee
Ltn Hahn ??		WIA
OffStv Fritz Meixner	FA48	POW, Bapaume
Oblt Friedrich Puckert	"	POW

3-4 April 1917

Nil

5 April 1917

Ltn Josef Flink	J18	WIA/POW; FTL Nr Neuve Eglise in Alb DIII 1942/16
Ltn Karl Hummel		Killed, Ghent
Gfr Simon Metzger		Killed, Mont d'Origny
Uffz Albin Nietzold		Killed, St Marie

6 April 1917

Uffz Ludwig Weber	J3	Alb DII 510/16, WIA nr Biache
Vfw Paul Hoppe	J5	Collided with Berr, N Noyelles; Killed
Oblt Hans Berr	J5	Killed – see above
Ltn Otto Splitgerber	J12	WIA over Thialt, 0825
Flg Josef Eichholz		Killed, Fampoux
Vfw Reinhold Wurzmann	J20	KIA, down in flames N Noyelles

Vfw Siegfried Thiele (P)	FAA233	KIA, 6 Armee
Ltn Karl Seyberth (O)	"	KIA, Lecluse
Ltn Walter Dieckmann	FAA243	KIA, Colmar
Ltn Hans Müller	"	KIA, Colmar
Uffz Rudolf Temler	FAA263	KIA, Quéant
Ltn Julius Schmitt	"	KIA, Quéant
Vfw H C F Donhauser	FA221	F/L – shot up
W Walter	"	"

7 April 1917

Gfr Schoop (P)	S7	MIA
Ltn Hupe (O)	FAA233	MIA, 6 Armee
Vfw Ludwig Müller	FA46	KIA, St Mihiel

8 April 1917

Ltn Wilhelm Frankl	J4	KIA, Alb DIII 2158/16.1415, N Vitry-en-Artois, 6 Armee
Ltn Roland Nauck	J6	KIA Villeveque, St Quentin, Alb DIII 2234/16 in Br lines
Flg Helmut Naudszus		Killed, St Quentin
Vfw Josef Schreiner		Killed, Amifontaine-Prouvais
Uffz Ferdinand Hinkemeyer		Killed, Cheret

9 April 1917

Ltn Schröder (O)	FA202	WIA, 6 Armee
Uffz Eugen Reuter (P)		KIA, Vitry
Ltn Rudolf Müller (P)	FAA276	Killed, Manningen by Metz
Ltn Max Trautmann (O)		Killed
OffStv Franz Hermann		Killed, Le Thone
Gfr Oskar Weller		Killed, Cheppy

10 April 1917

Flg Adam Diewald		Killed, Ghent
Gfr Karl Steecher		Killed, Montmédy

11 April 1917

Vfw Karl Möwe	J29	KIA, Junéville Ardennes, between Auberive & St Souplet
Ltn Heinrich Karbe	J22	Slightly wounded

12 April 1917

Ltn Adolf Schulte	J12	KIA in Alb DIII 1996/16 N Barelle, Rumaucourt
Gfr Richard Streubel		Killed, Asfeld la Ville

Flg Max Vogl	FA46	Killed, Jarny
Flg Paul Weiss		Killed, Cohartville
Ltn Ernst Beltzig (O)	FAA272	KIA, Alincourt
Gfr Arno Rebentisch (P)	"	KIA, Alincourt

13 April 1917

Uffz Binder	SS24	Severely WIA; 6 Armee
Uffz Simon Ruckser	J37	Severely WIA

14 April 1917

Ltn Helmut Baldamus	J9	KIA over St Marie-à-Py
Vfw Paul Ruger (P)	KG4	KIA, Clermont les Ferme
Ltn Kurt Matthias (O)	KG4	KIA, Clermont les Ferme
Flg Johann Ploes		Killed, Manonvilliers
Ltn Heinrich Schönberg		Killed, Aisne-Champagne
Oblt Erich Schwidder (O)	FAA251	Killed, Pauvres (Wibeah Ferme)
Ltn August Schlorf (P)	"	Killed, Pauvres
Ltn Otto Weigel	J14	KIA, Craonelle
Ltn Fritz Grunzweig	J16	KIA after KB attack nr Ellbach, Obertraubach
Ltn Gerhard Anders	J35	WIA
Ltn Margraf	J35	WIA
Oblt Herbert Theurich	J35	KIA Alb DIII 2097/16 over Neubreisach
Uffz Hermann Jopp	J37	KIA by flak in KB attack nr Mont Toulin
Uffz Erich Hartmann (P)	FAA243	KIA, Elsass
Ltn Otto Druck (O)	"	KIA
Ltn Friedrich Bierling (O)	FAA253	KIA, W of Anizy le Château
Ltn Theodor Aichele (O)	FA14	Killed, Rusach, Alsace
Vfw L Demmel	SS2b	Killed, Neubriesach
Uffz Simon Stebel	SS2b	Killed, Neubriesach
Ltn Paul Otto	FAA224	WIA

15 April 1917

Ltn Paul Dörr (O)	FA45b	WIA by ground fire at Bouchain. DOW 17th. 6 Armee
Unnamed officer	FAA242	WIA

16 April 1917

Ltn Hans-Olaf Esser	J15	KIA, Laon
Vfw Rieger	J17	MIA

Uffz Hans Precht		Killed, Aisne-Champagne
Ltn Hugo Sommer		Killed, Chivy
Ltn Hans Strathmeyer		Killed, Chivy
Uffz Walter Köppen (P)	FAA248	KIA, Villers Franqueux
Ltn Heinrich Wecke (O)	FAA248	KIA, Villers Franqueux
Ltn Walter Utermann (O)	FAA228	Killed, Juvincourt nr Verdun
Ltn Hans-Jorgen Kalmus (O) FA208		Killed, Liesse

17 April 1917

Flg Johann Schönhofer		Killed, Douai
Ltn Karl Helbig	FA278	KIA, Aisne-Champagne (or 16th?)

18 April 1917

Vfw Bernard Schattat (one aircraft of FA17 lost to infantry fire)		Killed, Dailly Ferme

19 April 1917

Ltn Paul Herrmann	J31	KIA over Bois Malvel
Uffz Friedrich Schneider (O)	SS28	KIA, Warmoville, Prosnes Gfr Hermann Brauer OK but he will be KIA 27 July

20 April 1917

Vfw Viktor Hebben	J10	WIA

21 April 1917

Ltn Günther v d Heyde	J9	KIA, over Nauroy
Ltn Gustav Nernst	J30	KIA in Alb DIII 2147/16, Arras
Ltn Oskar Seitz	J30	Brought down unhurt
Ltn R Wichard	J24	POW in 'VERA' 2096/16
Uffz Brosius	SS11	? 6 Armee
Ltn Koehler	"	?
Flg Julius Oettinger	FA275	DOW, Zeithain
Ltn Karl Schäfer	J11	Brought down by ground fire – safe

22 April 1917

Uffz Gustav Richter (P)	FA212	Killed, Chevigny
Ltn Erich Bersu (O)	"	Killed, Chevigny
Flgr Albert Karzmarek		Killed, Oulcherwald
Uffz Karl Schulz		Killed, Oulcherwald
Ltn Martin Möbius (P)	FAA211	WIA, Oppy
Ltn Goldhammer (O)	"	safe

23 April 1917

Vfw Arno Schramm	J7	KIA over Montfaucon
Hpt Paul v Osterroht	J12	KIA 1800, nr Écoust St Mein, Cambrai. 6 Armee
Uffz Nauczak	J33	Severely WIA over Quéant
Ltn Eberhard Stettner		Killed, Monceau
Oblt Heinrich Möller (O)		Killed, Monceau
Ltn Werner Steuber (O)	KG4	Killed, Monceau
Uffz Fritz Bruno		Killed, Monceau
Ltn Fritz v Massow (P)		Killed, Monceau
Ltn Karl Schweren Ltn Otto Wirsch OffStv Alfred Hecher	KG3/15	All POWs; Gotha GIV G610/16, Montreuil, nr Vron
Uffz Kaiser	SS7	crash-landed
Flgr Adam Föller	"	" " (killed 1 May 1917)
Oblt Georg Schmidt (O)	FAA254	KIA, Seclainvillers, Somme

24 April 1917

Oblt Rudolf Berthold	J14	WIA with a Caudron
Ltn Fritz Kleindienst	J18	Down in flames, N of Comines
Rittm Karl v Grieffenhagen	J18	Crashed after combat
Vfw Rudolf Rath	J35	Alb DIII 2020/16, KIA over Hagenbach, cr at Altkirch
Ltn Franz Blum	FA46	WIA by flak over S St Mihiel. Armee Det 'C'
Ltn Werner Hecht (P)	FAA222	Killed, Coney le Château
Ltn Hugo Schneider (O)	"	Killed, Coney le Château
Flg Josef Reuber		Killed, Sissone
Vfw Otto Hartung (P)	FA252	Killed, Nauroy
Ltn Friedrich Krowolitski (O)		Killed, Nauroy
Ltn Walter Rudatis (P)		Killed, Allemont, Laon
Ltn Karl Jaeger (O)	FAA253	Killed, Allemont, Laon
Ltn Karl Schmidt (O)	FAA251	Killed, Clemont
Ltn Hans Huppertz	FA18	POW, Béthune 6 Armee
Ltn Friedrich Neumüller	"	POW
Uffz Max Haase (P)	FA26	WIA/POW. DFW CV 5927/16: brought down at Havrincourt
Ltn Karl Keim (O)	"	DOW
Ltn Karl Timm (O)	FFA235	KIA Acheville
Ltn Richard Zeglin (P)	"	KIA, 6 Armee
Uffz Otto Haberland (P)	FAA227	KIA, over Armentières

Ltn Henrich Klofe (O)	"	KIA, nr Lille
Vfw Max Wackwitz	J24	F/landed damaged at Bignicourt
Vflgmt Josef Wirtz	MFJ1	Killed, Becelaere. Collided with FE2d over Polygon Wood in Alb DIII 2281/16
OfStv Rudolf Weckbrodt	J26	WIA

25 April 1917

Vfw Sebastian Festner	J11	KIA, Gavrelle, Alb DIII 2251/16
Flg Kurt Hebel		Killed, Lille
Ltn Werner Kachler (O)	KG5	KIA, Verdun

26 April 1917

Vfw Emil Eisenhuth	J3	KIA, Alb DIII 2207/16, nr Hayencourt, NW Cambrai
Oblt Max Reinhold	J15	KIA, over Lierval, Laon
Ltn Traugott Milbrandt (O)	FAA255	Killed, Cerny
Ltn Franz Blum (O)	FA46	Killed, Chambley (see 24 Apr)
Ltn Sigismund Steinfeld (O)	FAA271	Killed, Ripont
Ltn Friedrich Feldmann (O)	FAA252	DOW, Prosnes WIA 24 April

27 April 1917

Ltn Herbert Zimmermann (P)	FA14	POW/DOW; Bogeien, Gerardner
Ltn Ernst Naumann (O)		KIA, Gerardner
Ltn Eissfeldt	J10	Severely WIA
Ltn Friedrich Vonschott	J14	Severely WIA over Montchâlons, DOW 14 May
Flg Alfred Huherman		Killed, Bergnicourt
Ltn Rudolf Hepp	J24	Damaged Alb DII 1731/16, and crashes in flames at Lefricourt

28 April

Nil

29 April 1917

Ltn Peckmann	J15	WIA
Ltn Ludwig Dornheim	J29	KIA, over Beine
Vfw Rener (P)	FAA48	WIA
Ltn Alois Stegmann (O)	"	KIA, over Carvin
Flg Ernst Deutchmann	SS22	Killed, Braye-en-Laonnois
Ltn Bruno Kittel (P)	FAA45	KIA, Baralle, NW Cambrai
Ltn Hermann Waldschmidt (O)		KIA
Ltn Erich Bamm (O)	FAA201	KIA, Marchais, Liesse
Oblt Georg Krafft (O)	FA4	KIA Arras

Ltn Adolf Frey	J9	KIA in flames nr Nauroy
Ltn Friedrich Mallinckrodt	J20	Severely WIA. 2 Armee
Vfw Max Reichle (P)	FA259	POW, Heudicourt
Ltn Erich Hampe (O)	"	POW
Vfw Max Baatz (P)	FAA204	KIA, Houplines/Armentières
Ltn Alexander Schleiper (O)		POW/WIA; Albatros C captured
Ltn August Rodenback (O)	FAA233	KIA over Oppy. 6 Armee
Ltn Hermann Benckiser	FAA238	KIA over Rocourt. 6 Armee
Ltn Werner Marwitz	J9	KIA Nauroy
Ltn Ernst Poetsch (O)	KG2	KIA, Aussonce-Reims
Ltn Karl Beckmann (P)	"	KIA, Reims

Assessment

The main feature of Bloody April was the casualties inflicted on the Royal Flying Corps, and to a lesser extent on the French Air Service. Over the years numbers have been talked about or published, but at this distance it is difficult with any real certainty to be exact in this numbers game.

One established figure of RFC losses gives 316 British aviators killed or missing for this month and we would not argue with this. What we can show is that according to research into surviving loss records, operational casualties were some 245 aircraft destroyed as a direct result of air actions. Others of course were written off in crashes, many not in any way attributable to operations, even though they might be taking off or returning from an operational duty. In other words, the 245 aircraft were as a direct result of enemy action, both by German aircraft or German ground fire.

In the RFC's Summary of Work for April 1917, the list of casualties, claims and hours flown indicates the following:†

Date	Hrs flown	Missing	Enemy Casualties			
			Dest	OOC	DDD	KB‡
1st	517	not recorded	not recorded			
2nd	517	"	"			
3rd	753	"	"			
4th	517	"	"			
5th	1,358	"	"			
6th	1,279	17	34			1
7th	605	not recorded	2			1
8th	1,735	10	22			2
9th	941	2	11			
10th	480	–		1		
11th	720	10	11			
12th	395	3	1	4		
13th	1,250	14	5	5		
14th	1,363	10	18			
15th	346	–	–			
16th	917	5	5			
17th	38	–	–			
18th	47	–	–			
19th	379	–	–			

Date	Hrs flown	Missing	Enemy Casualties			
			Dest	OOC	DDD	KB‡
20th	829	2	1			
21st	708	4	4	6		
22nd	1,663	5 (+5 KBS)	6	15		7
23rd	1,966	2	10	19		
24th	2,202	6	10	19	14	2
25th	1,047	3	4	1	2	
26th	1,017	6	3	1	2	1
27th	1,274	4	5	11	4	
28th	1,082	3	3	2		
29th	1,814	15	7	12	10	
30th	1,842	10	8	19	20	

† The RFC day, for official purposes, ran from 6 pm to 6 pm, which can confuse issues when
  something happens after 6 pm on, say, the 21st and appears to be recorded as the 22nd.
‡ As claimed by RFC pilots and aircrew. Detailed breakdown between those destroyed, out
  of control and driven down damaged not given until later in the month.

Remarkably this only shows a total of 131 aircraft missing and five balloons. Perhaps it only indicated truly 'missing' aircraft, and did not include those known to have been lost? The figures given for claims against the Germans speak for themselves.

Another interesting statistic in this summary is the RFC strength. This is shown on 1 April as being 821 available aircraft, with 70 more unserviceable and 849 pilots available, 496 of which were actually flying (operational?). At the end of April, the figures showed 761 aircraft available, 148 being u/s. Pilot strength was 854, with 745 actually flying.

Figures, of course, can be manipulated to show almost anything that their author(s) wish to present, but here we are just showing the figures that seem to apply here from our researches. The loss of flying men – the often quoted 316 – is not that far out from our research. Our breakdown is 211 killed, missing or died of wounds, plus 108 taken prisoner. That makes 319. To this figure must be added several who were killed or injured in crashes and accidents, although it is not clear if the original 316 figure included those killed in this way. In addition, around 116 pilots and observers were wounded, not taking into account those captured men who were also wounded. (As a comparison, the RFC lost 499 pilots and observers between 1 July – the opening of the Somme offensive – and 22 November 1916; i.e. in four and a half months.)

As a matter of academic interest, the breakdown of the 245 aircraft by types known to be lost directly to enemy action shows the following:

BE2	75	Martinsyde G100	5
FE2	58	Sopwith Triplane	4
Nieuport Scouts	43	Morane Parasol	3

RE8	15	DH2	2
Sop 1½ Strutter	14	AWFK8	2
BF2a	9	SE5	1
Spad VII	8	Sopwith Baby	1
Sopwith Pup	7	Handley Page 0/100	1
DH4	6	Nieuport XII	1

Staying for a moment with the losses, the known French losses, which cannot be said to be 100% accurate, give figures of 55 aircraft lost, 63 airmen killed, missing or died of wounds, with at least 11 more prisoners and 55 wounded. The breakdown of aircraft types shows:

Spad VII	18	Morane Parasol	2
Nieuport Scout	12	Salmson-Moineau	2
Caudron G4	11	Voisin	1
Farman	4	Nieuport XII	2
Sop 1½ Strutter	2	Letord	1

As can readily be seen, the British Corps (observation) aircraft suffered severely, whether engaged on pure Corps work – contact patrols, reconnaissance or artillery patrols and registration missions – or bombing. These types (BE, RE8, Parasol, and 1½ Strutters) totalled 107, or just about one third of all losses. However, it is acknowledged that some FEs were also engaged on photo and recce work, as well as escort duties, while some Strutters were used on fighting patrols.

Pure fighting aeroplanes (Nieuport, Spad, Pup, Triplane, SE5) lost 65 of their number, but again, some of the FE2s would also come into this category and so, one supposes, did the new Bristol Fighters.

The overwhelming feature, however, has to be the Corps aircraft, sent out daily to gather photographs, help range guns, locate enemy artillery positions or to make contact with a fluid battle front. In poor aircraft they were shot to ribbons and anyone with less than reasonable front-line experience was easy prey to the Albatros and Halberstadt fighter pilots of the German Jastas.

This was nothing new, of course, and is emphasised by the Arras Battle, which just happened to come with the culmination of the spring weather, a spring offensive and a meeting head-on with the newly formed Jastas, whose pilots had been eagerly awaiting just this sort of confrontation since the previous autumn (fall).

An analysis of the Jasta pilots' claims is of interest. Some Jastas of course were very active and in the forefront of the battle areas, while others were not. But a full breakdown of individual unit claims for this month are:

Jasta 1	0	Jasta 13	6	Jasta 26	6
Jasta 2	21	Jasta 14	7	Jasta 27	0

Jasta 3	10	Jasta 15	2	Jasta 28	3
Jasta 4	16	Jasta 16	0	Jasta 29	0
Jasta 5	32	Jasta 17	6	Jasta 30	7
Jasta 6	0	Jasta 18	6	Jasta 31	4
Jasta 7	0	Jasta 19	12	Jasta 32	0
Jasta 8	5	Jasta 20	2	Jasta 33	1
Jasta 9	10	Jasta 21	5	Jasta 34	7
Jasta 10	0	Jasta 22	4	Jasta 35	2
Jasta 11	89	Jasta 23	1	Jasta 36	12
Jasta 12	23	Jasta 24	2	Jasta 37	1

(Jasta 25 is not shown for they were operating in Macedonia, not on the Western Front.)

Total claims were 298, which is not a bad average alongside the known losses of both British and French aircraft – 299 – although one has to remember a number of the Allied losses were to ground fire or anti-aircraft defences. German claims would also include balloons, which are not part of the 299 loss figure. (German pilots were credited with 34 balloons.)

The top four scoring Jastas – 11, 5, 12 and 2 – claimed 55% of these victories (165). Of the successful German aces in April, 14 scored five or more kills, the top being Kurt Wolff, and in total they accounted for 155 Allied aeroplanes and balloons. These 14 men claimed:

Kurt Wolff	Jasta 11 – 23	Sebastian Festner	Jasta 11 – 10
Manfred v Richthofen	Jasta 11 – 22	Edmund Nathanael	Jasta 5 – 9
Karl Schäfer	Jasta 11 – 21	Hans Klein	Jasta 4 – 9
Lothar v Richthofen	Jasta 11 – 15	Paul v Osterroht	Jasta 12 – 6
Otto Bernert	Jasta 2 – 15	Wilhelm Frankl	Jasta 4 – 6
Heinrich Gontermann	Jasta 5 – 11	Erich Hahn	Jasta 19 – 5
Kurt Schneider	Jasta 5 – 10	Karl Dossenbach	Jasta 36 – 5

Of these, nine had or would receive the Pour le Mérite, two were killed during April and only two would survive WW1 – Klein and Lothar von Richthofen.

Just why were the German fighter pilots so successful? Mention was made earlier of experience. The policy of the day for the British Royal Flying Corps and Royal Naval Air Service – and a policy which remained virtually unchanged for the whole war – was that pilots and observers were thrust into front-line squadrons as demands to replace casualties increased, often straight from flying schools. Total flying time, in most cases, could be counted in a few modest hours, perhaps 40 or 50 if they were lucky. Others may, of course, have had more, especially if they had been fortunate enough to be retained as instructors, or test pilots and so on, or even been lucky enough to get to the front at a quiet period, during which they might be able to gain extra flying hours without having to cope with the demands of an offensive. (Some Naval pilots were fortunate enough to go via No. 12 Naval Squadron which was a training unit formed in this April at St Pol, where they could acclimatise to France and prepare for war flying.)

This was as true for Corps or bombing pilots, as it was for fighter pilots or scouts as they were called in WW1. The Germans, on the other hand, generally came to the Jastas after a period as a two-seater pilot, having spent some months, certainly several weeks, at the front in this capacity. Having shown a desire or an aptitude for single-seat fighter work, they could volunteer to be transferred to fighters, and after a brief period at one of the Jastaschules, be assigned to a fighter unit, if the school instructors approved. In this way, therefore, the new Jasta pilot was already something of a front-line veteran, and at the very least knew what it was all about and had acquired a degree of battle experience, as well as the 'feel' of air fighting. Having, therefore, flown two-seaters, and now faced with, in the main, two-seater opponents, he knew exactly what it was like to be engaged by a fighter and in consequence how to approach and attack two-seat opponents.

In contrast, his opposite number, flying a Nieuport, a Pup or such like, was just about competent enough to take off and land, and fly his aircraft straight and level. To be thrust into the maelstrom of a whirling air-battle was often something which the embryo scouting pilot did not survive.

The two-seater Corps pilots too were just as inexperienced, and very often their observers were former artillery men, who had either asked or been asked to transfer to flying because they knew about artillery firing and the fall of shot. But if they became too embroiled in watching the ground, that is when the German air fighters were upon them before they knew the danger was close.

The RFC was still lacking an adequate fighting aeroplane to counter the new Albatros Scouts or the Halberstadts. Experienced Nieuport or Pup pilots had a reasonable chance against them in a fight, and the new Sopwith Triplanes were a good match, but the FE8 and DH2 pusher-types were now on their way out, and while the FE2 crews could give a good account of themselves, they were beginning to take heavy punishment, as the April losses show. The Spad wasn't bad – with experience – but the Bristol Fighter had proved a disaster and only with new tactics and an aggressive attitude would it become a deadly opponent in the future.

What made the success achieved by the German fighter pilots even more remarkable, despite their superior equipment, was their comparatively few numbers. On the actual Arras battle front there were only six fighting Jastas, increased to only eight after 12 April.

The nominal strength of a Jasta was 12 aircraft and 14 pilots, although this figure was rarely if ever reached or even approached, owing to losses and the slow rate of production in Germany which delayed the replacement of lost or damaged machines.

The average Jasta aircraft strength on any one day was about seven fit to fly; thus at Arras, for the period 1 to 11 April, there were no more than 42 operational German fighters, increased to just 52 from 12 April. The mistake made by the British and French in estimating the German strength as higher than it was, was due mainly to the devotion by both the German air and ground personnel, the former willing to fly three or four times a day, the latter working round the clock to ensure every possible aircraft was serviceable and ready for combat.

Perhaps the fact that Allied formations often reported far more hostile aircraft in an air fight than could possibly be there, had something to do with being unwilling to accept that they could lose so many men and machines to a much smaller number of opponents. But this is purely an observation and may be unfair in fact. However, having studied some of Jasta 11's fights, whereas Richthofen would often report flying with just three or four of his men (his average aeroplane strength in the last week of April was only seven) his opponents' combat reports often stated the enemy strength as anything up to 20 to 30. Even if a second Jasta was in evidence, it would be rare for such numbers to be available.

The Germans had long since ended the practice of flying defensive patrols, being considered useless, and wasteful of resources. Generally speaking, the single-seater fighters would be sent into action only at such times when the Allied flyers seemed especially active. These Allied activities were watched and monitored by special air protection officers – Luftschutz Offizier – situated just behind the front, who had at their disposal observation and signalling equipment. Reports from these officers, via air unit commanders at Corps HQ, gave the HQ staff a good picture of events from which they could decide or not to get fighters into the air, and in what opposing strength.

As the German fighter pilots' main task was to gain mastery over the front, a move was made to try and group some Jastas together. Jastas 3, 4, 11 and 33 were among the first, which later led to the formation of von Richthofen's Jagdesgeschwader Nr.1 in the early summer (Jastas 4, 6, 10 and 11).

However, during the Arras battle, no central command had overall control of the fighters, this being left to the air unit commanders at Corps HQ. Their fighter zones generally coincided with the close reconnaissance areas of these Corps.

Turning to the question of claims made by British and French airmen, although to some degree we do not fully understand what losses the Germans incurred, it appears obvious that they did not sustain anything like the losses the two Allied sides were claiming. It would seem fair to assume that German official 'losses' were more associated with men than aircraft, but we are just not certain. But knowing what the fighter pilot losses were in relation to killed, taken prisoner and wounded, we can say that personnel casualties in the Jastas were not as high as Allied claims would tend to indicate. Unfortunately two-seater losses are recorded even less accurately, or records have not survived.

However, by analysing the British and French claims and showing them next to known or admitted 'losses', we can see that at best the Allied flyers were overclaiming.

	Destroyed	OOC	KBs	
RFC claims for April	126	206	16	
French claims	70	–	8	
Totals:	196	206	24	(not including AA or Corps two-seater claims)
Known German losses	76	N/A	7	(to air combat actions)

In a post-war study into claims and losses, the German Air Ministry provided figures to the British Air Ministry for the VIth Army zone. The ones relevant to this period indicate the following:

	Total Br Losses	In German Lines	German Personnel			Aircraft
			Dead	Miss	Wounded	
31 March to 7 April 1917	37	32	2	1	3	2
8 April to 14 April 1917	47	31	2	2	2	3
15 April to 20 April 1917	17	12	1	–	1	–
21 April to 26 April 1917	37	11	7	7	1	11
27 April to 3 May 1917	40	26	12	6	6	10

The VIth Army boundaries on 9 April were Wervicq-Cassel-Boulogne in the north, Bullecourt-Ervillers-Acheux-Canaples-Condé-Folie in the south, and the coast to the mouth of the Somme in the west.

The Battle of Arras ended on 4 May, following a third Battle of the Scarpe two days earlier. All that had really been achieved was the important capture of Vimy Ridge, and the centre of activity soon shifted to the Flanders front further north, for the start of another scheme. This one was designed to free the Belgian coast by pushing the Germans back to the Scheldt River. It didn't work. On the French front, Nivelle's failure at Champagne effectively stopped all French offensive action for the rest of the year, the British having to take the brunt of the fighting on their northern and central sectors. There followed the Battle of Messines (7 to 14 June); Battle of Ypres (31 July to 10 November including the Battle of Passchendaele – 12 October to 10 November); then the Battle of Cambrai (20 November to 3 December).

Meantime, the new SE5 fighter became established, 56 Squadron merely being the forerunner of some 14 squadrons on the Western Front by 1918. The other new fighter was the Sopwith Camel, which arrived in France during June 1917.

Index

French